Introduction

Battles of the US Marine Corps

The US Marine Corps is America's foremost elite fighting force with a distinguished history stretching back to 1775.

As the corps celebrates its 250th anniversary this year, it is an ideal time to look back at some of its most iconic battles, which played a central role in establishing its unparalleled reputation for combat success.

Over its long history, the US Marine Corps has always played a leading role in America's wars, from its struggle for independence against Britain through to the recent 'Global War on Terrorism'.

The names of those battles have a become a watch-word for American heroism.

Belleau Wood in World War One, Guadalcanal and Iwo Jima in World War Two, Inchon and Chosin Reservoir in Korea, Khe Sanh and Hue in Vietnam.

In this century, the corps led America's wars in Afghanistan and Iraq, where another generation of US Marines have carved new chapters of history.

As well as its battlefield bravery, the US Marine Corps has an unprecedented reputation for tactical and technical innovation. Heroism is often not enough to bring victory, so far-thinking US Marine Corps officers have always looked for new ways to defeat America's enemies and give their marines battlefield advantage.

Battles of the US Marine Corps concludes with a profile of the US Marine Corps today, looking at its tough training, equipment, organisation and global deployments.

We hope you enjoy *Battles of the US Marine Corps*

Semper Fidelis

Tim Ripley
Editor
July 2025

ABOVE: The US Marine Corps now operates hundreds of attack and transport helicopters. (USMC)

LEFT: Landing at Inchon. The US Marine Corps amphibious assault in September 1950 turned the tide of the Korean War. (USMC ARCHIVE)

LEFT: The US Marine Corps Memorial in Washington DC honours the generations of fallen marines. (FAMARTIN)

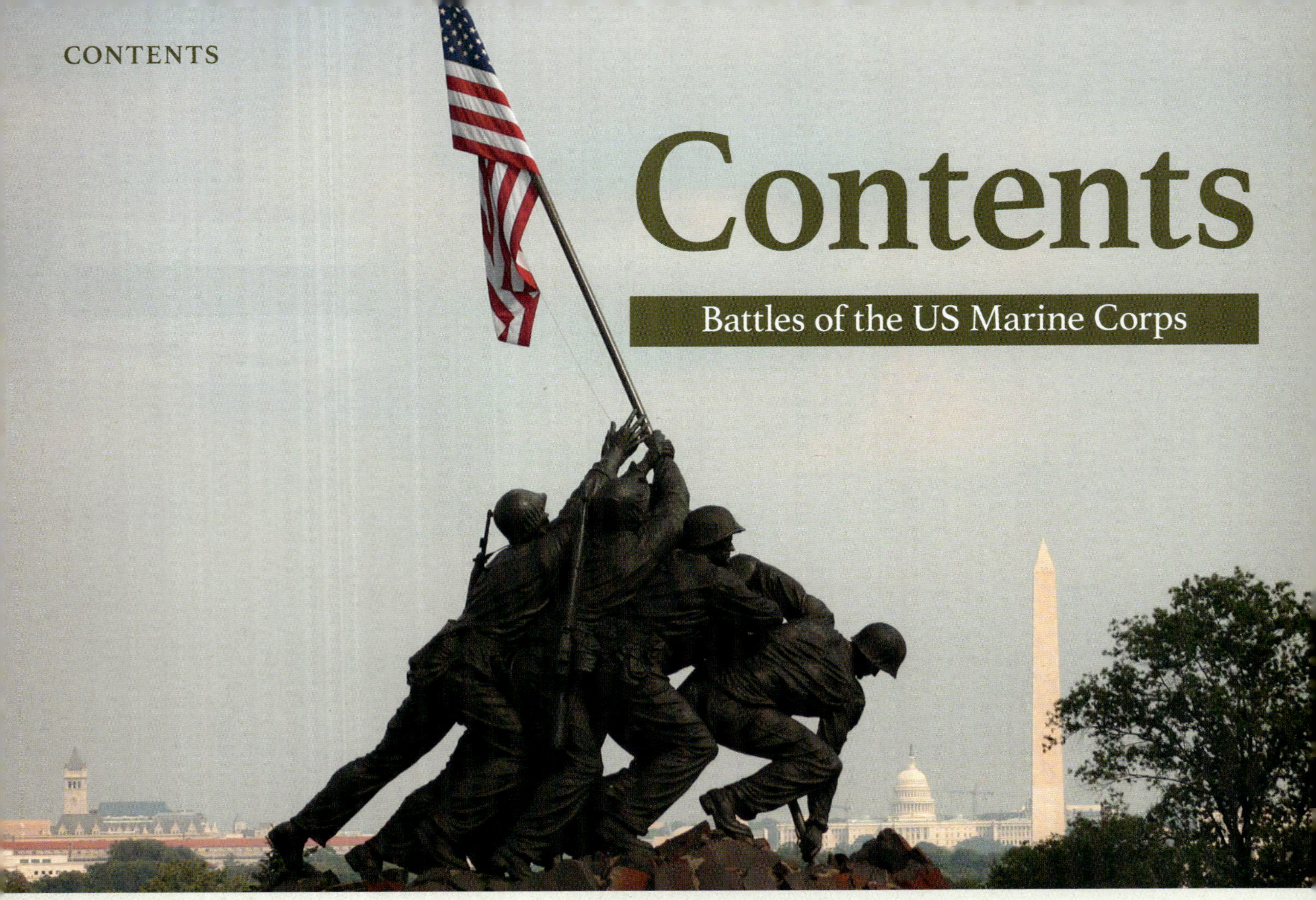

Contents

Battles of the US Marine Corps

ABOVE: The Battle of Iwo Jima in 1945 was the pinnacle of the US Marine Corps 'island-hopping' campaign across the Pacific. (DAVID B KING)

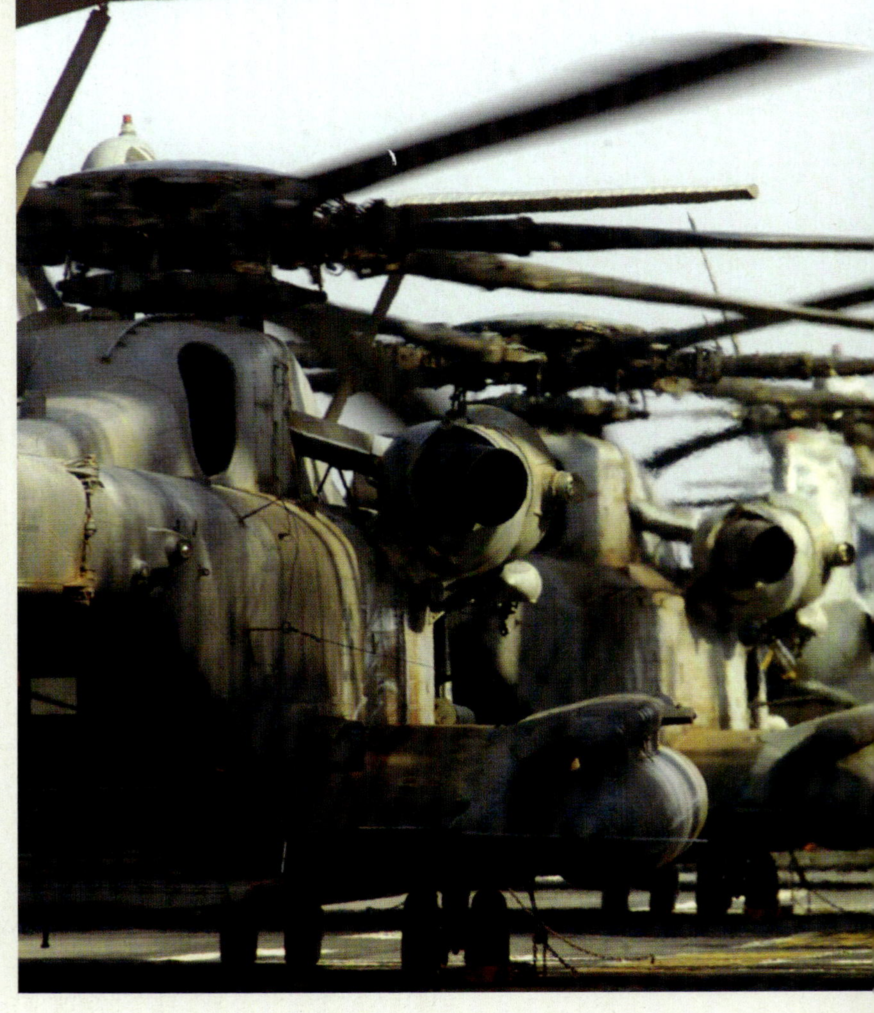

RIGHT: Since the Korean war, the US Marine Corps has flown into battle by helicopter. (USMC)

ABOVE LEFT: To defeat the communists in Hue, US Marines had to rapidly learn street-fighting skills. (USMC ARCHIVE)

ABOVE RIGHT: Amphibious warfare has always been the core skill of the US Marine Corps. (USMC ARCHIVE)

LEFT: The modern US Marine Corps was forged in fire against the Japanese in World War Two. (USMC ARCHIVE)

LEFT: The US Marine Corps spearheaded the 'shock and awe' drive on Baghdad that defeated Saddam Hussein's army. (USMC)

ISBN: 978 1 83632 132 3
Editor: Tim Ripley
Data and photo research: Joe Ripley
Senior editor, specials: Roger Mortimer
Email: roger.mortimer@keypublishing.com
Cover Design: Steve Donovan
Design: SJmagic DESIGN SERVICES, India
Advertising Sales Manager: Sam Clark
Email: sam.clark@keypublishing.com
Tel: 01780 755131
Advertising Production: Becky Antoniades
Email: Rebecca.antoniades@keypublishing.com

SUBSCRIPTION/MAIL ORDER
Key Publishing Ltd, PO Box 300
Stamford, Lincs, PE9 1NA
Tel: 01780 480404
Subscriptions email:
subs@keypublishing.com
Mail Order email:
orders@keypublishing.com
Website: www.keypublishing.com/shop

PUBLISHING
Group CEO: Adrian Cox
Publisher: Steve O'Hara

Published by
Key Publishing Ltd, PO Box 100,
Stamford, Lincs, PE9 1XQ
Tel: 01780 755131
Website: www.keypublishing.com

PRINTING
Precision Colour Printing Ltd, Haldane,
Halesfield 1 Telford Shropshire. TF7 4QQ

DISTRIBUTION
Seymour Distribution Ltd, 2 Poultry Avenue,
London, EC1A 9PU
Enquiries Line: 0274 294000.

America's Elite Warriors

When looking at the world's elite fighting forces, the US Marine Corps is up there with other legendary units – the French Foreign Legion, Nazi Germany's Waffen-SS, Napoleon's Old Guard or the legions of Imperial Rome.

The US Marine Corps' 250-year history of unprecedented battlefield heroism and combat success can be attributed to the fighting qualities of its troops. While tactics and technology have changed since the days of muskets and sailing ships, modern day marines still share the mindset of their illustrious predecessors.

At the heart of the ethos of the corps is its training that moulds young men and women into marines. Apart

from a few brief periods in World War One and Two, as well as during the Vietnam conflict, the US Marine Corps has always been a professional service. Marines chose to join this elite band of warriors.

It is during their training that the marines learn the ethos of their calling. Honour, courage and commitment are the core values of the US Marine Corps. There have been several Hollywood movies based on marine basic training, with the 1980s film *Full Metal Jacket* catching the spirit of life at a recruit training depot during the Vietnam era.

While the content of US Marine Corps training has changed dramatically over the past century, there are some core elements that have remained constant and ensured continuity in building future generations of marines. The biggest change is that women can now serve in all roles in the corps and today's marines are far better educated than their predecessors. The days of recruits painting rocks white, for the sake of it, are long gone. Every part of the marine training syllabus serves a purpose.

Some things have remained the same. Would-be marines still train

at recruit depots at Parris Island in South Carolina and San Diego in Southern California. The inside of the barrack blocks still look as they did in the 1950s and 1960s. Drill instructors still wear their distinctive 'campaign hats' and bark orders at hapless recruits from the moment they get off the bus at the base. At the heart of their training is the idea that every marine has to be trained as a rifleman, so if necessary, they can take the fight to the enemy with rifle and bayonet in hand. The Rifleman's Creed (see box) started to be taught to marines in 1942, as General Alfred M Gray, 29th Commandant of the Marine Corps famously said: "Every Marine is, first and foremost, a rifleman. All other conditions are secondary."

This remains the case, even though the corps has entered the era of drone and cyber warfare. Specialised training comes later in a marine's career, but having those core military skills marks the US Marines out from many other military organisations.

Modern marine basic training is 13 weeks long and every recruit has to pass for the privilege of

The Rifleman's Creed

"This is my rifle. There are many like it, but this one is mine. My rifle is my best friend. It is my life. I must master it as I must master my life.

Without me, my rifle is useless. Without my rifle, I am useless. I must fire my rifle true. I must shoot straighter than my enemy who is trying to kill me. I must shoot him before he shoots me. I will …

My rifle and I know that what counts in war is not the rounds we fire, the noise of our burst, nor the smoke we make. We know that it is the hits that count. We will hit …

My rifle is human, even as I [am human], because it is my life. Thus, I will learn it as a brother. I will learn its weaknesses, its strength, its parts, its accessories, its sights and its barrel. I will keep my rifle clean and ready, even as I am clean and ready. We will become part of each other. We will …

Before God, I swear this creed. My rifle and I are the defenders of my country. We are the masters of our enemy. We are the saviors of my life. So be it, until victory is America's and there is no enemy, but peace!"

Major General William H Rupertus
Marine Corps Chevron on March 14, 1942

LEFT: The entrance to the Marine Corps Recruit Depot at Parris Island makes it clear that would-be marines are joining an elite fighting force. (USMC)

BELOW: For more than 100 years, generations of marines have learnt their trade at Parris Island. (USMC)

wearing the corps' Eagle, Globe and Anchor insignia.

The first phases of this training are aimed at turning civilians into marines and making them eat, drink and sleep together as marines; making platoons work as a team to achieve common objectives.

Platoons have limited contact with the outside world; recruits have to leave their old lives behind and become immersed in corps life. They are issued with their uniform, equipment and rifle, before learning how to keep them in fighting order, in all circumstances and environments. Recruits have to deal with food rationing, sleep deprivation, rigorous day and night-time marches, assault course races, close order drill and days on the rifle range. On top of this, they have daily room and uniform inspections.

By working as a team, marines learn to complete their tasks with confidence and resilience. Once they have completed the first phase of training, there are challenges

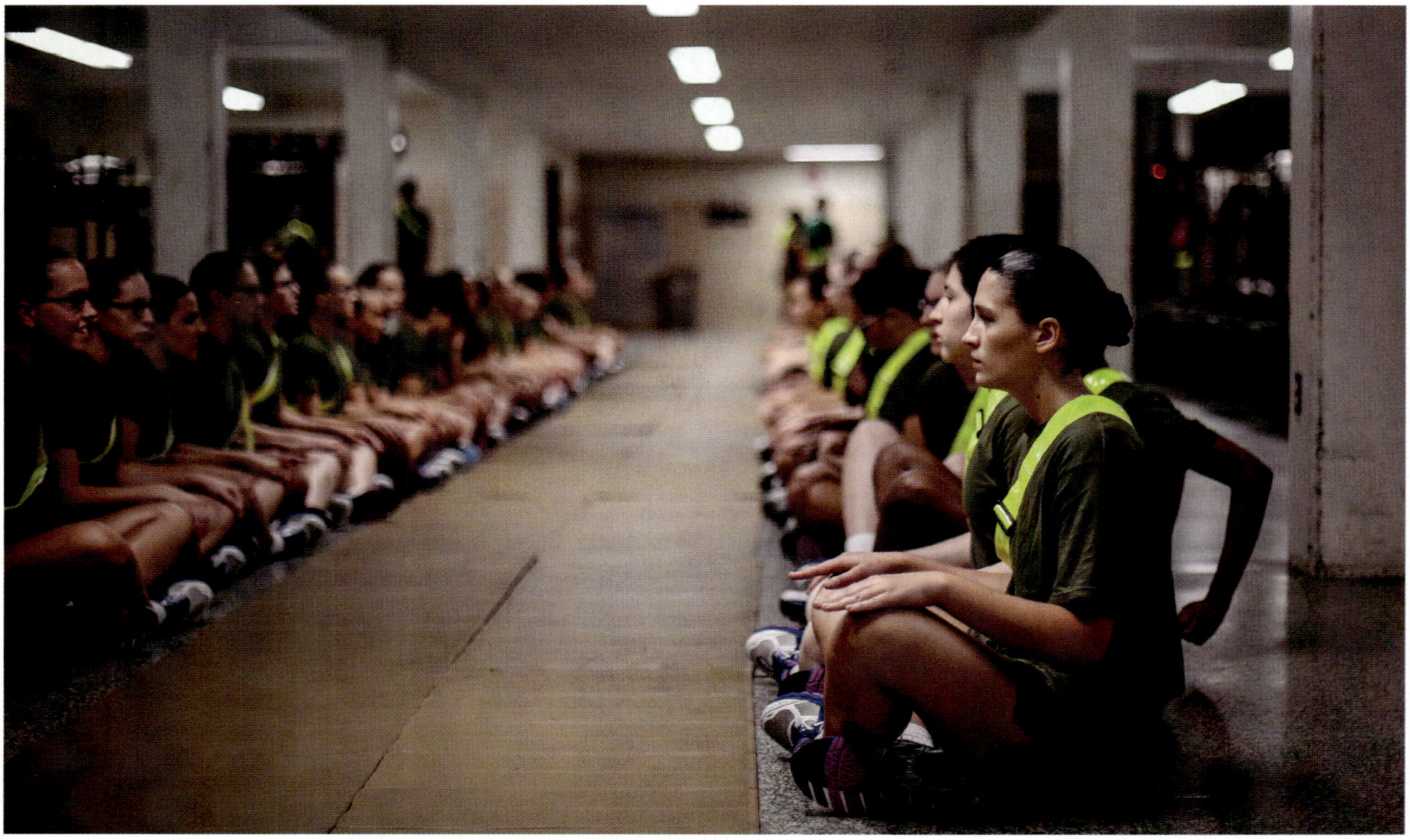

ABOVE: Women can serve in every branch of the US Marine Corps and undergo training alongside their male counterparts at its two recruit depots. (USMC, SGT DANA BEESLEY)

that require more commitment and more endurance as the intensity of the training increases, including in combat water survival, physical and combat conditioning and martial arts.

As the course comes to its close, field combat skills take centre stage, along with more advanced marksmanship training. Recruit training ends with a 54-hour-long test of endurance, known as 'the crucible'. The participants have to get by on little sleep and food, while being tested to see how they react and respond to conditions of stress and simulated combat. The recruits have to work together, connected by a common cause and refusal to quit.

According to the US Marine Corps, once they pass this "demanding phase of recruit training", they will "feel immense purpose and unmistakable pride" in displaying that they have what it takes to be a United States Marine. The corps continues: "The Eagle, Globe and Anchor emblem represents the culmination of every hardship endured and every battle won during recruit training. Earn it, and it will forever serve as a testament to true purpose found coming together for a common cause, pointing to your place among the few who fight and win for our nation as United States Marines."

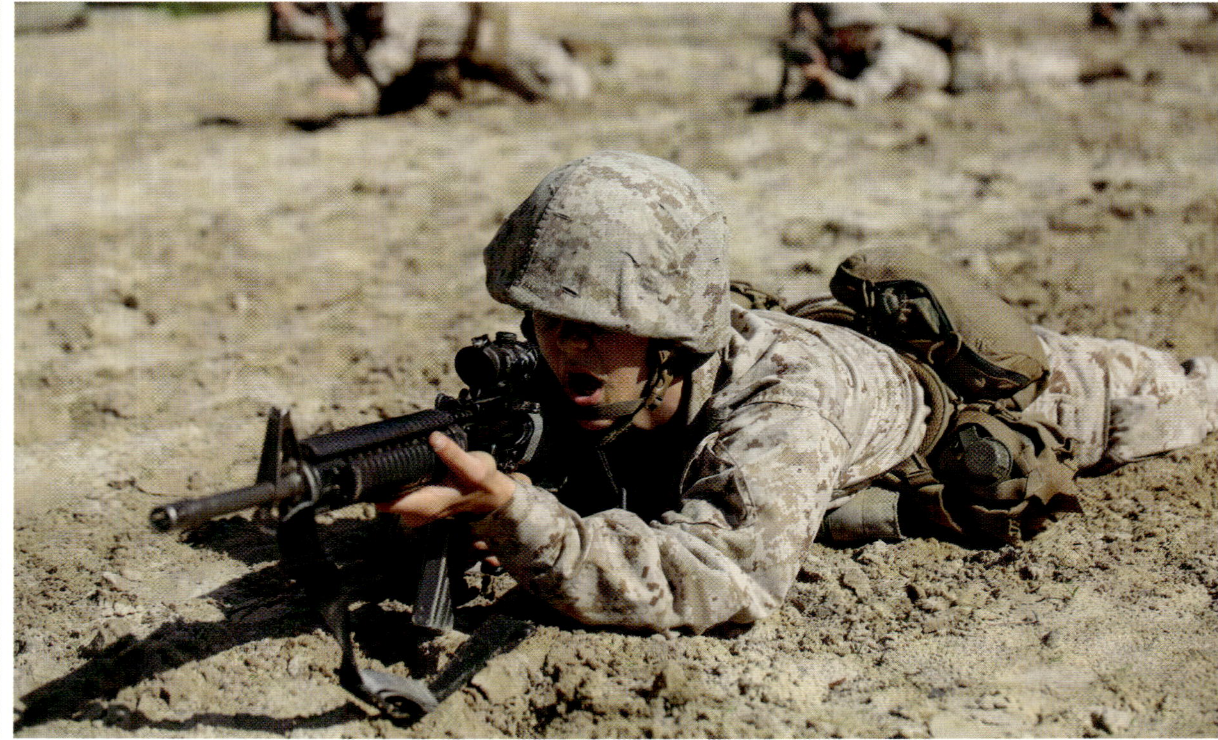

RIGHT: Marksmanship continues to be central to marine basic training. (USMC)

ABOVE: Physical fitness is a core skill for marines, and the corps maintains strict standards to ensures its marines are fit to fight at all times. (USMC)

LEFT: After 13 weeks of basic training, marines get to parade in front of their families and friends at the graduation parade. (USMC)

Founding the US Marines

250 years of history

The US Marine Corps traces its history back to November 10, 1775, when the Revolutionary Congress authorised the formation of the first units of Continental Marines to fight against the British in the American War of Independence. At the end of the war, the marines and other American military units were disbanded because the new United States did not want to pay for a standing military. This changed in August 1794, when US Congress recreated the regular US Navy and ordered the formation of the first marine units to protect America's maritime trade interests. Four years later, the US Marine Corps was formally established by an Act of Congress.

At that time, ship-borne troops were often known as 'sea soldiers' or 'maritime infantry' but in America they were soon known as 'marines'.

BELOW: The Battle of Derna was the first land battle waged by the United States on foreign soil after the American War of Independence. It saw a contingent of US warships and marines dispatched to the Mediterranean to take on the Barbary pirates, who had been staging attacks on American merchant shipping. (COLONEL CHARLES WATERHOUSE, US MARINE CORPS ART COLLECTION)

ABOVE: Samuel Nicholas was commissioned as a 'Captain of Marines' by the Second Continental Congress, November 28, 1775, and he played a prominent role in the Battle of Nassau. As a result, on June 25, 1776, Congress placed Nicholas "at the head of the Marines with the rank of Major". (MAJOR DONNA J NEARY, USMCR)

They were long-service professionals who made a career of their time in uniform. From 1834, the US Marine Corps formally fell under the jurisdiction of the Department of the Navy and since then its personnel have been members of America's Naval Service.

In the era of sailing ships, the corps traditionally served on US Navy warships, enforcing discipline among the crews, acting as marksmen to protect ships from boarding parties and leading expeditions ashore.

Detachments of marines served on US Navy ships throughout the 18th and 19th centuries in continuing clashes with British, Spanish and French ships. When America fought a war with Barbary pirates in North Africa, US Marines landed in Libya to earn their famous battle honour, Tripoli, that is immortalised in the corps hymn.

US Marine Corps Hymn

From the Halls of Montezuma
To the shores of Tripoli
We fight our country's battles
In the air, on land and sea
First to fight for right and freedom
And to keep our honor clean
We are proud to claim the title
Of United States Marine.

Our flag's unfurled to every breeze
From dawn to setting sun
We have fought in ev'ry clime and place
Where we could take a gun
In the snow of far-off Northern lands
And in sunny tropic scenes
You will find us always on the job
The United States Marines.

Here's health to you and to our Corps
Which we are proud to serve
In many a strife we've fought for life
And never lost our nerve
If the Army and the Navy
Ever look on Heaven's scenes
They will find the streets are guarded
By United States Marines.

As the 19th century progressed, the United States embarked on its expansion into its 'Wild West' and sought to increase its influence in central and south America. The US Marines were in the centre of this action.

In the 1847 American-Mexican war, marines led the US advance on Mexico City and stormed Chapultepec Castle to raise the Stars and Stripes over the fortress. The heavy losses are memorialised in the 'blood stripes' of the corps' blue dress uniform trousers. This campaign led to the opening line of the corps hymn, with its reference to the 'Halls of Montezuma'.

The 1898 Spanish-American war proved to be a real watershed for the US Marine Corps. This conflict saw the United States seize the remaining chunks of the Spanish Empire in the Caribbean and the Pacific. Cuba, Puerto Rico, Guam and the Philippines all fell under US control, creating what in effect was a colonial empire.

To control this new empire, the US Navy needed to establish naval and refuelling bases across the Caribbean and Pacific. In the wake of the conquest of the Philippines, the US seized Hawaii to enable a naval base to be permanently established on the islands to allow the US Navy to dominate the central Pacific.

In this new era of global engagement, the US Navy looked to its marines to take on roles such as the seizing and holding of naval bases on foreign shores. This was the true genesis of the US Marine Corps as America's dedicated amphibious force.

In the run-up to the Spanish-American war, a marine expeditionary battalion, backed up by an artillery battery, was formed at Key West and it trained to be landed from US Navy warships on hostile shores. The First Marine Battalion was the first US unit to land in ➤

ABOVE LEFT: A US naval detachment and a contingent of 234 marines under the command of Captain Samuel Nicholas landed at Nassau in the British-controlled Bahamas on March 3, 1776. The expedition led to the capture and destruction of British arms, supplies and naval vessels, and is credited as the first successful engagement of the newly formed US Marines. (V ZVEG, US NAVY ART COLLECTION)

LEFT: US Marines embarked on the USS *Wasp* played a prominent role in the naval battle that led to the capture of HMS *Reindeer* in the English Channel in June 1814. They defeated British boarding parties before turning the tables and forcing the surrender of the Royal Navy vessel. (STAFF SGT JOHN F CLYMER, US NATIONAL MUSEUM OF THE MARINE CORPS)

RIGHT: US Marines played an important role in the defence of the American legation in the Chinese capital Peking, during the 1900 Boxer Rebellion, holding out six weeks until an international relief force that also contained a contingent of US Marines was able to fight its way to the city. (US NATIONAL ARCHIVES)

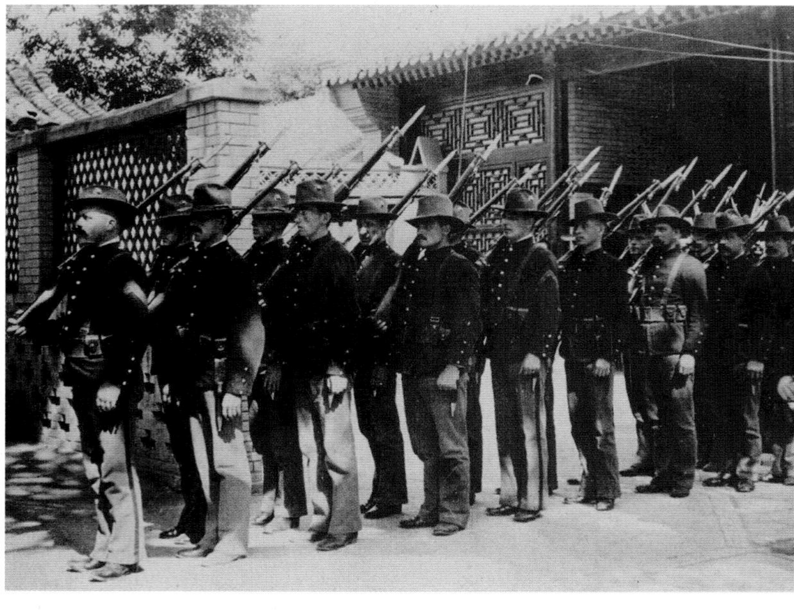

Cuba and successfully captured Guantánamo Bay on the island's southern coast. This soon became the US Navy base in the heart of the Caribbean and allowed American warships to dominate the region.

This success set in train the events that led to the US Marine Corps being built up as America's expeditionary combat force, trained, equipped and configured to project power around the world.

In World War One, marine units were landed in France to serve on the Western Front as part of the American Expeditionary Force. They were soon in the thick of the action and this significantly enhanced their reputation as an elite fighting force. At the Battle of Belleau Wood in June 1918, the marines held their ground in the face of a German offensive in response to the rallying cry, "Retreat, hell! We just got here!"

During the 1930s, the corps underwent a major re-organisation to turn it into a specialist amphibious force, under the Fleet Marine Force initiative. This saw the expansion of the corps into the air, land and sea organisation that exists today, the first specialist landing craft were developed and marine aviation units were expanded.

After the Japanese surprise attack on the US Pacific fleet at Pearl Harbor on December 7, 1941, the corps was expanded to spearhead the US island-hopping campaign across the Pacific. US Marines stormed ashore on several heavily defended Japanese islands and fought bloody battles to capture them. The names of these occupied islands – Guadalcanal, Iwo Jima, Peleliu, Tarawa, Saipan, and Okinawa – are now immortalised as corps battle honours and several US Navy amphibious ships have borne their names. The heroism of those who fought in those bloody battles put the corps on the map. Navy Secretary James Forrestal famously commented that the Marine flag-raising on Iwo Jima in 1945 meant there would be "a

BELOW: When the US Navy transitioned from sail to steam, the US Marines had to adjust their role as the need for marksmen on warships disappeared. The US Marines began to focus on leading landings and expeditions in foreign countries. (NATIONAL MUSEUM OF US NAVY)

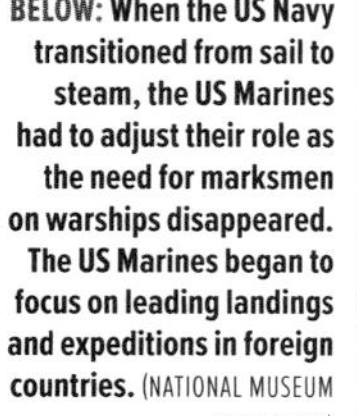

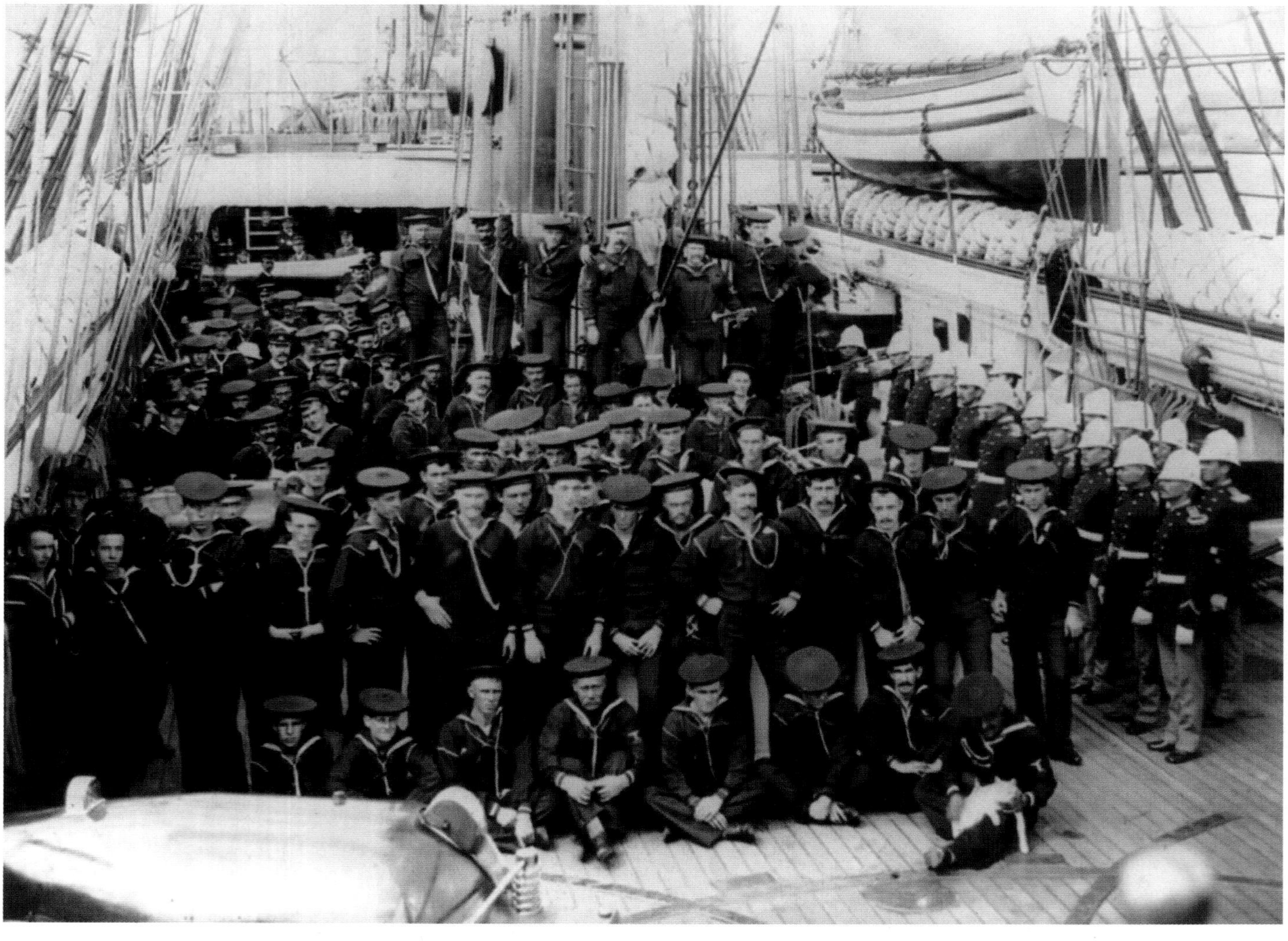

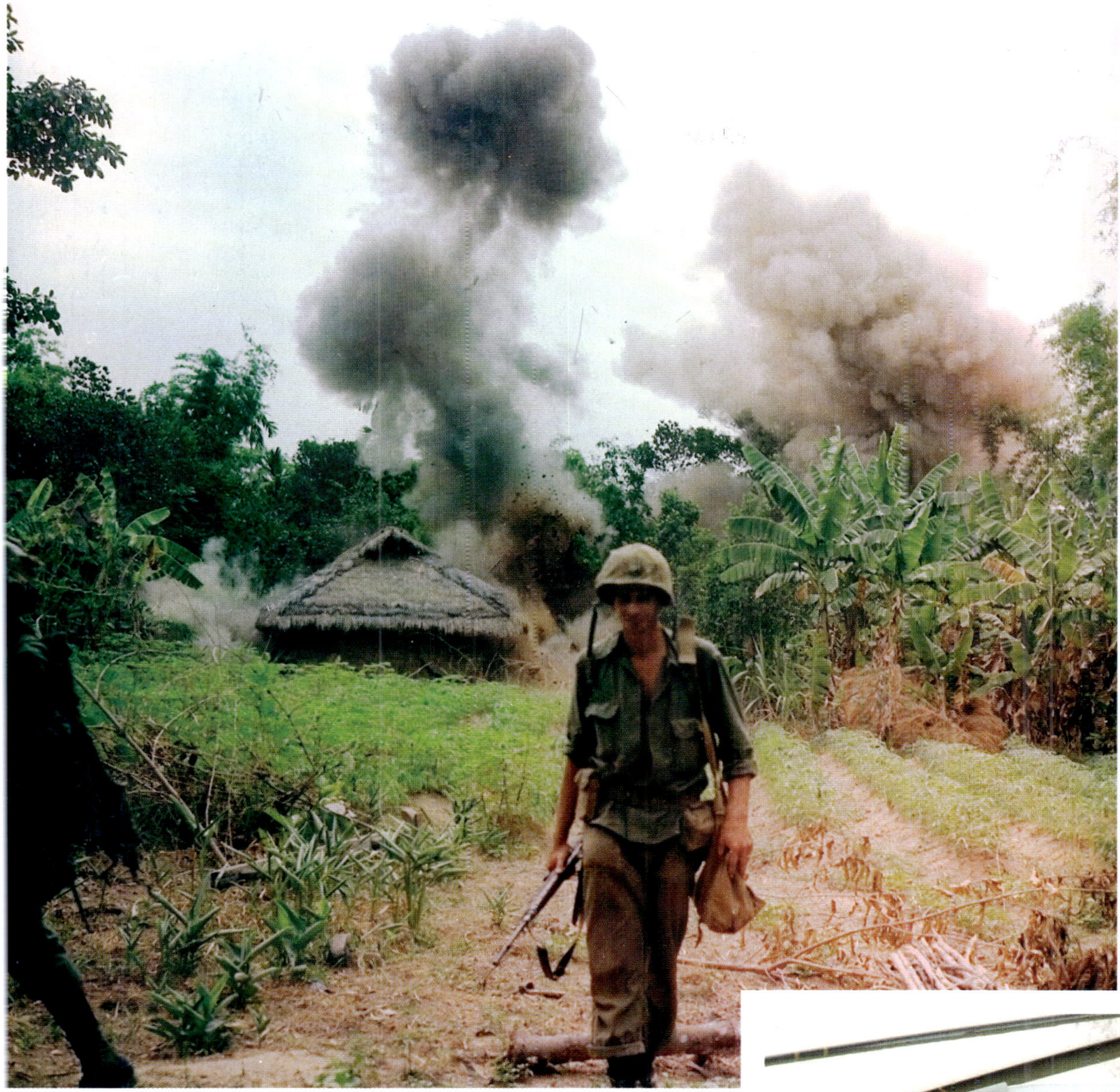

LEFT: In the 1960s and 1970s, the US Marines played a prominent role in the Vietnam War. (USMC ARCHIVE)

BELOW: The US Marine Corps now has important ceremonial roles in Washington DC, as well as being responsible for the safe transport of US presidents by helicopter in 'Marine One'. Here, President Ronald Reagan and Nancy Reagan arrive on the White House Lawn. (WHITE HOUSE PHOTOGRAPHIC COLLECTION)

Marine Corps for the next five hundred years".

There was an ill-fated move in the aftermath of World War Two by the US Army to grab the US Marine Corps from the US Navy, but public and congressional opposition meant the corps was left alone. It was legally confirmed as America's fourth military service in 1947 in the military shake-up that led to the creation of the US Air Force as an independent air arm separate from the US Army. The heroism of US Marines in Korea put an end to any attempts to cut the corps down to size.

Today, the corps has several prestigious roles in the life of Washington DC and plays an important function representing the United States of America overseas at the country's embassies.

The Marine Band, dubbed the 'President's Own' in 1801 by President John Adams, had long been famous for performing 'Hail to the Chief' during state functions in the White House. Ceremonial companies perform at state functions and provide burial parties for marines being interned at Arlington National Cemetery. Since 1954, the US Marine Corps has provided the helicopters that fly the president and vice-president onto the lawn of the White House. The helicopters of Marine Helicopter Squadron One, HMX-1, use the famous radio callsigns 'Marine One' and 'Marine Two', respectively, because of their high-profile passengers.

Since the United States started to set up embassies in foreign countries, the Secretary of State – America's top diplomat – has called on the US Marine Corps to provide ceremonial and security roles in diplomatic outposts. These embassy security detachments are now the most overt America military presence around the world.

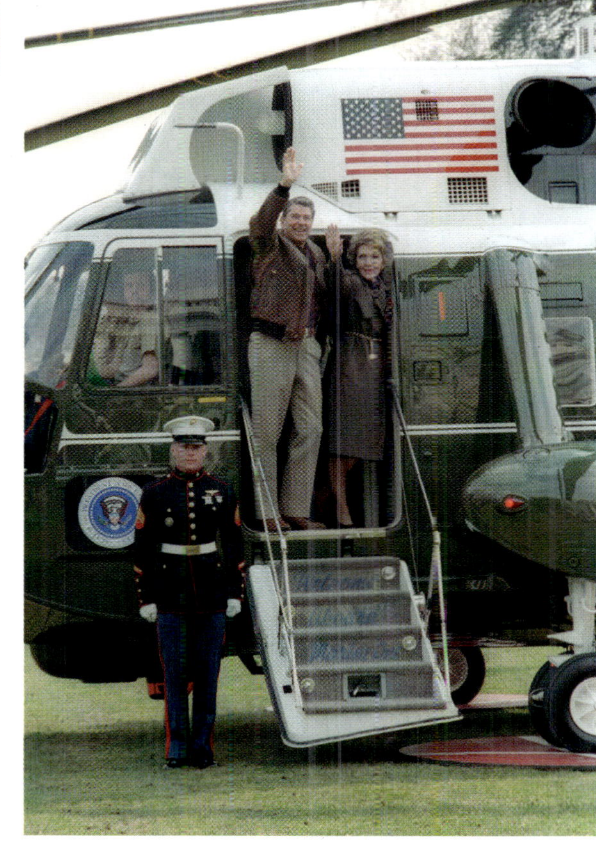

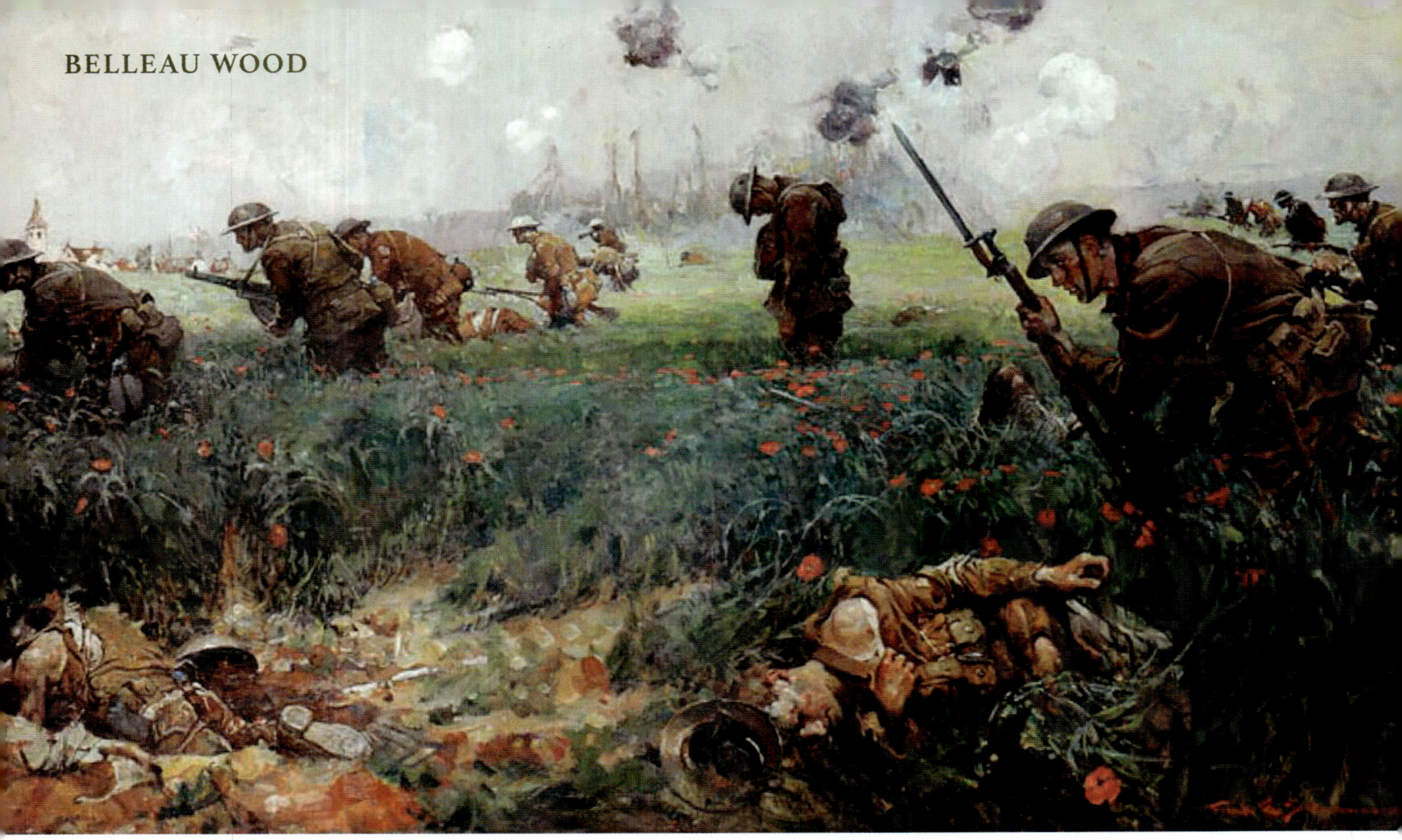

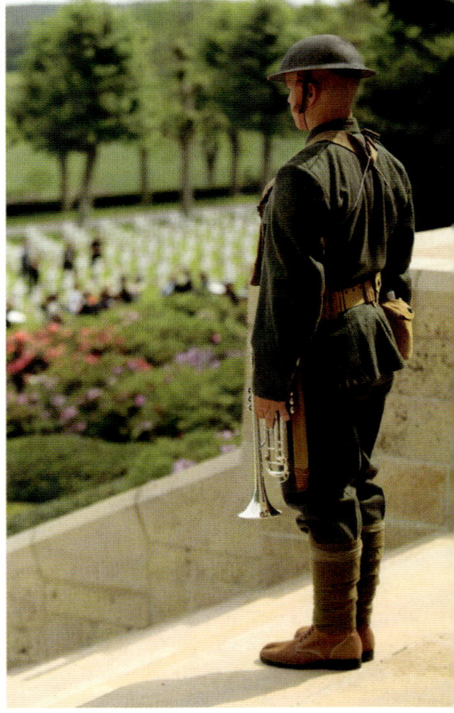

Battle of Belleau Wood

Birth of a legend

ABOVE: The heroism of the 4th Marine Brigade at the Battle of Belleau Wood was immortalised in a series of paintings, created in the aftermath of the battle. (USMC, FRANK SCHOONOVER)

When America entered World War One on April 6, 1917, its military was not ready to fight European armies equipped with machine guns, artillery, poison gas and fighter planes. A crash programme was launched to get the American Expeditionary Force (AEF) ready ship out to France to fight on the Western Front.

A key ingredient that was missing was officers and soldiers with combat experience. This was the chance for the US Marine Corps to show what it could do. From the turn of the century, the marines had led a series of interventions in Central America, known as the 'Banana Wars', because they were aimed at securing US control of trade in the region, particularly banana plantations. US Marines fought in Mexico, Panama, Cuba, Veracruz, Haiti, Santo Domingo and Nicaragua, so almost every marine officer and non-commissioned officer had seen action. To support its interventions, marine regiments were equipped with modern weapons and had their own independent logistics. The marines had also formed their own aviation units and practised air-ground co-operation under battle conditions.

To speed the formation of the AEF, the 17,725-strong corps embarked on a rapid expansion of its fighting strength. By the end of the war, the corps would be more than 70,000-strong. A first wave of volunteers was soon on the way to the Parris Island depot in South Carolina to begin ten weeks of tough training to turn them into marines. By the spring of 1918, the 4th Marine Brigade was in France serving as part of the US Army's 2nd Infantry Division and getting ready to go into the line against the German army.

A huge German spring offensive soon had the French reeling. In a bid to save Paris, the AEF was dispatched to plug a gap in the line. On June 2, the 4th Marine Brigade marched ten kilometres to set up an improvised defence line south of Belleau Wood to blunt the German drive on Paris. By early morning, the marines were in position and had just managed to dig a series of shallow firing posts using their bayonets. Brigade commander US Army General James Harbord famously ordered his marines to "hold where they stand".

During the afternoon of June 3, the Germans surged forward again and moved towards the marines' lines. The German spearhead battalions

RIGHT: A US Marine Corps bugler with the 2nd Marine Division Band, in period uniform, stands waiting for his cue to begin playing taps at Aisne-Marne American Cemetery and Memorial in Belleau in May 2014, to celebrate Memorial Day and mark the 96th anniversary of the battle. (DOD, MASTER SGT CHAD MCMEEN)

advanced across waist-high wheat fields and were unaware that the marines were blocking the way.

Marine commanders let the Germans advance to within 100 metres of their lines before letting their troops open fire, taking the Germans by surprise. Hundreds of Germans were killed or wounded in a few minutes. Reeling from the accurate and sustained marine fire, the Germans were soon retreating.

Captain Lloyd W Williams of the 5th Marine Regiment, was heard encouraging his marines to hold fast, telling them: 'Retreat, hell! We just got here.'

For two more days, the Germans surged towards the marine lines in a desperate bid to break through. The marines held their lines.

On June 6, the marines and their French allies launched a counter-attack to turn back the Germans. A battalion of the 5th Marines was assigned to attack Hill 142, and advanced across the wheat fields with fixed bayonets. The marines ran into a nest of German machine guns, which mowed down hundreds of them. The survivors held off furious German counter-attacks, fighting hand-to-hand. Gunnery Sergeant Ernest Janson won the first US Marine Corps Medal of Honor of World War One in this fighting for killing two Germans at bayonet point. By the end of the afternoon, more than 332 marines were dead or wounded, but the survivors held their positions.

More marine battalions were thrown into the fight to capture Belleau Wood. The attacking units suffered grievous casualties as they launched bayonet charge after bayonet charge across the wheat fields. First Sergeant Dan Daly was heard to encourage his men forward by shouting: "Come on, you sons of bitches. Do you want to live forever?"

The marines eventually fought their way into Belleau Wood and pushed back the German defenders. They suffered 1,087 killed or wounded in the course of the battle, making this the highest-ever number of casualties suffered by the US Marine Corps in a single day at that time.

For the next two weeks, the marines and Germans fought over Belleau Wood. Day after day, each side would launch attacks, which were driven back with heavy losses. It was not until June 26 that the marines were able to report that the last Germans had been driven from the wood. In just over three weeks of fighting, the Americans suffered 9,777 casualties, including 1,811 killed.

Although the heavy casualties were attributed to poor tactics, including attacks in the open with bayonets fixed, the Battle for Belleau Wood was a major success of the 4th Marine Brigade. It kept fighting in the face of horrendous ➔

RIGHT: The countryside around Belleau Wood was shattered by intense artillery fire and illustrated the intensity of the fighting. (USMC ARCHIVES)

BELOW: The 1st Marine Division commemorated the 97th anniversary of the Battle of Belleau Wood with colours flying and a parade in full dress blue uniforms. Generations of marines have paid tribute to their illustrious forefathers who fought in the World War One battle. (USMC)

casualties and eventually captured its objective. The French, British and Germans were very impressed with the fighting qualities of the marines. Back home, the American media and politicians rushed to praise their bravery and heroism. One US newspaper reported that Germans had nicknamed them 'Teufel Hunden', or 'devil dogs', because of their reckless attacks. There is no evidence that the Germans actually used the term to describe the marines, but it quickly entered corps folklore.

A grateful French government renamed the forest as 'Bois de la Brigade de Marine', 'Wood of the Marine Brigade'. Both the 5th and 6th Marine Regiments were awarded the Croix de Guerre decoration three times each. They still wear its insignia on the left shoulder of their blue dress and service uniforms.

The battle was a huge boost to American morale, prompting the AEF's commander General John Pershing to declare: "The deadliest weapon in the world is a United States Marine and his rifle."

While the 4th Marine Brigade was rightly praised for its exploits, it was not the only marine unit to reach France. Soon, the 5th Marine Brigade arrived in France and was assigned to protect Allied supply lines.

The 1st Marine Aviation Force flew fighter and bomber missions over the Western Front during the final months of the war. Its squadrons had managed to fly 57 missions, including 43 in co-operation with the British Royal Air Force and 14 on their own.

The marines dropped more than 33,000lb of bombs and counted four confirmed kills of German fighters and eight 'probables'. Four marine aviators were killed and one pilot and two gunners wounded.

The US Marine Corps' brief exposure to modern warfare in France in 1918 was a crucial event in its development. Many veterans of the war would rise to high command in World War Two. More importantly, the American public came to love and respect their marines as some of the country's most fearsome warriors. That reputation remains to this day, but was earned in blood. Out of the 32,000 marines who served in France, 11,366 became casualties, including 2,459 killed or missing in action.

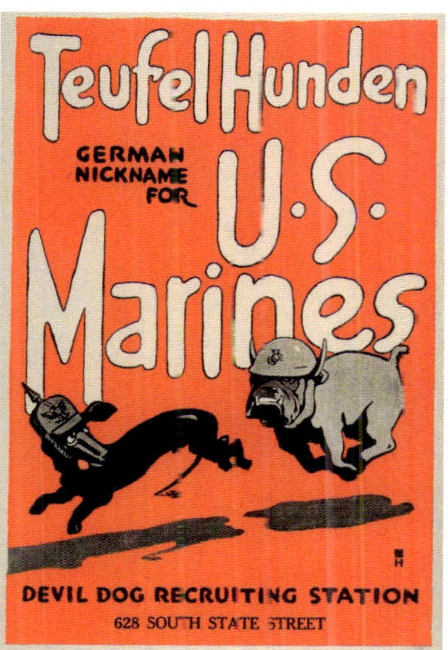

LEFT: After the Battle of Belleau Wood, the legendary 'Teufel Hunden' – 'Devil Dogs' – nickname was adopted in US Marines recruiting posters. (USMC)

ABOVE: Assistant Commandant of the Marine Corps General Gary L Thomas salutes during the Anniversary of Belleau Wood Memorial Ceremony in Belleau Wood, May 26th, 2019. (USMC, SGT WESLEY TIMM)

SUBSCRIBE TODAY!

Amphibious Marines

Getting Ready for the Pacific Campaign

The US Marine Corps 'island-hopping' campaign in the Pacific during World War Two saw some of the biggest amphibious operations ever undertaken and led to major tactical innovations.

In the 1920s, US Marine Corps officers had begun to think seriously about developing a modern amphibious warfare doctrine. Young officers, including Major Earl 'Pete' Ellis, had studied the disastrous British landings at Gallipoli in 1915 and were instrumental in developing ideas about how to conduct amphibious landings against well-prepared enemy defences – in the era of aircraft carriers, long-range bombers and submarines. They identified that America's main enemy would be Japan if war should break out and the conflict would revolve around the control of key islands in the centre of the Pacific. America would have to be able to control these islands to allow the establishment of air and naval bases, which could eventually be used to strike at the Japanese homeland and win the war.

The concept of the Fleet Marine Force (FMF) was developed from 1934 and this envisaged establishing permanent units trained for amphibious operations, supported by purpose-built landing craft and other specialist equipment that could operate across the expanse of the Pacific.

Work to design specialist landing craft started to enable squads of infantry, tanks, vehicles and supplies to be landed across beaches, when harbours were not available. Development began of the Amphibious Vehicle, Tracked (LVT), also known as the Alligator, which was an armoured tractor capable of carrying a squad of marines off ships and then driving over the coral reefs that surrounded many Pacific islands.

At the same time, far-thinking marine officers were working to develop a new doctrine for amphibious warfare. This was aimed at turning the FMF concept into reality, allowing the formation of dedicated amphibious units and the training of specialist personnel.

Firstly, the new doctrine outlined the command relationship between the landing force, naval support and air units. Procedures were developed to call in naval gunfire support from warships against enemy defences along beaches. A key ingredient was setting up a structure to efficiently call in close air support from US Marine Corps aviation

BELOW: A whole family of specialist landing craft was developed by the US Marine Corps in the run-up to World War Two as part of the drive to transform the corps into a specialist amphibious force. (US NATIONAL ARCHIVE)

ABOVE: Amphibious training exercises were carried out at Cape Cod to practise the procedures to land on opposed beaches in 1942 to prepare for the war in the Pacific. (US NATIONAL ARCHIVE)

BELOW: Bringing field guns and other heavy equipment ashore on hostile beaches from landing craft required marines and sailors to learn new skills. (US NATIONAL ARCHIVE)

units. Forward air controllers with radios were assigned to frontline marine units, so they could guide attacking aircraft to their targets. Marine aviators were trained to fly their aircraft off US Navy aircraft carriers to forward airstrips inside bridgeheads ashore. Navy 'Seabee' engineer units were provided with bulldozers and other equipment to allow them to carve runways and dispersal ramps in jungles and other harsh environments.

The 1920s and 1930s saw a rapid expansion of marine aviation units, so by the time the US entered World War Two, the corps had fighter, ground attack, reconnaissance, observation and torpedo bombing squadrons.

Working with the US Navy, marine officers devised the procedure to 'combat load' troop transports – equipment and vehicles needed in the first wave of any amphibious landing were loaded last so they could be off-loaded first, with minimum confusion.

Considerable effort was put into developing procedures to control ship-to-shore movement by large numbers of landing craft, so they could be directed to the right landing beach and their approach synchronised with naval gun fire and air support. Buoys and picket boats were organised to mark the approach routes for waves of landing craft.

On landing beaches, special command teams known as shore parties and led by 'beach masters' were set up. It was their job to take control of beaches and ensure assault troops moved in-land quickly and follow-up supplies were directed to supply dumps. Teams of engineers and pioneers were assigned to the shore parties to construct routes off beaches, build supply dumps and unload supplies into them.

A dedicated amphibious training centre was set up and USMC units were rotated through it to build up experience and expertise. Regimental combat teams (RCT), trained and equipped for amphibious assaults, were set up in the Atlantic and Pacific fleets. As well as infantry elements, each RCT also contained light artillery, logistic troops, engineers, anti-aircraft and signal communication troops, so they could operate independently. From 1935, a series of Fleet Landing Exercises were held to trial these new ideas. In June 1941, the Amphibious Corps consisting of the 1st Marine Division, the 1st Army Division, marine and army air components, commanded ➤

time, the US Marines had much of their specialist equipment and new shipping. The Japanese were waiting and only the lavish use of naval gunfire and air support neutralised the defenders. It took the Americans three days to clear the island. When the battle was over, only 17 Japanese were captured alive.

As the Americans' island-hopping offensive continued, the Japanese put up determined resistance so ever-larger assault forces were needed. The success of the amphibious campaign depended on the organisation skill of the US Navy to pre-load ships with marines, equipment and supplies at the home ports on the west coast of America or Hawaii, before the long voyage to the combat zone. 'Combat trains' of supply ships kept the marines on shore fully stocked with ammunition, food and fuel.

In February 1945, the US Marines embarked on their toughest test yet when they stormed Iwo Jima. More than 21,000 Japanese were dug in on the island when 70,000 marines of the V Amphibious Corps attacked.

by Major General Holland Smith, was set up. He would later command several of the most important amphibious assaults during the Pacific war. At the heart of the Amphibious Corps concept was the integration of air, land and naval forces under a single commander to ensure battlefield success.

The 1st Marine Division and its support units staged a series of divisional level landing exercises on the South Carolina coast in the summer of 1941 to give its commanders and troops experience of large-scale amphibious operations.

The US Marines put their amphibious warfare doctrine to the test on a large scale for the first time during the Guadalcanal campaign in the summer and autumn of 1942, when they were sent to seize the southern Solomon Islands. This saw the 1st Marine Division sail from New Zealand to land on Guadalcanal in August 1942. It did not have much of the new equipment and specialist shipping so still relied largely on open-top motorboats to come ashore from converted troop transport ships.

By the following year, the Americans were taking the offensive in the central Pacific in their drive towards Japan. The first island to be assaulted by the US Marines was Tarawa in November, which was defended by nearly 5,000 well-prepared Japanese forces, dug into deep bunkers and surrounded by minefields. This

The finale of the American drive on Japan was Operation Iceberg to capture the island of Okinawa, which is only 500 kilometres from the Japanese mainland. This required a 180,000-strong American invasion force, made up of the US Marines III Amphibious Corps and US Army soldiers, under the command of the 10th US Army. More than 70,000 Japanese troops and tens of thousands of armed civilians were dug-in as defenders. To protect the island the Japanese deployed 5,500 kamikaze (suicide) aircraft in a bid to destroy the American fleet carrying the assault force. It took more than two months of heavy fighting to clear Okinawa and the last resistance was recorded on July 2. American losses were 49,451, including 12,520 dead or missing and 36,631 wounded. The Japanese lost approximately 110,000 killed, and 7,400 taken prisoner.

Operation Iceberg was the most demanding US amphibious operation of the Pacific campaign and it is all the more remarkable because it was begun even before resistance ended on Iwo Jiwa. The near-simultaneous execution of two massive amphibious operations, on the far side of the Pacific, was testament to the organisation ability of the US Navy and US Marines Corps to marshal amphibious forces on a scale never seen before.

ABOVE: Air support for amphibious landings across the Pacific was provided by US Navy aircraft carriers. (US NATIONAL ARCHIVE)

BELOW: US Marines use an inflatable boat to move casualties out to hospital ships during the Battle of Tarawa in 1943. The ability to 'adapt, improvise and overcome' was central to the ethos of marines fighting in the Pacific. (US NATIONAL ARCHIVE)

Battle of Guadalcanal

The first land victory over Japan

ABOVE: US Marines storm ashore on Guadalcanal, August 7, 1942, to open the way for the first land victory over the Japanese of the war in Pacific.
(US NATIONAL ARCHIVES)

On August 7, 1942, thousands of US Marines waded ashore on beaches along the northern coast of Guadalcanal to open a new front against Imperial Japan. The 1st Marine Division found the beaches undefended, but days later the Japanese mustered thousands of troops to launch furious 'Banzai charge' counter-attacks with fixed bayonets to try to drive the Americans back into the sea.

For six months, the marines battled the Japanese and eventually emerged victorious to inflict the first land defeat of World War Two on Tokyo's army.

This victory turned the tide in the Pacific campaign and opened the way for the US Marine Corps to storm island after island to bring Allied forces within striking distance of the Japanese homeland.

The Battle of Guadalcanal had its origins in decisions by the Japanese to attempt to isolate Australia by capturing the Solomon Islands. This followed weeks of debate in Tokyo over war strategy. The Japanese navy had just been rebuffed at the Battle of Midway, losing four aircraft carriers in a major clash with the US Navy.

RIGHT: US Marines and soldiers bring supplies ashore during the Battle for Guadalcanal.
(US NATIONAL ARCHIVES)

Army leaders proposed adopting a defensive strategy to allow the Japanese Empire to consolidate its strength to withstand the inevitable American counter-attack. This view was opposed by the Japanese navy, which wanted to maintain the strategic initiative and keep the Allies on the run; giving the Americans a chance to rebuild their strength would be fatal, said Tokyo's admirals.

In the early summer of 1942, the decision was made by the Japanese to launch a new offensive to seize the Solomons, a chain of islands 1,700 kilometres off the northeast coast of Australia. Once they had taken these islands and started building air and naval bases, it would have been very difficult for the US to supply Australia and would therefore open the way for a Japanese invasion of the Commonwealth country.

The Allies did not have enough troops and naval forces to try to hold the Solomons, but left a network of coast watchers to monitor Japanese movements. These were former colonel officials, traders and plantation owners, who retreated into the jungle to operate observation posts linked by radio to Allied intelligence headquarters in Australia.

ABOVE: Controlling Henderson Field was central to the 1st Marine Division's successful defence of their embattled enclave on Guadalcanal. (US NATIONAL ARCHIVES)

LEFT: In an unprecedented move, General Alex Vandegrift was awarded the US Medal of Honor "for outstanding and heroic accomplishment above and beyond the call of duty as Commanding Officer of the 1st Marine Division in operations against enemy Japanese forces in the Solomon Islands during August to December 1942". (US NATIONAL ARCHIVES)

In the middle of June, they started reporting that the Japanese had begun to build an airfield on the island of Guadalcanal, in the centre of the Solomons. Soon a garrison of 3,000 Japanese troops were spotted on the island and the coast watchers reported signs that the work on the airfield would be completed soon, to allow aircraft to start arriving.

In Washington DC, the head of the US Navy Admiral Ernest King rapidly realised that the Japanese threat ➤

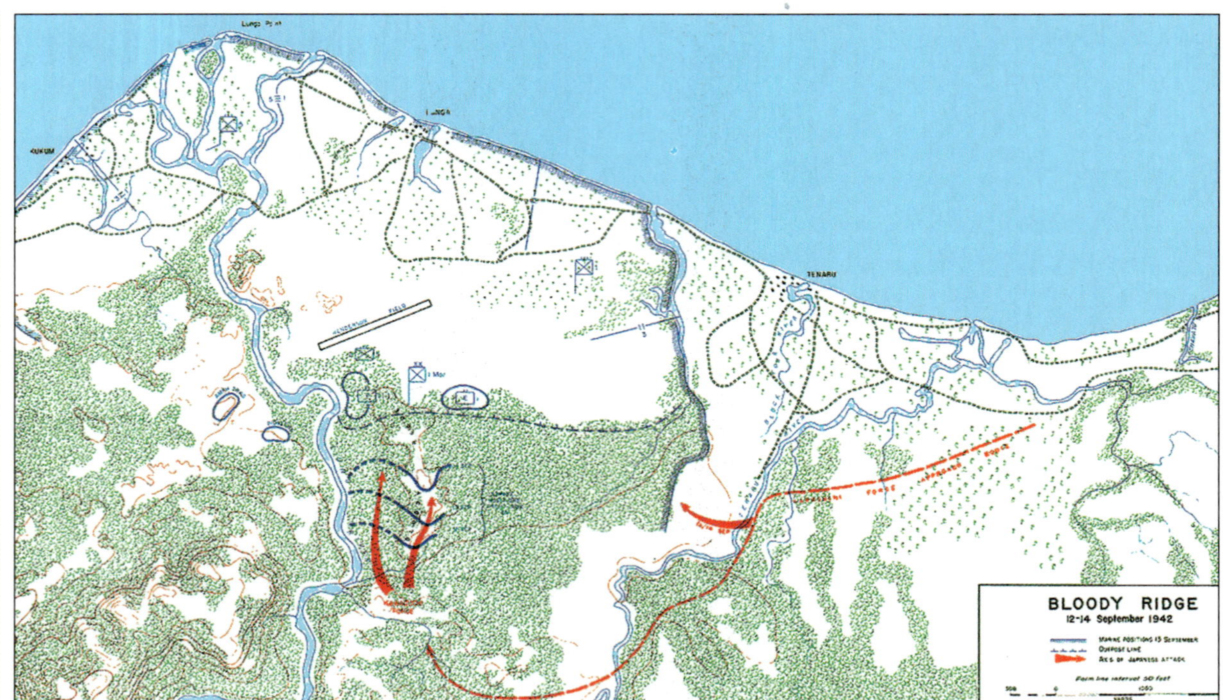

RIGHT: Steamy rainstorms were as much a challenge for General Vandegrift and his marines as the Japanese army: thousands fell victim to tropical diseases during the fighting on Guadalcanal. (US NATIONAL ARCHIVES)

BELOW: Japanese reinforcements marched for days with little food and water before launching frantic Banzai charges against the US lines around Henderson Field. (US NATIONAL ARCHIVES)

to Australia had to be neutralised. Air or commando raids would not be enough. King wanted Guadalcanal to be captured and held to turn the tables on the Japanese. This was to be a job for the 1st Marine Division, under the command of Major General Alexander Vandegrift, which was in the process of relocating from North Carolina to New Zealand, where a US fleet was mustering.

Vandegrift was a veteran professional marine officer, who had played an important role in the development of amphibious warfare tactics. His division was far from ready to go to war; it had

only just been expanded to wartime strength with new recruits who had only signed up in the days after the Japanese attack on Pearl Harbor in December 1941. There were shortages of vital equipment, weapons and ammunition, including landing craft and communications gear to call in naval gunfire support from US Navy warships. More importantly, the division had yet to carry out a full-scale amphibious exercise to test its ability to land on enemy shores. Few of Vandegrift's marines had seen the inside of a landing craft and none of his officers had organised a real landing on an enemy-held beach.

When Vandegrift was briefed on the Guadalcanal operation on June 25, 1942, the general realised his marines would face huge challenges. D-Day for the landing was only five weeks away. On top of this, apart from the reports from the coast watchers there was a huge intelligence void; there were not even any up-to-date maps of the island.

All these deficiencies were recognised by senior Allied naval officers, but they hoped they could take the Japanese by surprise by making a rapid dash to the north coast of Guadalcanal to land Vandegrift's marines. They would then make a rapid advance to capture the strategic airfield, allowing Allied aircraft to fly in air support, allowing the Allies to dominate the skies and seas to prevent Japanese reinforcements being put ashore. Vandegrift's division was reinforced by units of elite marine parachute and raiding battalions to beef up his 'green' force with more experienced personnel.

The Allied fleet and amphibious forces gathered off Fiji in the last week of July and held a brief 'rehearsal', but this did not include a full practise beach landing. The fleet then set sail for the Solomons, aiming to land on Guadalcanal on August 7. In the early hours, the landing force sailed in the channel between Guadalcanal and the neighbouring small islands of Tulagi, Gavutu and Tanambogo. A screen of cruisers and destroyers cleared a route to the landing beach, then put down a barrage on suspected Japanese positions just before dawn. The attack took the enemy by surprise, leading to the few Japanese defenders on the coastline retreating inland.

By complete accident, the beach selected by the Americans for the main body of the 1st Marine Division's landing was completely undefended. This was a stroke of luck. Thousands of marines then scrambled down nets from their transport ships to climb into rudimentary landing craft and other boats to make the brief trip to the shore.

The landing craft hit sand bars some distance out and the marines had to wade ashore, carrying their rifles above their heads. Once on land they fanned out into the jungle >

to secure the beachhead, making room for the follow-up waves of landing craft carrying tanks, artillery, ammunition and supplies. Now the lack of experience and training came into play and soon the beaches were engulfed in chaos as stores were unloaded in no particular order and there was no one on the beaches to receive and organise them.

Vandegrift was determined to exploit his success by advancing five kilometres through the jungle to seize a half-completed airstrip. On the morning of August 8, the first US patrol had pushed through the jungle and reached the airstrip to find it abandoned. The Japanese construction unit had fled the day before, leaving their cooking pots and rice bowls behind. Soon Vandegrift's marines had set up a defensive perimeter and started to move their supplies inland from the beachhead.

The Americans then suffered their first setback of the campaign – a strong Japanese cruiser squadron appeared and drove off the Allied naval force, leaving Vandegrift and his marines isolated ashore.

The general and his marines were determined to hold out and soon set to work to fortify their positions. Marines took over abandoned Japanese engineering equipment to finish off the runway to allow the first contingent of US Marine Corps fighter aircraft to be flown ashore from US Navy aircraft carriers.

After their naval success, the Japanese were able to land reinforcements on the island to start an offensive to destroy the American incursion. A regiment under Colonel Kiyonao Ichiki was put ashore on August 18, 20km to the east of the American bridgehead. Rather than wait for the full Japanese army force to land and attack with overwhelming strength, Ichiki, who held the Americans in contempt, decided to launch an attack with his 2,000-strong regiment, despite being outnumbered by the marines.

The attack force marched through thick jungles to reach their start line on the eastern flank of the American bridgehead. There were no roads, so the Japanese artillery and much of the ammunition had to be left behind. As a result, Ichiki launched his men into action on the morning of August 21 without any effective artillery barrage being put down on the American positions. Ichiki just lined up his men, ordered them to fix bayonets and then led them in a Banzai charge into the face of American defences. It was slaughter.

Marine machine guns, artillery and mortars mowed down hundreds of Japanese attackers. The surviving Japanese troops were pinned down on the edge of American lines for the rest of day, trading fire with the marines. Vandegrift launched flanking attacks that eventually trapped Ichiki and his troops in a small 'pocket'. Aircraft from the airstrip, which had now been renamed Henderson Field, joined the battle flying strafing missions against the trapped enemy. A tank attack was organised to complete the defeat of Ichiki's decimated force. The Japanese colonel managed to escape during the night and, as per the Japanese military's code of honour, he set fire to his regimental colour and then committed hara-kiri, or suicide, with his sword.

This success was not the end of Japanese attempts to capture Henderson Field. A larger force was landed during the final days of August and began massing within

striking range of Vandegrift's enclave. US warships were still unable to get through to land reinforcement and supplies. Extra aircraft were flown in from US Navy aircraft carriers to bolster air cover over Vandegrift's marines, who were surviving on limited food supplies and were having to ration their ammunition. Tropical diseases were starting to take their toll and the 'walking wounded' were rapidly

discharged from field hospitals to go back to foxholes around the perimeter. To try to disrupt the Japanese build-up, the special operations Marine Raiders staged a night attack on the suspected Japanese headquarters, recovering important intelligence.

The Japanese build-up continued and culminated on September 12, when an all-out attack was launched against the southern sector of the

American bridgehead, known as 'Bloody Ridge'.

This time, the Japanese were more respectful of the Americans. Japanese warships cruised off-shore and bombarded the marine positions to cover a night infiltration attack. Small groups of Japanese troops crawled through the bush and jungle towards American foxholes. They managed to take several isolated marine positions and ended up surrounding a platoon of Marine Raiders, who had to fight their way back to American lines.

During the evening of September 13, three battalions of 2 000 Japanese were launched forward in a Banzai charge against Bloody Ridge in a bid to overrun Marine Raiders' lines, while Japanese warships bombarded the American positions. The marines' firepower inflicted huge casualties, but the marines had to pull back up the ridge. Further attacks were pressed home during the night and by dawn the Japanese were within 1,000 metres of Henderson Field's runway.

Now, Vandegrift decided to attack. Marine fighters took off to strafe the surviving Japanese, as artillery and mortars pounded their positions. Exposed on the open ridge, the Japanese could not hold on to their gains and were soon retreating back into the jungle. The marines counted the bodies of more than 1,200 dead ➤

LEFT: Evacuating a wounded marine from the jungle during the Battle for Guadalcanal. (US NATIONAL ARCHIVES)

BELOW: Colonel Evans Carlson led the 2nd Marine Raider Battalion, famously known as Carlson's Raiders. His Raider unit launched several daring missions behind Japanese lines to keep the enemy off balance and collect valuable intelligence. (US NATIONAL ARCHIVES)

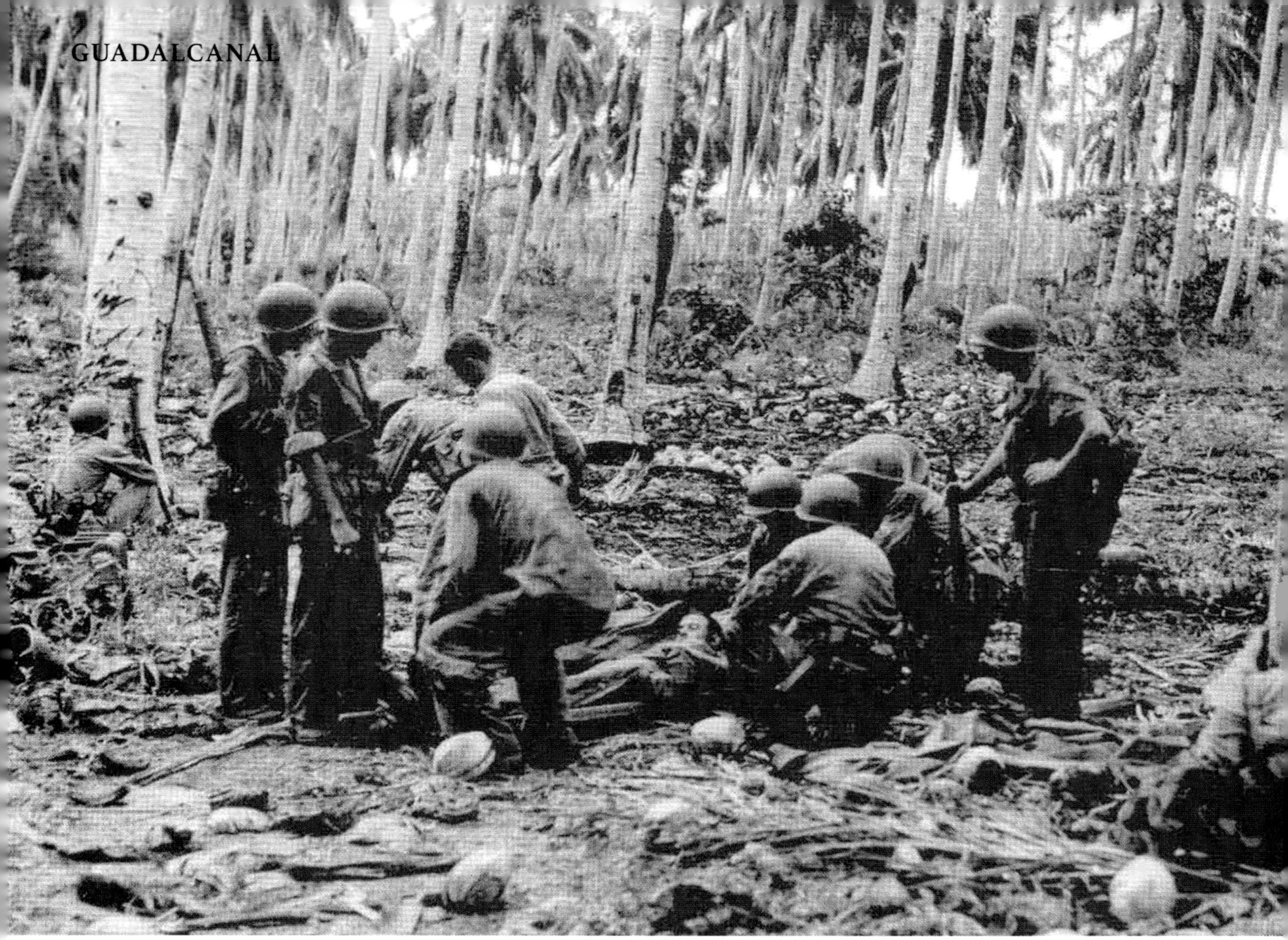

ABOVE: As the Japanese retreated in the latter half of 1942, there were several determined rearguard battles against pursuing marines.
(US NATIONAL ARCHIVES)

Japanese when they edged forward to inspect the carnage. American losses were just as bad with more than 400 killed or wounded in the battle.

Over the next month, both the American and Japanese fleets were able to dodge past each other to land reinforcements: Vandegrift received more than 6,000 extra marines and US Army soldiers; the Japanese put ashore 20,000 fresh troops and a contingent of tanks.

The Japanese managed to trek through the jungles to launch one final attack on the American bridgehead on October 23. Over two days, the Japanese launched massive attacks involving more than 5,000 troops at a time. US artillery, mortars and aircraft inflicted thousands of casualties. American firepower won the day, and the Japanese assault soon faltered, leaving behind 3,500 dead.

RIGHT: Marine mortar crew provided invaluable fire support during the vicious battles with the Japanese on Guadalcanal in 1942.
(US NATIONAL ARCHIVES)

The Japanese retreated back into the jungle and called for reinforcements to renew the attack. American naval and air forces were now cruising around Guadalcanal in strength and managed to intercept the Japanese convoy carrying the reinforcements, sinking six out of the 11 troops transports. Only 2,000 Japanese soldiers managed to get ashore. At the end of December 1942, the Imperial General Staff in Tokyo realised the game was up and ordered the surviving 11,000 Japanese troops to fall back along the western coast of Guadalcanal to be evacuated.

By the first week of February 1943, all the Japanese survivors had been lifted off the evacuation beaches at night. Vandegrift and his 1st Marine Division had by now been replaced by US Army units and the 2nd Marine Division.

The Battle of Guadalcanal had blunted the Japanese bid to isolate Australia and turned the tide in the Pacific. Vandegrift and his marines proved more than a match for the Japanese, despite their lack of time to prepare for their missions. Their victory was a major boost to US morale, at home and across the

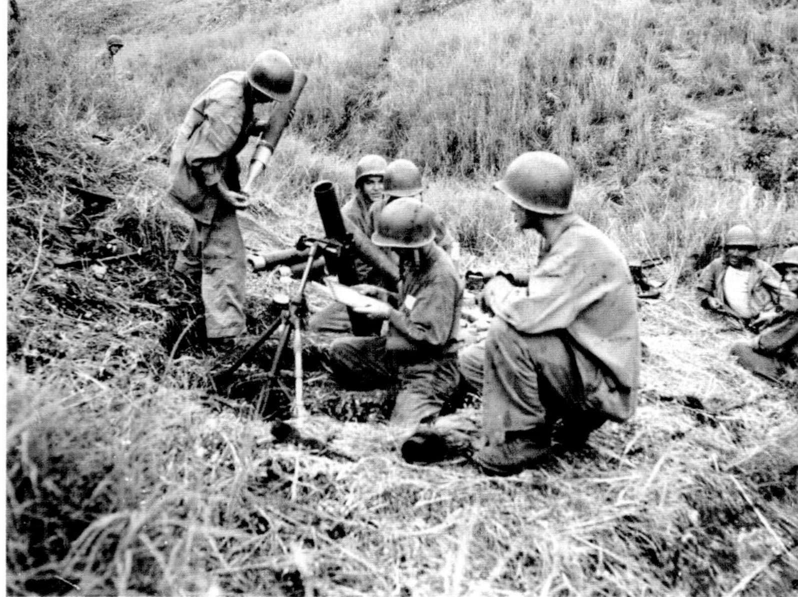

ABOVE: Columns of marines pursued the Japanese across Guadalcanal, fighting through thick jungles to keep the enemy on the run. (US NATIONAL ARCHIVES)

Pacific theatre. No longer would the Americans be on the defensive: Guadalcanal was the first US Marine Corps victory of World War Two; its marine riflemen had shown they could fight and its officers, aviators, artillery gunners and supply troops had demonstrated that they could work together to achieve victory.

Today's marine air-ground task force concept has its roots in the defence of Henderson Field in August 1942.

The 1st Marine Division paid a heavy price for its victory, losing 650 killed in action, 1,278 suffering battle wounds, a further 8,580 contracting malaria and 31 missing in action. Its enemy's losses dwarfed those numbers, with the Imperial Japanese army suffering 19,000 casualties, including 8,500 killed in action.

LEFT: The Japanese transport 'Kinugawa Maru' lies beached at Guadalcanal in November 1943, symbolising Japan's first major defeat or land in World War Two. (US NAVY)

Iwo Jima

Amphibious victory

The image of US Marines raising the Stars and Stripes over Iwo Jima's Mount Suribachi is iconic. It was soon reproduced on newspaper front covers around the world. After World War Two, it was the inspiration for the building of the United States Marine Corps War Memorial in Arlington Ridge Park, just outside Washington DC.

Iwo Jima has a special place in the history of the US Marine Corps. The bloody battle cost its V Amphibious Corps 26,000 casualties, including 6,821 dead. Twenty-two marines won the Medal of Honor during the campaign, representing 28% of the 82 distinguished medals awarded to marines in World War Two. Four US Navy medical corps personnel serving alongside the marines

also received America's highest decoration for their part in the land fight for Iwo Jima. The intensity of the fighting is graphically illustrated by the Japanese casualties: out of the 21,000 defenders, just over 1,000 survived; the rest died while resisting the Americans.

As a result, the top marine commander in the Pacific, Lieutenant General Holland 'Howlin' Mad' Smith, said: "This fight is the toughest we've run across in 168 years."

The flag-raising generated huge excitement among the marines fighting to capture the island and is credited with boosting morale at a key part in the battle. It also cemented the corps' reputation as America's most effective fighting force. Famously, Smith was accompanying Secretary of the Navy James Forrestal ashore at Iwo Jima at the time of the flag-raising. He remarked to Smith: "Holland, the raising of that flag on Suribachi means a Marine Corps for the next five hundred years."

In October 1944, the US Navy commander of the Pacific theatre, Admiral Chester Nimitz ordered Smith and his marines to capture Iwo Jima because of its strategic position, just three hours flying time from Tokyo. Seizing the two airfields on the island would allow US Army Air Force Boeing B-29 Stratofortress heavy bombers to divert if they ran into trouble during their trips to attack the Japanese capital from airfields on the Mariana Islands. American strategists also wanted to deny the Japanese the chance to use the airfields to strike at US bombers as they flew to their targets. ❯

ABOVE: The first wave of marines arrived on Iwo Jima in hundreds of LVT(A) vehicles that were known as Alligators to the marines.
(US NATIONAL ARCHIVES)

LEFT: US Navy warships and aircraft bombarded Iwo Jima for weeks ahead of the landing by V Amphibious Corps. The barren and featureless terrain convinced American air and naval commanders that few Japanese defenders could have survived the bombardment. Mount Suribachi is at the bottom of the island.
(US NATIONAL ARCHIVES)

ABOVE: As the assault waves of LVT(A) went ashore, US Navy destroyers close to the coast put down naval gunfire on suspected Japanese positions. (US NATIONAL ARCHIVES)

RIGHT: Follow-up waves by landing craft behind the LVT(A) enabled marine infantry to secure the beachhead. (US NATIONAL ARCHIVES)

RIGHT: Once the main landing beaches were secured, marines backed by LVT(A) tried to push inland, but quickly ran into fierce resistance from the dug-in Japanese defenders. (US NATIONAL ARCHIVES)

battle. He dubbed them the 'Courage Division' and ordered them to "use every moment you have, whether during air raids or during battle, to build strong positions that enable you to smash the enemy at a ratio of ten to one".

Iwo Jima's area is less than 20 square kilometres and in 1945 it was largely devoid of trees or other vegetation. The small civilian population had long been evacuated to allow the build-up of the island's defence to be accelerated. Weeks of air and naval bombardment added to the impression that Iwo Jima was a desolate rock: it appeared to be little more than one big beach, with the

A few weeks later, US warships started to bombard the island to clear a path for the invasion. Battleships and cruisers made regular forays to blast at any sign of Japanese activity. In the middle of November 1944, B-29s joined the bombardment. Soon, American intelligence analysts were reporting that every building or man-made structure on the island had been destroyed. Air and naval commanders confidently predicted that defences had been smashed and that the Japanese would put up minimal resistance. Smith and his marines were not convinced; their experience of fighting the Japanese over the past two-and-a-half years told them they could expect fanatical resistance when they went ashore.

Since June 1944, the Japanese commander of the island, Lieutenant General Tadamichi Kuribayashi, had been preparing his troops for

Iwo Jima to begin intensifying the bombardment. Still the Japanese held their fire. On February 17, a flotilla of US small craft made a foray towards the island to drop off frogmen to swim towards the landing beaches to identify minefields and underwater obstacles. This convinced the Japanese that the invasion was under way, and their coastal gun batteries opened fire. This revealed their position and allowed the American warships to blast many of them.

The main landing was confirmed for two days' time on beaches on the southeastern coast of the island, just to the north of Mount Suribachi. Immediately behind the beach was Airfield No 1. Eight marine battalions were to be landed in the first wave of the assault, carried by a fleet of 482 Amphibious Vehicle, Tracked – LVT(A) – or Alligators. These tracked armoured vehicles each carried a squad of 24 marines, others were fitted with rotating gun turrets to provide fire support. Two marine divisions would land on D-Day, the 5th Division on the left and the 4th Division on the right.

On the morning of D-Day, the US fleet moved to 4,000 metres off the invasion beach and began launching the LTV(A) in waves of 60-80 vehicles at a time. In 45 minutes the first marines were ashore. Unlike in other Pacific Island battles, the Japanese decided to hold their fire to allow the Americans to land un-opposed.

Once the first Alligators were ashore, they unloaded their ➤

southern end of the island dominated by Mount Suribachi.

Kuribayashi determined that his troops would stand no chance against the Americans if they fought in the open and ordered his men to start digging. For months they built concrete pillboxes, trenches, foxholes and artillery bunkers. These were all linked by kilometres of tunnels, to allow the defenders to retreat safely underground for protection against American bombardments. In the north of the island, the Japanese fortified a network of deep caves, turning them into underground headquarters, supply dumps, hospitals and artillery positions. The Japanese commander imposed tight fire discipline on his troops to prevent them opening fire until the main American landing force was within range.

Smith made equally meticulous preparations. The V Amphibious Corps was the best equipped formation the US Marine Corps ever sent into action. Its commanders and most of its marines were all experienced combat veterans. Nothing was left to chance, with a full-scale rehearsal taking place on an island with a similar shape and terrain to Iwo Jima. In an innovative move, Native Americans from the Navajo tribe were drafted as radio operators to be trained to call down naval gun fire. As no Japanese had ever learned the Navajo language, the Native American radio operators could send messages without requiring them to be coded, allowing calls for fire support to transmitted in a matter of seconds, rather than more than 30 minutes if they had to be encoded.

D-Day was set for February 19, 1944, and a few days earlier the fleet of 450 US Navy vessels appeared off

RIGHT: The marines paused on the edge of the landing beaches before moving inland to capture Airfield No 1.

marines who started to push inland to cross the 2,000-metre-wide peninsula to capture Airfield No 1. As they moved off and pushed 300 metres from the beach, the Japanese emerged from their tunnels to open fire. Taken by surprise, the marines dived for whatever cover they could find and started to return fire. It was difficult to work out where the Japanese were. One minute they would open fire, then they would disappear back underground. The only way to clear the enemy was to inch forward to drop demolition charges into the Japanese positions or use flame-throwers.

This battle went on for a full day before the marines managed to push through to the eastern shore of the island and isolated Mount Suribachi. It cost them hundreds killed and wounded.

For three days, the 5th Marine Division pushed south to clear Mount Suribachi. This would neutralise the peak that allowed the Japanese to rain fire on the landing beaches and prevented the operation of Airfield No 1.

On the morning of February 23, the famous flag-raising occurred. A 40-strong marine patrol penetrated Japanese lines and made it to the top of the peak. The incident is now the stuff of legend and involved two separate flag-raising events. At around 10am a platoon from the 2nd Battalion, 28th Marine Regiment got to the summit and raised a flag given to them by the crew of the USS *Missoula*. The flag-raising was seen on the landing beaches and immediately raised a cheer from the marines and sailors on the beachhead. However, it could not be seen on northern slopes of the island so a decision was taken to find a bigger flag. Navy Secretary Forrestal also wanted the flag as a souvenir, much to the fury of the marines on the mountain. So, the 2nd Battalion's commanding officer, Lieutenant Colonel Chandler Johnson, sent an officer out to the fleet to find a bigger flag – he came back with the famous flag that had been flying over a navy depot at Pearl Harbor on the day of the Japanese attack in 1941. By noon, the new flag had been carried to the summit and was raised in front

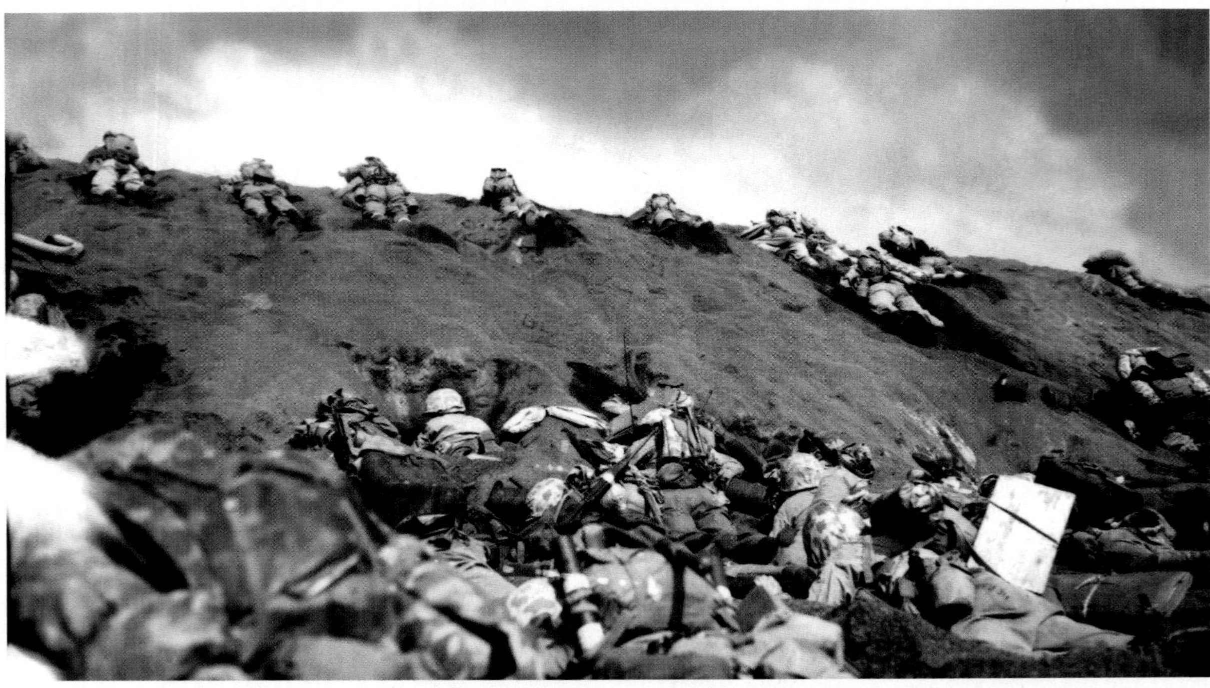

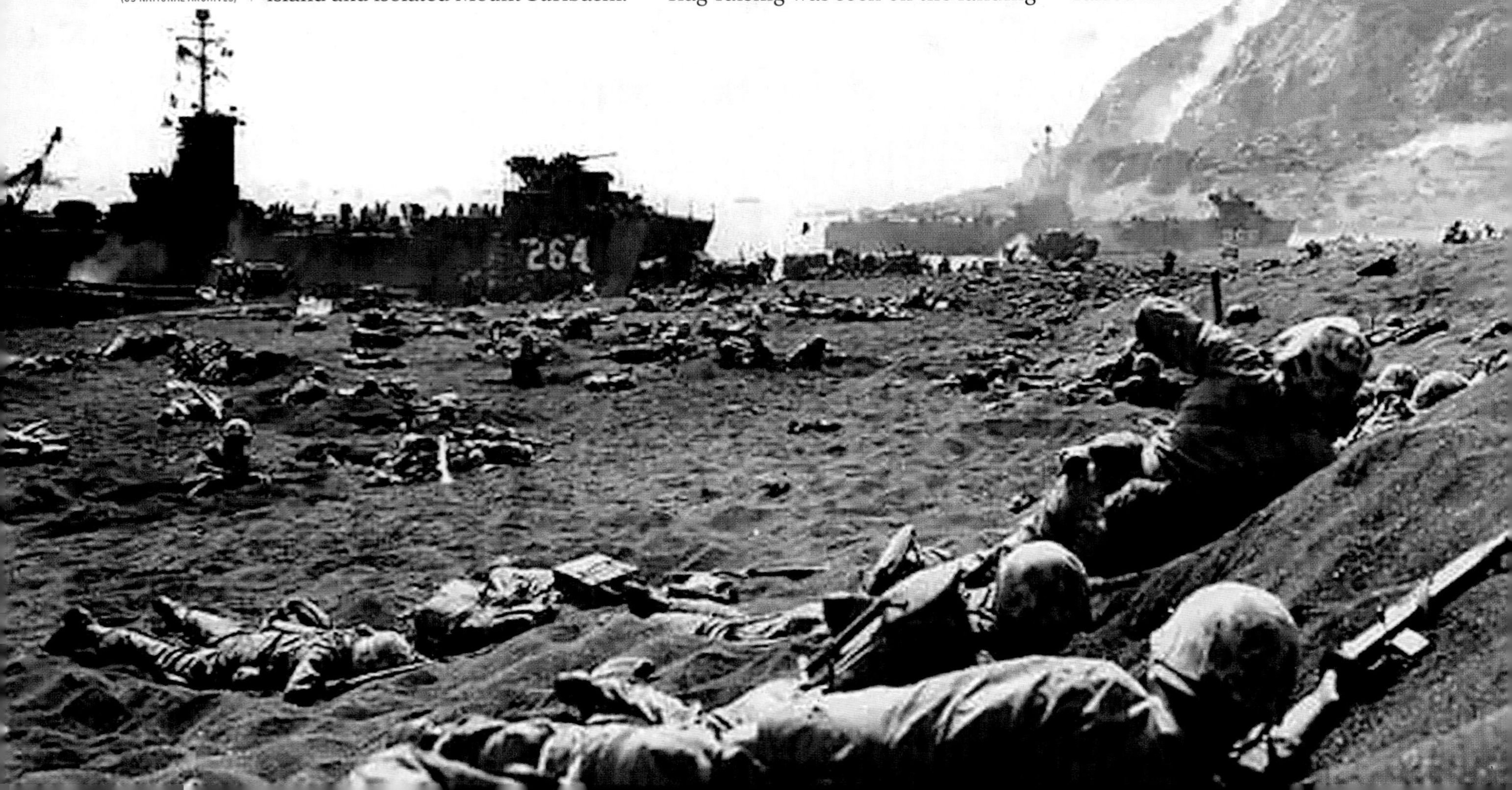

BELOW: Iwo Jima was covered in volcanic sand and there was little vegetation to provide cover to the marines as they awaited the order to move off the landing beaches. Mount Suribachi, which dominated the island, can be seen in the distance. (US NATIONAL ARCHIVES)

of Associated Press photographer, Joe Rosenthal. The rest, as they say, is history.

Although the flag-raising gave the impression of victory, the Battle for Iwo Jima was far from over.

The two marine divisions now swung round to sweep up the remainder of the island. To bolster the offensive, the 3rd Marine Division was brought ashore and positioned in the centre of the line, between the 5th and 4th Divisions.

By February 24, Airfield No 1 had been cleared, but the Japanese were making the Americans pay for every metre of ground. The Japanese tunnel network stretched back to the north coast of the island and there were still thousands of ardent defenders holding out.

Squads of marines had to crawl forward to clear every Japanese trench and bunker. The Navajo radio operators sent more than 800 messages to the fleet calling for gunfire support to blast Japanese positions.

Day after day, the advance struggled forward as position after position was cleared with grenades, demolition charges, flame-throwers or tank fire. The Japanese took a heavy toll, using their tunnels to stage hit-and-run attacks on the marines. Often, they would emerge behind the American lines to take marines by surprise.

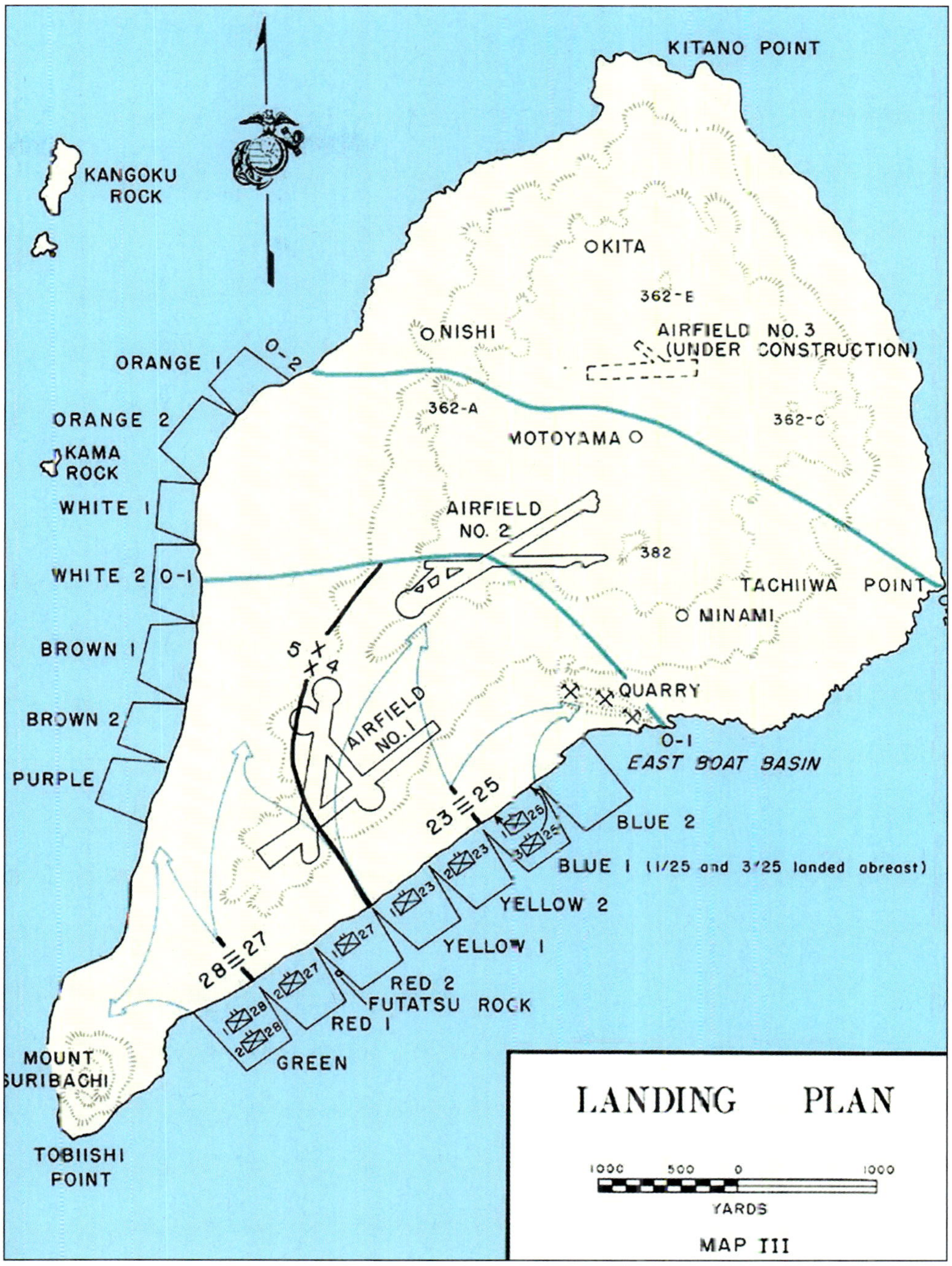

Some marine units were reduced by 50% casualties, but their commanders kept pressing the advance forward.

On March 9, a patrol from the 3rd Marine Division was able to push forward to reach the northern coast of the island effectively cutting the Japanese defenders in half. Now, the last Japanese survivors started to stage a series of desperate Banzai charges against the marines as they began to run out of food and ammunition. Rather than surrender, whole Japanese units would emerge from their tunnels and caves to rush at the marines with bayonets fixed, led by their officers waving ceremonial swords. Invariably, the marines just machine-gunned the Japanese by the hundred. In one position, the marines counted the bodies of more than 650 attackers. ➤

ABOVE: The small size of Iwo Jima constricted the US assault units, which landed on the southeastern side of the island, then moved north and south to destroy the last pockets of Japanese resistance. (USMC HISTORY DIVISION)

LEFT: A platoon of the 2nd Battalion, 28th Marine Regiment, raised the first Stars and Stripes on Mount Suribachi at around 10am on February 23. Later in the day, a second flag-raising event was immortalised by Joe Rosenthal's iconic photograph. (US NATIONAL ARCHIVES)

RIGHT: Flame-throwers were often the only way to halt Japanese soldiers resisting from within heavily fortified pillboxes, bunkers and caves.
(US NATIONAL ARCHIVES)

BELOW: After the marine infantry pushed forward, the landing beach was turned into a logistics zone, where food and ammunition were brought ashore and casualties evacuated out to the fleet.
(US NATIONAL ARCHIVES)

Resistance continued for almost two weeks, with a final surprise attack by 300 Japanese taking place against a marine bivouac area on the night of March 25/26, reputedly led by their commander, General Kuribayashi. The Japanese took the Americans by surprise and silently slashed tents, bayoneted sleeping men and lobbed hand grenades. For several hours, the Americans and Japanese fought hand-to-hand, but by dawn all the Japanese had been killed, including their general. His body was never identified as he had removed his rank insignia before emerging from his subterranean command post to lead his troops on their final foray.

It took another nine days for the marines to sweep Iwo Jima for the last holdouts of starving and demoralised Japanese; remarkably, the Americans rounded up 867 prisoners – mostly wounded – to join the 216 captured over the previous month. These were the only survivors from the 20,933 Japanese garrison.

Even before the last pockets of Japanese resistance were mopped up, US Navy Seabee combat construction engineers had set to work to repair Iwo Jima's airfields. On March 4, the first B-29 that was running short on fuel landed on the island – by the end of the war, 850 of the heavy bombers had used the island's airfields, saving the lives of more than 9,000 aviators and $1.5 billion worth of aircraft.

In April, the first long-range escort mission by North American P-51 Mustang fighters was flown over Japan from the island, further reducing losses among the American bomber crews.

The 34-day battle for Iwo Jima was the last amphibious assault of the Pacific campaign fought almost exclusively by the US Marine Corps. Its strategic significance was immediately apparent to the survivors of the battle who could watch the stream of B-29s arriving at the island's airfield. Little did they know that far away in Washington DC, President Harry Truman and his military advisors were shocked by the furious Japanese resistance and heavy American casualties. If this was how the Japanese fought on a small featureless island, what kind of fight would they put up to defend their home island when Allied troops launched a full-scale invasion?

Within weeks, Truman resolved to use the new atomic bomb as soon as possible to try to defeat Japan without the need for an invasion.

Landing at Inchon

Turning point of the Korean War

RIGHT: US Marines head for the landing beaches at Inchon as part of General Douglas McArthur's daring operation that turned the tide of the Korean war. (US NATIONAL ARCHIVE)

BELOW: Landing craft of the first and second waves approach Red Beach on September 15, 1950, while the destroyer USS *De Haven* provided covering fire. (US NAVY)

In September 1950, the American forces in Korea were on the ropes. Barely two months before, communist forces had launched a surprise attack across the 38th Parallel and chased US and South Korean troops down to the port of Busan (also called Pusan) in the southeast corner of the Korean peninsula.

The southern troops of the Republic of Korea (ROK) army had been decimated, losing more than 70,000 of their 90,000-strong army. When the US Army's 24th Infantry Division was dispatched from Japan to try to halt the advance by North Korean troops it was overrun, losing 36,000 dead and nearly 3,000 captured, including its commander.

Over August, US reinforcements stabilised the Busan bridgehead, but the commander of the US forces in the Far East, General of the Army Douglas MacArthur, said decisive action was needed to defeat the communist forces. A frontal assault out of Busan would take time and risk heavy casualties. He wanted to land US forces behind communist lines and try to cut off the bulk of their troops in the south, opening the way for the complete liberation of all of the Korean peninsula.

At a strategic level, the amphibious landing was very attractive, but making it actually happen was to prove more of a challenge. At the end of World War Two, the US Marine Corps had been downsized as part of the demobilisation of America's fighting forces. It was hoped that America's monopoly of atomic weapons would deter its enemies. As a result, the main amphibious formation in the Pacific, the 1st Marine Division was reduced to little more than a regimental combat team. Similar reduction took place in US Navy amphibious shipping and landing craft.

Gen MacArthur at first tried to mobilise US Army units in Japan for the invasion, but they were either unsuitable or tied up in the Busan bridgehead. However, the

leadership of the US Marine Corps was already thinking ahead and had started to bring the 1st Division up to combat strength.

Crucially, the marines decided to call up thousands of World War Two-era reservists to fill out the ranks of the 1st Division. A flotilla of amphibious ships set sail from the west coast of the continental US and the 1st Division's commander, Major General Oliver Smith, flew out to Japan to start working on the Inchon plan with MacArthur's staff. Smith was a military history enthusiast and former head of the corps' school at Quantico in Virginia. He was nicknamed the 'Professor' because of his thoughtful and careful planning of combat operations.

MacArthur picked the port of Inchon (now spelled Incheon) on Korea's west coast as the target for the landing. It was only 30 kilometres away from the South Korean capital, Seoul, and would allow US troops to rapidly advance to liberate it.

To reach the landing beaches, the amphibius fleet would have

ABOVE: General of the Army Douglas MacArthur watched the landings from the bridge of amphibious command ship USS *Mount McKinley*.
(US NATIONAL ARCHIVE)

sail through narrow channels that were swept by strong tides. This meant only a few days a month were suitable for the landing. This pointed to September 15 as the ideal date for the landing. If this was missed, the landing would be delayed for a month, and MacArthur's troops would have to conduct their offensive as winter was starting.

With time pressing to meet the deadline, the pressure was on Smith and his marines. Fortunately, almost all the senior marine officers were World War Two veterans and the 1st Division was full of experienced hands from the Pacific campaign. There was no time for a rehearsal and the invasion fleet had to sail without one. There were not enough landing craft to bring ashore all the division's three regiments in one wave, so the assault was divided into three phases on three separate beaches.

To try to ensure surprise, the main landing was to take place without a sustained bombardment to neutralise the communist beach defences and without navigation lights. A team of special forces operated at a key moment just after midnight on September 15 to guide the invasion force to the landing beaches.

The first landing was made on Green Beach on Wolmi Island, just off Inchon port, by the 3rd Battalion, 5th Marines. It caught the North Koreans off-balance and, by noon, they had cleared the island of the outnumbered communist troops. More than 200 North Koreans were killed and 130 captured; the

LEFT: (USMC HISTORY DIVISION)

ABOVE: Lieutenant Baldomero Lopez leading his platoon over the seawall that blocked Red Beach. Minutes later, he was killed trying to prevent his men being hit by a grenade, by lying on top of it as it detonated. He was posthumously awarded Medal of Honor for his bravery. (US NATIONAL ARCHIVE)

RIGHT: US Navy warships cruised offshore throughout the landings to provide naval gunfire support as the 1st Marine Division pushed inland. (US NATIONAL ARCHIVE)

BELOW: The first-wave landing craft carrying the 1st Marine Division approached Inchon in the early hours of September 15, 1950. (US NATIONAL ARCHIVE)

marines suffered just 14 casualties. Until the rest of the force was onshore, the 3rd Battalion set up a blocking position at the end of the causeway that connected the island with Inchon city.

As the tide came in later in the afternoon, the second wave of marines was launched to capture Red and Blue Beaches. By now the communist defenders were fully alerted. The landing craft and landing ship tanks (LSTs) heading to Red Beach carrying the other battalions of the 5th Marines came under machine gun and mortar fire. Gunners on the LSTs returned fire, allowing the assault marines to get off the beach and storm Cemetery Hill, which had been turned into a strong point by the communists.

A seawall along the beach temporarily delayed the advance. Improvised wooden ladders carried in the landing craft were now brought up to allow the marines to get off the beach. Communist troops contested this move and several fire fights started – a grenade was thrown at the assault troops, prompting Lieutenant Baldomero Lopez to dive on one

grenade to protect his troops. The officer was posthumously awarded the Medal of Honor for his bravery.

By the evening, marine spearheads had reached the end of the causeway, allowing the troops on Wolmi island to start moving inland.

The third landing of the day took place on Blue Beach to the south of Inchon, which involved the 1st Marine Regiment coming ashore from another flotilla of LSTs. Communist gunners initially put up strong resistance, hitting one LST hard and causing it to sink. US destroyers and aircraft were now called forward to silence the resistance. Once ashore, the 1st Regiment quickly cleared away the disorganised and demoralised North Korea defenders, who either retreated or surrendered whenever they were approached by the marines. For the marine veterans of the Pacific campaign, the lack of organised resistance was a big relief; the North Korean army was nowhere near as fanatical as the Imperial Japanese army.

By the evening of September 15, the 1st Marine Division was ashore in strength in Inchon. The city and its nearby port complex were being swept by marine patrols to round up communist stragglers. US Navy Seabee combat construction

engineers started to build a pontoon dock near Green Beach to allow LSTs to unload vehicles directly onto the harbour wall.

General MacArthur had watched the landing from the command ship USS *Mount McKinley* and was keen to get ashore to savour the success.

During the second day of the operation, MacArthur pushed Smith to move rapidly inland to capture Kimpo airfield, allowing Allied aircraft to begin reinforcing the marines' bridgehead. There appeared to be few communist forces near Inchon, so MacArthur wanted to capitalise his success. As the 5th Marines moved inland on September 16, they found their advance blocked by six Soviet-made T-34/85 heavy tanks. The marines went to ground and called up air support to see off the tank threat. Eight Vought F4U Corsairs of Marine Fighter Squadron VMF-214 appeared overhead and started to engage the tanks with cannons and rockets, knocking out two and forcing the rest to retreat. Now M26 Pershing tanks of the 1st Marine Tank Battalion arrived and finished off three more of the T-34/85s, allowing the 5th Regiment to continue its advance.

This was not the last of the communist tanks. In the early hours

LEFT: After pushing inland from their beachheads, the marines had to clear the Inchon port and town of pockets of North Korean resistance. (US NATIONAL ARCHIVE)

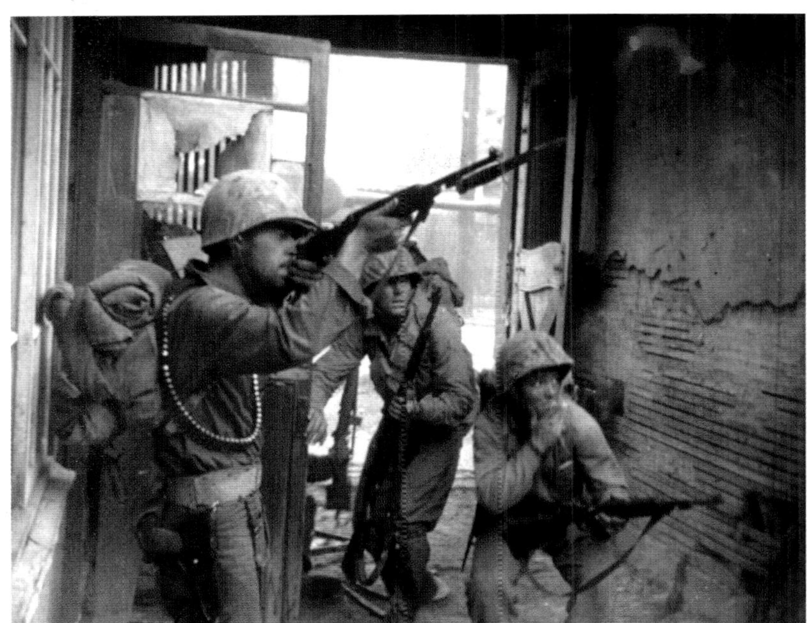

of September 17, another six-strong tank force, backed by more than 250 infantry, approached the 5th Marines in the dark. The tanks got to within 50 metres of the forward marine position before being detected. A quick-thinking marine, Private First Class Walter C Monegan, engaged the first tank with a bazooka, setting it on fire. As the tank commander tied to escape his burning turret, Monegan opened fire and killed him. The 1st Tanks now moved forward and engaged the rest of the T-34/82s, knocking out the rest. Marine infantrymen opened up on the communist troops, who fled leaving more than 100 dead behind.

Later in the day, the 5th Marines had captured Kimpo airfield and the road to Seoul seemed open. MacArthur and his senior commanders were now ashore and went forward to inspect the knocked-out communist tanks, which were the first heavy armour ever encountered by US Marines.

By now the US Army's 7th Infantry Divisions and a contingent of ROK Marines were coming ashore into Inchon harbour to allow the advance on Seoul to be accelerated.

Communist resistance stiffened as the American troops approached the city, and the 5th Marines were again counter-attacked by T-34/85s on September 20. Private Monegan again had to deploy his bazooka to engage three tanks at very short range. He knocked out two and was aiming at the third when he was cut down by machine gun fire. For his bravery in two battles with enemy tanks, Monegan was posthumously awarded the Medal of Honor. A second Medal of Honor was won on September 20, when Second Lieutenant Henry A Commiskey of the 1st Marines led his platoon in a full-frontal attack on an enemy-held hill. Unlike Lopez and Monegan, Commiskey survived the Battle of Inchon and eventually became a marine aviator.

On September 20, the first American troops entered Seoul and were quickly locked in fighting with pockets of communist troops, but tank support soon cleared

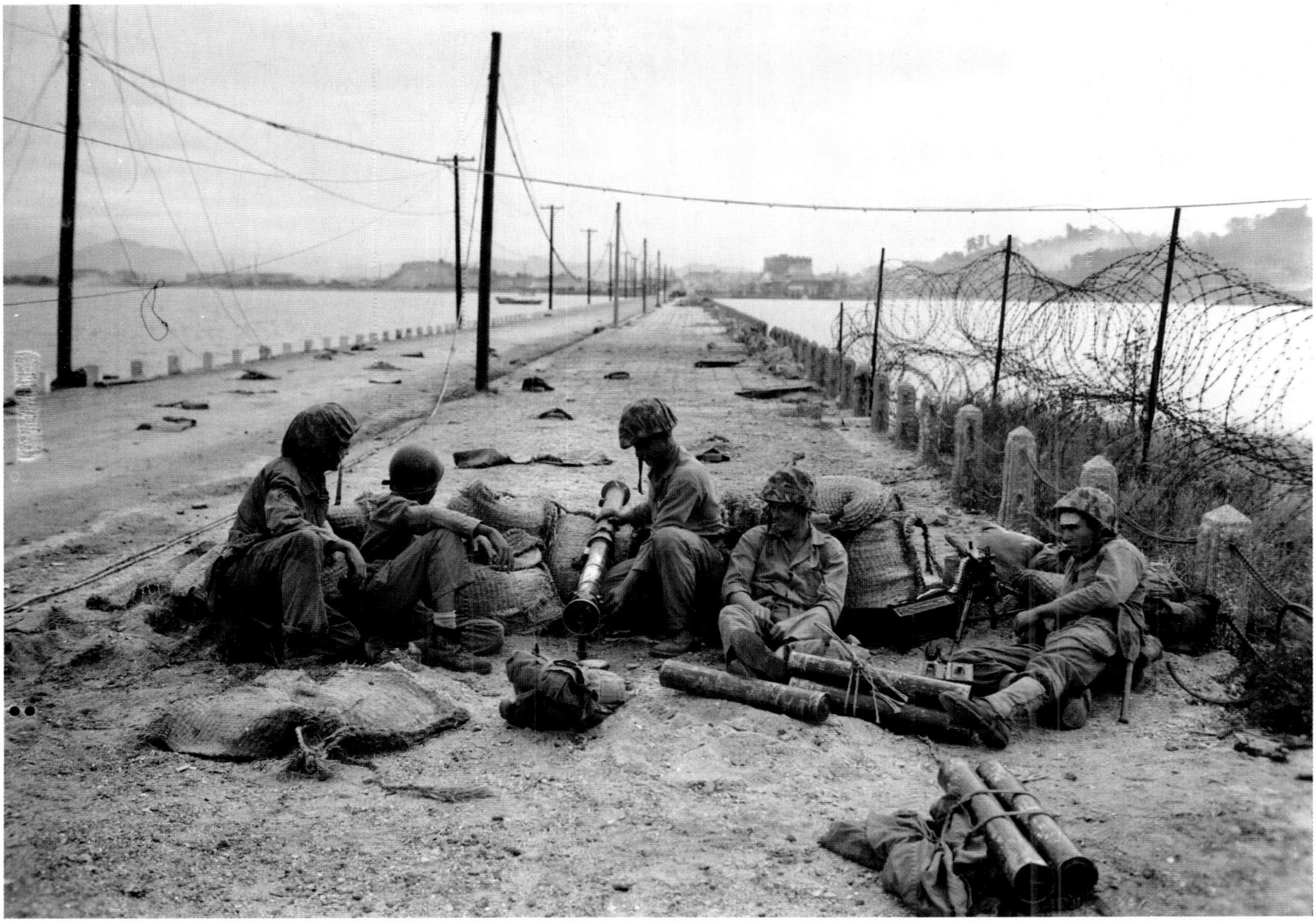

BELOW: The 5th Marine Regiment had to hold the causeway to Wolmi Island until Red and Green Beaches were secured. (US NATIONAL ARCHIVE)

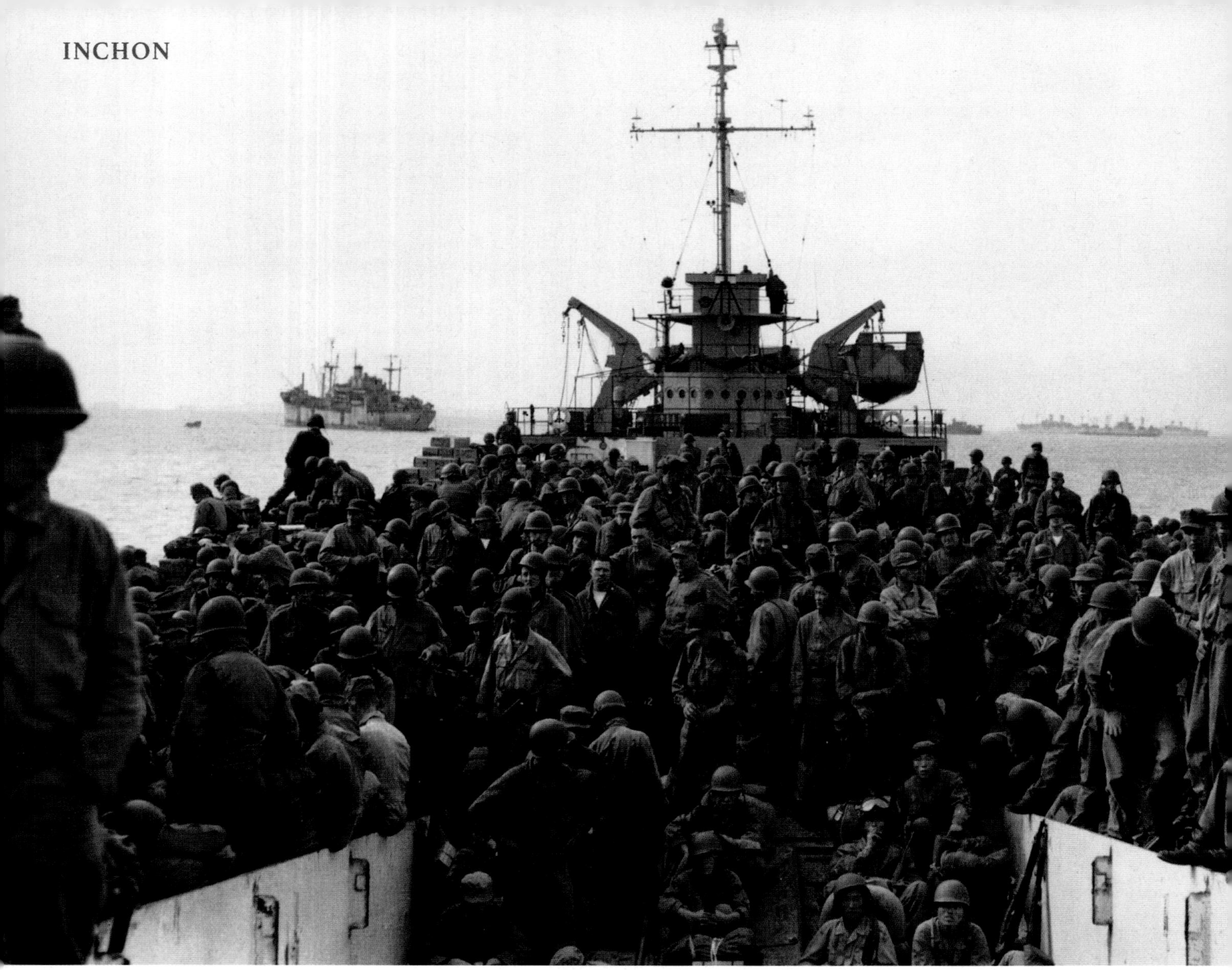

ABOVE: After the 1st Marine Division had secured Inchon, US Army soldiers of the 31st Infantry Regiment came ashore to join the drive on Seoul. (US NATIONAL ARCHIVE)

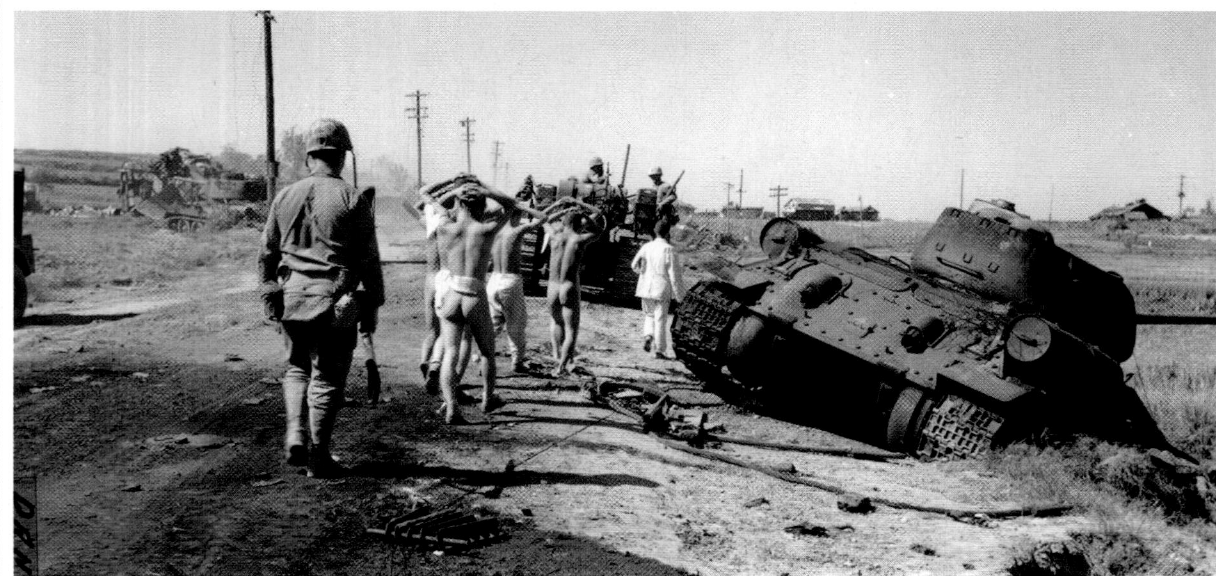

out the disorganised and dispirited defenders. On September 25, Seoul was cleared by MacArthur's divisions, but small pockets of enemy troops held out for three more days.

With 1st Marine and 7th Infantry Divisions now inside Seoul, the US troops in the Busan bridgehead started their own offensive.

The communist high command realised that unless they started a rapid retreat, their main force risked being cut off by the US troops advancing from Inchon. Soon, they were in full retreat.

General Smith and his marines were now pulled out of the battle to rest and reorganise. MacArthur wanted them to stage another amphibious landing on the east coast to trap retreating communist troops, but the enemy was moving too fast and escaped before the marines could come ashore.

The landing at Inchon had been a major success, changing the course of the Korean war and once again demonstrating the professionalism

RIGHT: North Korean prisoners of war are marched past a knocked-out T-34 tank, east of Inchon, on September 17, after the marines fought off an enemy tank attack. (US NATIONAL ARCHIVE)

ABOVE: **US Marine Corps M26 Pershing tanks helped clear Seoul in the weeks after the landing at Inchon.** (US NATIONAL ARCHIVE)

and fighting prowess of the US Marine Corps. US losses were small in the operation – some 145 killed and 900 wounded up to September 23; more than 1,000 communist troops had been killed and thousands more captured.

Crucially, Smith and his officers had managed to plan and organise a major amphibious operation with minimal time to prepare and execute the mission. By meeting McArthur's very tight time timetable, the marines demonstrated the value of having a dedicated amphibious force, ready to go at short notice.

Less than a year earlier, General Omar Bradley, Chairman of the Joint Chiefs of Staff had commented: "Large-scale amphibious operations such as those that occurred at Sicily and Normandy will never occur again." Amphibious bridgeheads were just too vulnerable to attack by atomic bombs, said the critics of the marines. The 1st Marine Division showed that the detractors of amphibious warfare were wrong.

LEFT: **The landings at Inchon turned the tide of the Korean war against the communists and allowed the US-led forces to drive north to the Chinese border.** (US NATIONAL ARCHIVE)

ABOVE: A column of marines and M26 tanks of the 1st Marine Division move through Chinese lines during their successful breakout from the Chosin Reservoir encirclement. (USMC, CORPORAL PETER MCDONALD)

Battle of Chosin Reservoir

The great escape

After the successful landings at Inchon in September 1950, communist forces were in full retreat across Korea. On October 1, the commander of the United Nations forces in Korea, General of the Army Douglas MacArthur, demanded that the North Korean forces surrender. They made no response. Days later, the US and Allied forces crossed over the 38th Parallel, which had previously divided the communist north from the pro-US south.

MacArthur was determined to drive up to the Yalu River that marked the border between Korea and Red China. The decision was controversial, as it appears that US President Harry Truman had not specifically signed off on the plan.

At first, US and Allied troops faced little resistance, so MacArthur was given the benefit of the doubt. The Chinese communist diplomats started to warn the Americans that if they advanced to the Yalu River, the People's Liberation Army (PLA) would intervene to drive the

RIGHT: Marines fought a series of running battles with Chinese troops to punch a corridor to safety during the Battle of Chosin Reservoir. (USMC, SGT FRANK C KERR)

American troops back from their border. McArthur was contemptuous of the Chinese threats and kept his troops advancing during October and November 1950.

Freezing winter weather now gripped Korea, inhibiting US troops' movements and interfering with Allied air support. In November, the first Chinese troops crossed into Korea and staged a series of counter-attacks that halted the US advance. MacArthur ordered a new offensive to complete the drive to the Yalu.

By the last week of November, MacArthur's troops had their

ABOVE: Major General Oliver Smith was the unflappable commander of the US 1st Marine Division as it fought its way out of encirclement in November and December 1950.
(USMC ARCHIVE)

objective in their sights, and he started to talk about the first US soldiers being home for Christmas.

In the eastern sector, Major General Oliver Smith's 1st Marine Division was operating around the Chosin Reservoir under the command of X Corps. The region was shrouded in heavy snow drifts and criss-crossed with deep mountain valleys, making life miserable for the marines as they shivered in foxholes to hold their sector of the front.

Smith's 25,00 marines were positioned to the west and south of the frozen Chosin Reservoir, with the bulk of the division's combat units – the 5th and 7th Marine Regiments – positioned around the town of Yudami-ni. The divisional headquarters was positioned at Hagaru-ri, at the southern edge of the reservoir, along with a collection ❯

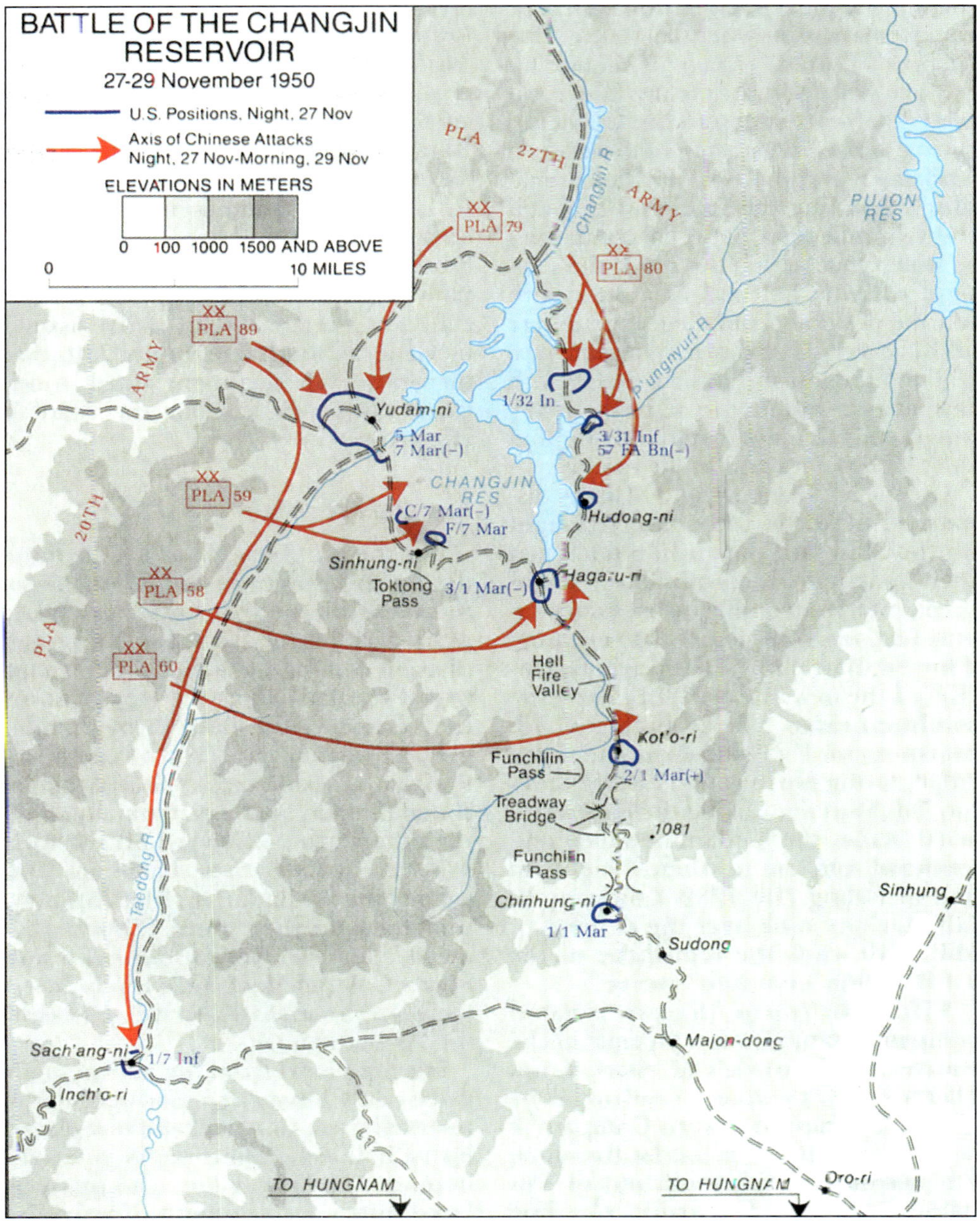

ABOVE: (USMC HISTORY DIVISION)

LEFT: US Marines fight a rear-guard action during their retreat from Chosin Reservoir to the coast and safety from Chinese encirclement

of US Army and Marine Corps engineers and rear support units. US Navy Seabee combat construction engineers were in the process of building an airfield close to the town. Further south at Koto-ri, the 1st Marine Regiment was in reserve.

Ten kilometres to the north on the eastern side of the reservoir were 2,500 US Army soldiers from Regimental Combat Team 31 (RCT-31) at Sinhung-ni.

Over a two-day period from November 25, the PLA launched its general offensive along the length of the Allied front. Very soon, several Republic of Korea (ROK) and US Army units crumbled in the face of charges by Chinese troops; the front line started to break. In the 1st Division's sector, the marines held firm thanks to their professional officers and strong morale.

Over the next few days, Smith began to realise his division was in mortal danger as the Allied units on its flanks started to retreat. Soon, 120,000 Chinese troops were surging forward and within days they had swept around behind the marines, cutting their main supply route to the coast.

The 89th and 79th PLA divisions attacked the marine regiments around Yudami-ni trapping them in a pocket, after the 59th PLA Division cut the road south to Hagaru-ri. Another PLA division was rapidly advancing towards Hagaru-ri, threatening to overrun Smith's headquarters and logistic base.

As disaster threatened, Smith gathered his commanders and ordered a major re-organisation to allow his division to fight off the Chinese. A battalion of the 1st Regiment was rushed north to secure the divisional headquarters, arriving just in time to set up a perimeter as the first Chinese troops appeared on the mountain ridges around the base. Other Chinese troops marched south of the town and cut the road to the Koto-ri. The bulk of the 1st Division was now surrounded.

Over several days, the marines fought off furious attacks. Marine artillery men at Hagaru-ri turned their field guns on the Chinese, firing directly at the attackers in the fields

around the town. The marine infantry then counter-attacked to drive back the Chinese and keep them at a safe distance from the airstrip, which was the only lifeline to the outside world. A shuttle of US Air Force and marine transport aircraft, as well as newly introduced helicopters, were now bringing in supplies and evacuating wounded marines.

General Smith now set about bringing his two regiments safely back from Yudami-ni, so his division could march south to the coast.

He was determined to make sure no tanks or artillery were left as trophies for the communists, so the 1st Division could get back in the fight once it had escaped the trap.

The 5th and 7th Regiments were ordered to break out from Yudami-ni starting on December 1. A battalion of the 7th Regiment opened the breakout with an attack to capture two hills overlooking the main road south. Once the route was secured, the main column set off, led by a single Sherman tank. Aircraft of the 1st Marine Air Wing circled overhead to be ready to strike at any Chinese troops that opened fire on the marines.

Over four days, the marines marched south through the freezing snow. Units were only allowed brief halts to rest and sleep before the officers and senior NCOs roused them to keep marching. All the wounded were loaded on ambulances and trucks that weaved down the icy road, along with the last remaining artillery pieces.

By December 4, the column reached Hagaru-ri complete with their artillery and wounded. The frozen marines were sheltered in tents and fed warm food from field kitchens, before being sent back into the line around the town. The retreat became legendary when Smith heard criticism of the withdrawal and remarked: "Retreat, hell! We're not retreating, we're just advancing in a different direction."

As the marine regiments started their retreat, RCT-31 at Sirhung-ni, which had been put under Smith's command, was hit by a full Chinese division and was swiftly threatened with being overwhelmed. Its commander ordered a withdrawal, ➤

LEFT: Wet, stinging snow and ice made the retreat from Chosin Reservoir one of the most iconic battles in the history of the US Marine Corps. (USMC ARCHIVE)

BELOW: Sikorsky HO3S helicopter crews from Marine Observation Squadron VMO-6 made heroic flights into the besieged enclave around the Chosin Reservoir to bring out badly wounded marines to hospitals on the Korean coast. These successful missions convinced the leadership of the US Marine Corps that helicopters could transform warfare. (USMC ARCHIVE)

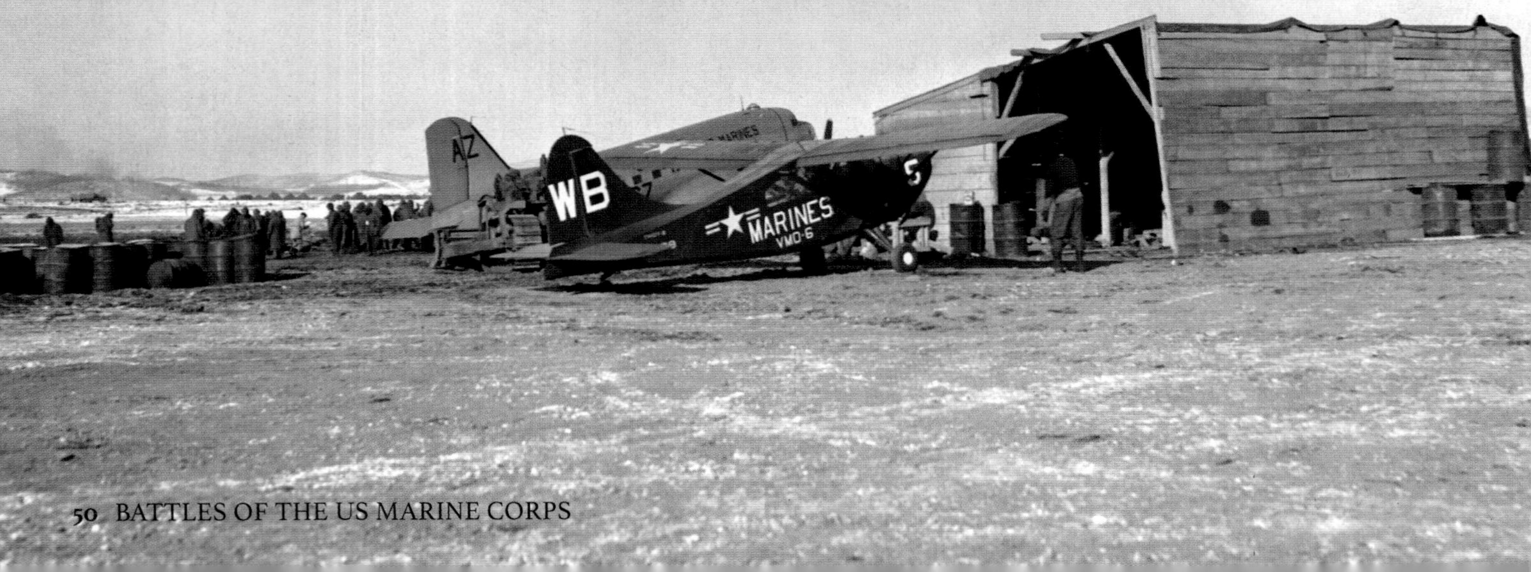

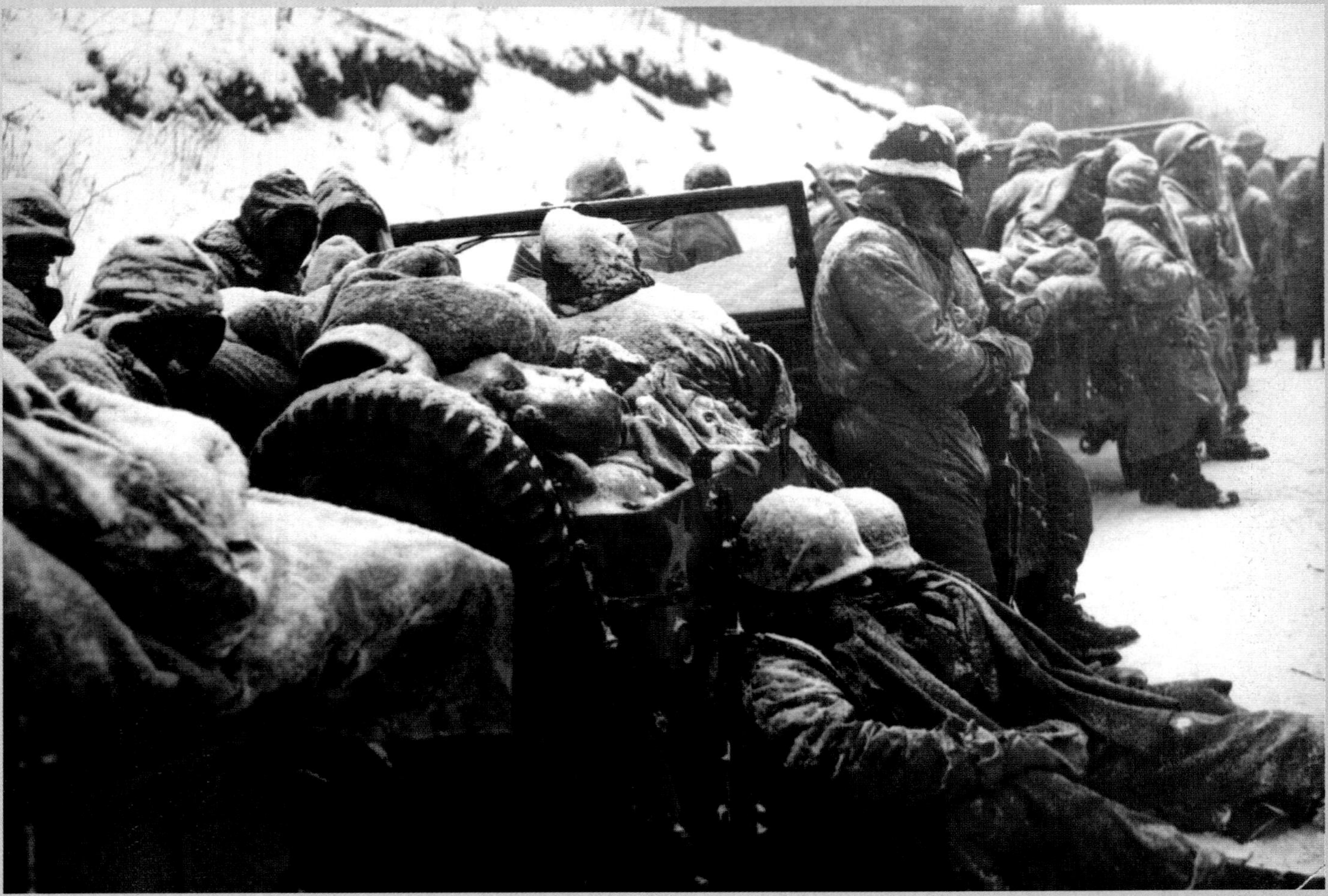

ABOVE: Marines halted in freezing conditions on the road south of Hagaru-ri waiting for a Chinese roadblock to be cleared to allow the retreat to the coast to continue. (USMC ARCHIVE)

but its retreat was blocked by Chinese troops. Only an airstrike with napalm by marine aircraft cleared a way through the encirclement. More Chinese troops attacked the US Army convoy, and it soon collapsed into chaos. Some US soldiers headed out across the frozen reservoir and others dispersed in small groups to find a way through Chinese lines. Out of the 1,000 soldiers who eventually made it to Hagaru-ri, fewer than 400 were fit to continue fighting.

General Smith now set about organising the next phase of his withdrawal. More PLA divisions were massing to attack, so the marines needed to head south quickly to avoid being overrun.

The 7th Regiment set off first, with the mission to capture a series of hills overlooking the road south to Koto-ri on December 6. Once they had confirmed the road was secure, the main convoy carrying the American wounded, artillery and other combat equipment set off south. The 5th Regiment was the rear guard, holding Hagaru-ri until the last vehicles had left.

A Chinese division tried to attack the retreating column in what became known as Hell Fire Valley, but the 7th Regiment fought them off to allow the column to reach Koto-ri on December 7.

The Chinese troops holding the Funchilin Pass were ordered to fight to the last to stop the Americans escaping. A key bridge was blown up by the Chinese. Two battalions of marines and the remnants of RCT 31 were ordered forward to clear a route through. One Chinese battalion fought to the last man. Another communist unit was found frozen to death in the foxholes.

Although the pass was now secure, the downed bridge was blocking the vehicles moving south; the US Air Force started to parachute sections of a portable bridge to the marine engineers, who set to work repairing the escape route. The temporary bridge opened on December 9 and over the next two days the column was clear of the pass and heading for the coast

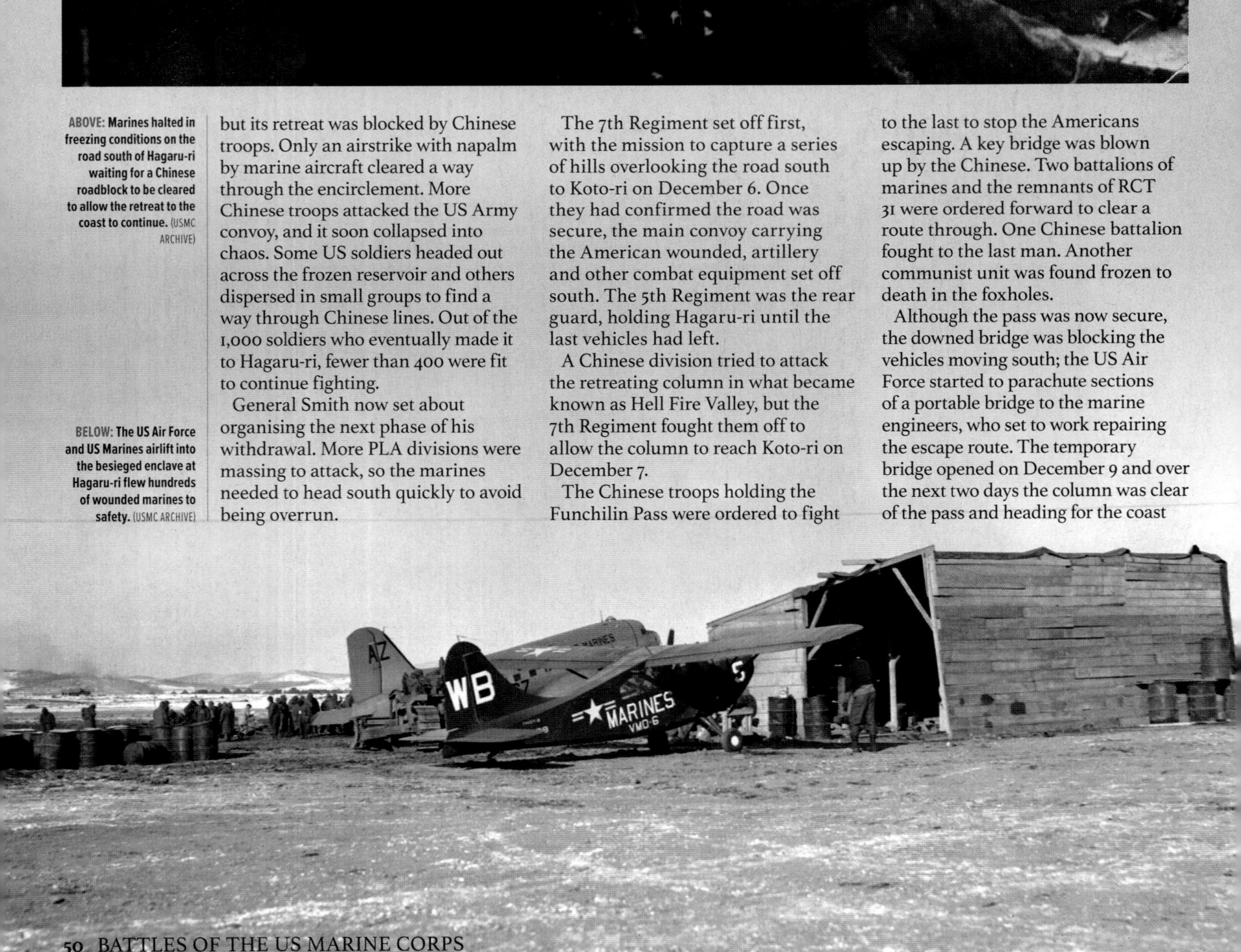

BELOW: The US Air Force and US Marines airlift into the besieged enclave at Hagaru-ri flew hundreds of wounded marines to safety. (USMC ARCHIVE)

LEFT: General Smith used his small number of M26 Pershing tanks to protect his columns of marching marines and to punch routes through the communist encirclement around Koto-ri. (USMC ARCHIVE)

and safety at Hungnam. Over the next two weeks, the 1st Marine Division and survivors of X Corps, along with the ROK I Corp were safely evacuated by a 193-ship armada.

The epic retreat of General Smith's command is credited with breaking the back of the Chinese offensive and preventing the PLA sweeping down to the sea. Chinese historians later reported that the PLA's 9th Corps, which had battled the 1st Marine Division, suffered more than 50,000 casualties or a third of its total strength during the fighting around Chosin Reservoir. Out of the 25,000 US Marines under Smith, 4,385 were killed or wounded and 7,338 more fell victim to cold-related injuries, including frostbite. Despite suffering nearly 50% casualties, the marine division safely evacuated all its wounded and heavy equipment. After only a few months resting and refitting it was ready to be sent back into action again.

The Battle of Chosin Reservoir has been described as the most brutal in American history, due to heavy casualties, extreme weather conditions and intensity of the fighting over the course of 14 days. More decorations for bravery were awarded than in any other engagement, bar the 1944 Battle of the Bulge in the Ardennes.

Fourteen marines, two soldiers and one navy pilot were awarded the Medal of Honor for bravery during those days in November and December 1950. A further 78 service cross medals were awarded, this compared with 20 and 83 Medals of Honor and service cross medals, respectively, during the Battle of the Bulge.

When General Smith and his men reached the coast, they found they were celebrities: all America was captivated by the story of the beleaguered division As reports emerged that the marines were trapped, the nation feared the worst. But when they marched to safety, there were celebrations and relief. The marines who served at Chosin were nicknamed 'The Chosin Few' in honour of their bravery and fortitude.

BELOW: The 1st Marine Division marched down the road between Funchilin Pass and Chinhung-ni to freedom between December 9 and 11, 1950. (USMC ARCHIVE)

Helicopter Marines

A new era in warfare

RIGHT: The US Marines used helicopters in combat for the first time in the Korean war and, in the decade after that conflict, invested heavily in new rotorcraft. (USMC ARCHIVE)

In the aftermath of the Korean War, the US Marine Corps set in motion a major re-organisation to make it more able to rapidly intervene in crisis zones around the world.

This was the era of the Cold War, with the US military garrisoned around the world to stop the spread of communism, inspired by Moscow and Peking. America's nuclear arsenal deterred major military action by the communists against US allies in Europe, the Middle East and Asia. Checked by this nuclear stalemate, Washington DC feared that the communists would try to achieve their objectives by fermenting revolution and insurgency across the world. These so-called 'bush fire wars' required the rapid intervention of highly trained elite units to support allies and ensure stability.

The US Marine Corps and US Navy saw this as an opportunity to build up forces for these types of conflicts. With the US Army and US Air Force pre-occupied with nuclear weapons and global conflict against the Soviet

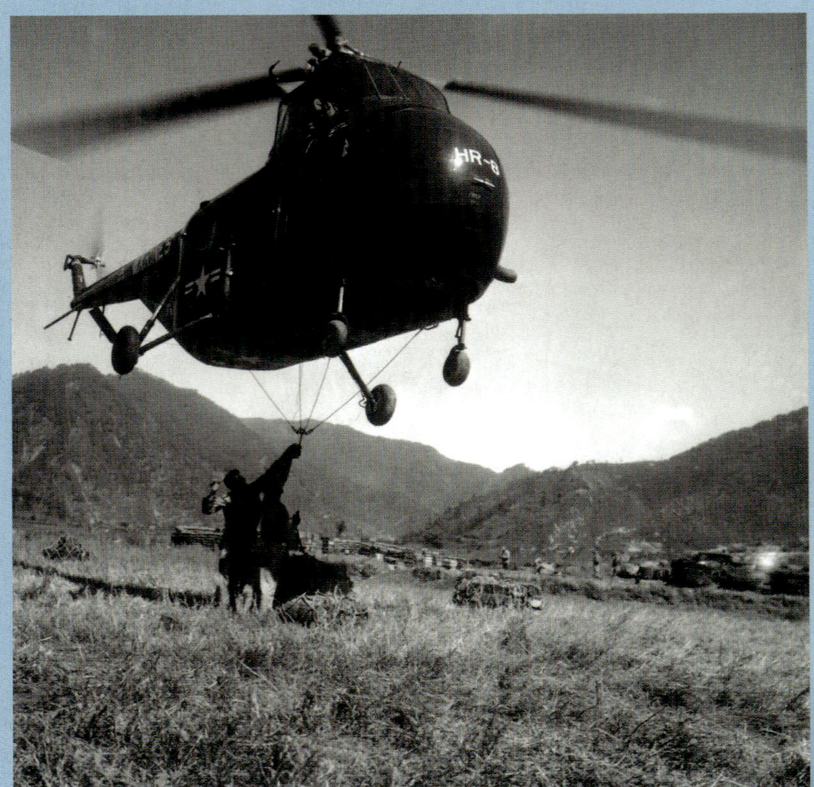

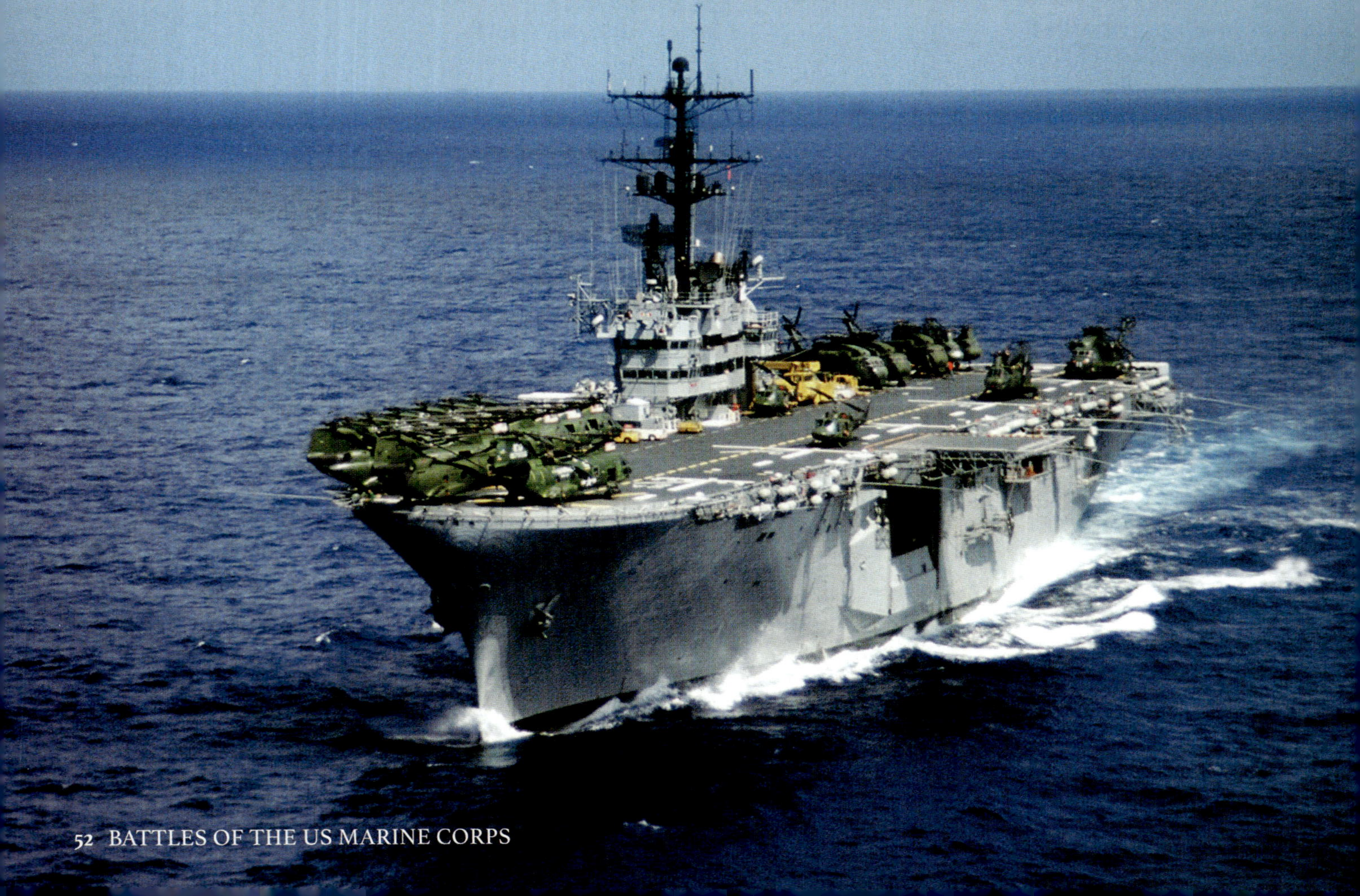

BELOW: The USS *Iwo Jima* was the first amphibious assault ship to be designed and built from the keel up as a dedicated helicopter carrier. (USMC)

Union and Red China, there was a gap in the market for a '911 force' that could rapidly move to intervene if a crisis threatened.

The potential for integrating air, land and sea elements into a single force had long been recognised by the US Marine Corps, but the decisive role in close air support in the Korean War led the corps' leadership to take the idea further. During the late the 1950s, the Marine Air Ground Task Force

(MAGTF) concept started to take shape. This envisaged air, land and naval elements, plus logistics support being combined under the command of a single marine headquarters, to better exploit the potential of each component. Starting in the early 1960s, the headquarters at corps, brigade, regiment and battalion level were progressively re-configured so they had the personnel and communications equipment to

take under command a spread of capabilities, to operate across multiple domains. This had long been the way the US Marine Corps had fought, but now the concept was formalised and moved on from the World War Two-era structures that had persisted through to the Korean war. Senior marine officers then set about buying the equipment needed to turn their vision into reality.

Marine chiefs were keen to learn the lessons of the Korean conflict and exploit the potential of many of the new weapons and equipment that first saw service in that war. The battlefield utility of helicopters to move troops, supplies and equipment ashore as well as to evacuate casualties was embraced by the US Marine Corps leadership. Fleets of helicopters were ordered and requirements for new designs sent out to the American aerospace industry.

By the time the marine units went ashore in Vietnam in 1965, they were supported by armed Bell UH-1 Huey gunships, Boeing CH-46 Sea Knight and Sikorsky UH-34 HUS transport helicopters. They were soon joined by the Bell AH-1 Cobra gunship and the Sikorsky CH-53 Sea Stallion heavy-lift helicopters. Marine units ➤

ABOVE: The old Essex-class aircraft carrier was reclassified in 1959 as an amphibious assault carrier or LPH-5. It was designed to carry enough helicopters to put ashore a marine battalion so they could conduct 'vertical envelopment' by landing marines behind enemy beach fortifications. (USMC ARCHIVE)

LEFT: The July 1958 Lebanon crisis saw thousands of US Marines land around Beirut to protect American interests in the Middle East country, setting the scene for further interventions around the world. (USMC)

The assault ships of the Iwo Jima-class were all named after US Marine Corps battle honours – *Iwo Jima, Okinawa, Guadalcanal, Guam, Tripoli, New Orleans* and *Inchon* – signalling the prestige of the corps in 1960s. (US NAVY)

in Vietnam could carry out air assault operations, just like the US Army's air cavalry, from shore bases or ships.

The US Marine Corps and US Navy began experimenting in 1957 with the concept of a carrier loaded with enough helicopters to land a full battalion of embarked marines in one lift. Experiments with the USS *Boxer* involved the ship working alongside landing ship tanks (LSTs), to test new helicopter-based amphibious tactics. After the success of these trials, three other surplus World War Two Essex-class flattops were converted into the first US Navy landing platform helicopters (LPH).

In 1959, the first of seven Iwo Jima-class LPHs were laid down and they entered service over the next decade. The USS *Iwo Jima* was the lead ship of her class and was the first amphibious assault ship to be designed and built from the keel up as a dedicated carrier for helicopters and embarked elements of what was then called a Marine Amphibious Unit (MAU).

USS *Iwo Jima* saw action off Vietnam in 1965, acting as a base for helicopters supporting marines fighting ashore.

The success of the Iwo Jima-class prompted the development of the new

BELOW: A marine brigade landed at Da Nang in March 1965 to begin the decade-long involvement of the Corps in America's wars in Southeast Asia. (USMC ARCHIVE)

Tarawa-class of landing helicopter assault (LHA) ships, which could carry marines and helicopters and launch landing craft out of a 'well deck'. The first of these ships entered service in 1971 and heralded a new era in amphibious warfare, giving marine commanders unprecedent tactical options in a range of scenarios.

Across the corps, World War Two and Korean war-era equipment was steadily replaced during the late 1950s and early 1960s. The old 'Alligator' landing vehicle, tracked (LVT) was replaced by the bigger and better-armoured LVTP-5 (landing vehicle, tracked, personnel) from 1956.

US Marine Corps aviation units first used jet strike aircraft and by the time of the Vietnam conflict, the iconic Douglas A-4 Skyhawk light attack jet, Douglas F-4 Phantom fighter-bomber and Grumman A-6 Intruder were in widespread use. These powerful and effective aircraft bore the brunt of close air support work for marines fighting in the Vietnamese jungles. Even before the Vietnam war was over, marine aviation commanders were looking to future ways to put fixed-wing airpower ashore on beachheads without requiring airfields to be captured or runways to be built, as was needed for its existing A-4 Skyhawk light attack jets. As a result, the marines ordered the British-designed Harrier jump jet in 1969 and, two years later, the first US-assembled McDonnell Douglas AV-8A Harriers were delivered to the corps.

The MAGTF-era saw the US Marine Corps transformed into a fighting force fit for the latter half of the 20th century. In 1965, the commitment of a corps-sized MAGTF to fight around Da Nang in Vietnam saw the marines put their new concept into action. Over seven years, marines in Vietnam fought a new type of warfare that showed the corps was at the cutting-edge of developing innovative tactics, combat organisations and equipment. As well as fighting hard, the US Marine Corps had learnt to fight smarter.

Khe Sanh

Marines under siege

There was "light at the end of the tunnel" in November 1967 according to General William Westmoreland, the top American commander in Southeast Asia. He was just one of a stream of senior US military commanders and intelligence experts who were now reporting steady progress in the Vietnam war.

The 'body count' of Vietcong insurgents and North Vietnamese Army (NVA) regulars claimed killed by US forces was at a record high. US troops and their South Vietnamese allies, the Army of Republic of Vietnam (ARVN) had communist forces on the run, or so said the Pentagon.

This positive outlook felt rather out of touch for the US Marines holding the Khe Sanh combat base in northwest Vietnam. As they sheltered in their bunkers and trenches from NVA mortar, rocket and artillery fire, the communist threat did not seem to be diminishing.

Life or death in the remote garrison of the 26th Marine Regiment was

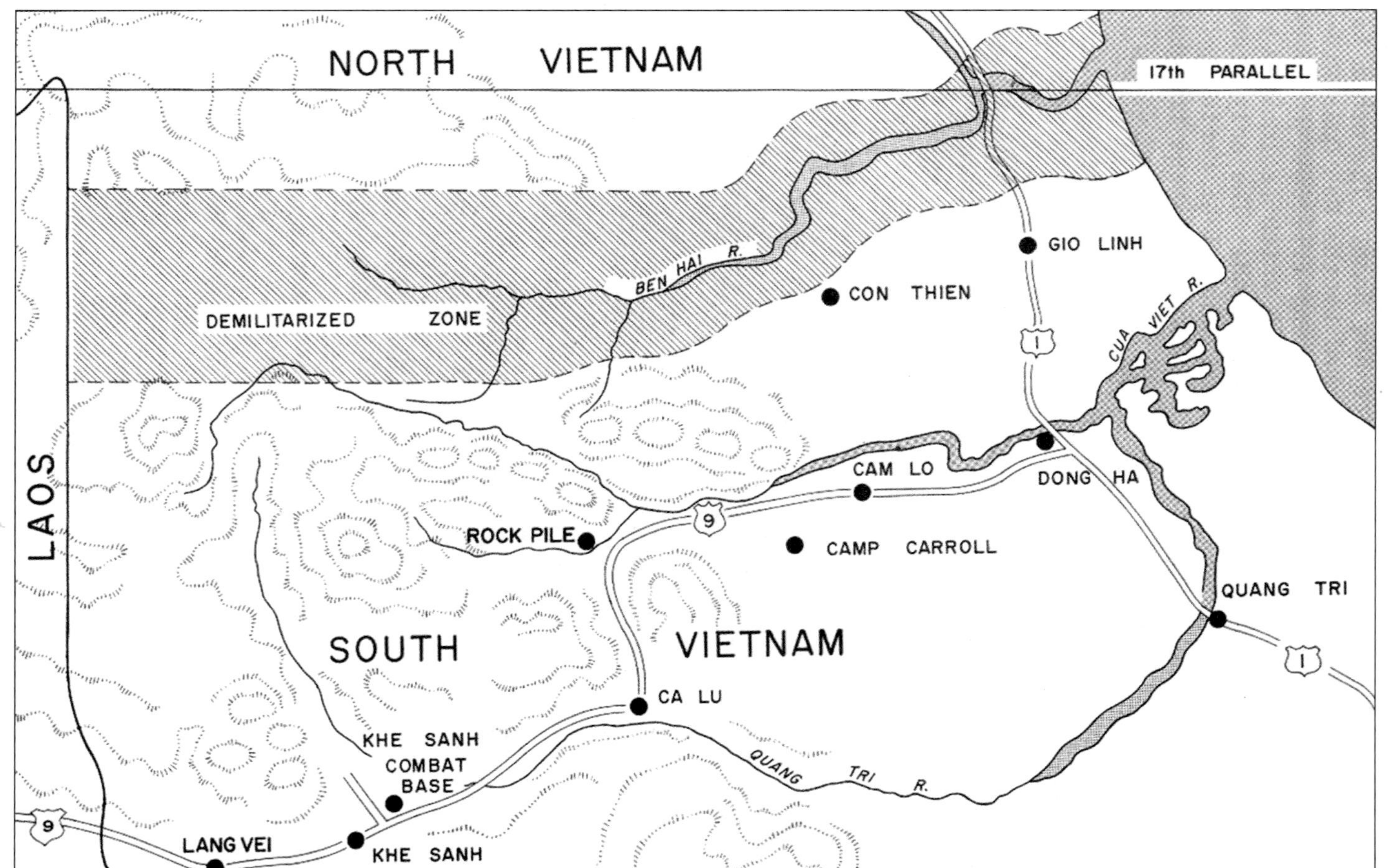

LEFT: US Marine Corps sniper teams stayed on alert monitoring enemy movement around the perimeter of the Khe Sanh combat base. (US NATIONAL ARCHIVES)

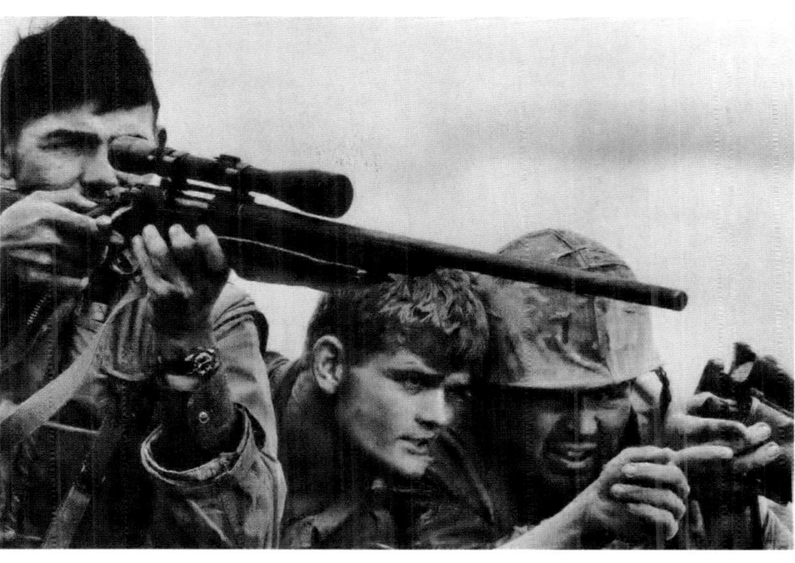

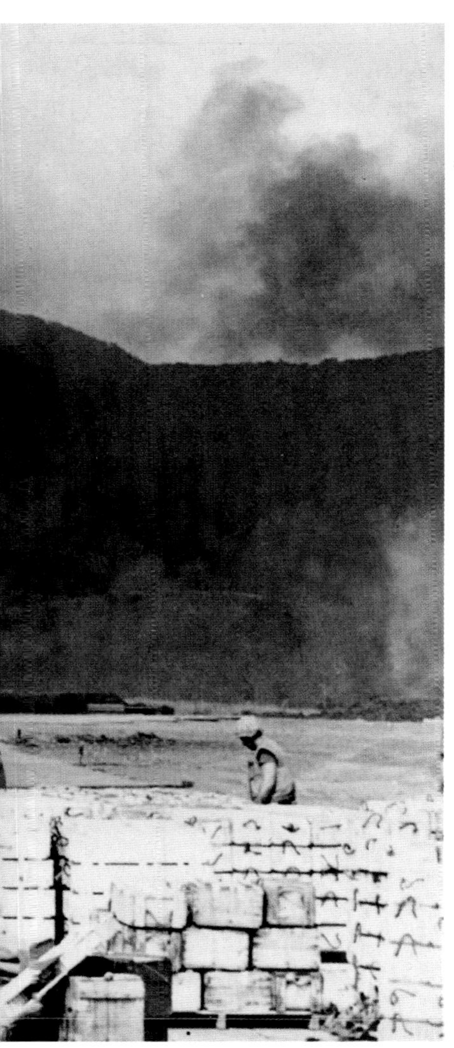

random. Shells and rockets were a daily hazard in the two-and-a-half months up to April 1968 as the siege of Khe Sanh was at its peak.

The US military first opened the base at Khe Sanh in 1962 to allow a contingent of US Army Special Forces 'Green Beret' advisers to help locally recruited militia to monitor communist infiltration into Quang Tri province across the border from Laos, only 12 kilometres away. Westmoreland was determined to beef-up the effort to close the border to prevent communist troops and supplies entering South Vietnam from the so-called Ho Chi Minh Trail. The logistic route was protected from aerial surveillance by the thick jungle canopy, so having 'boots on ground' near the Laotian border was a top priority.

During 1966, the first US Marine Corps contingents arrived at Khe Sanh and began to expand the base. Eventually, an airstrip was constructed and a series of defensive positions established around the site. Marine commanders used the site as a base to launch patrols into the jungle to find communist infiltration routes. The 'Green Beret' advisers had built two camps nearby, where they trained tribal militia loyal to the

BELOW: Helicopters and aircraft on the Khe Sanh airstrip were at risk of communist shelling whenever they tried to land at the base. (US NATIONAL ARCHIVES)

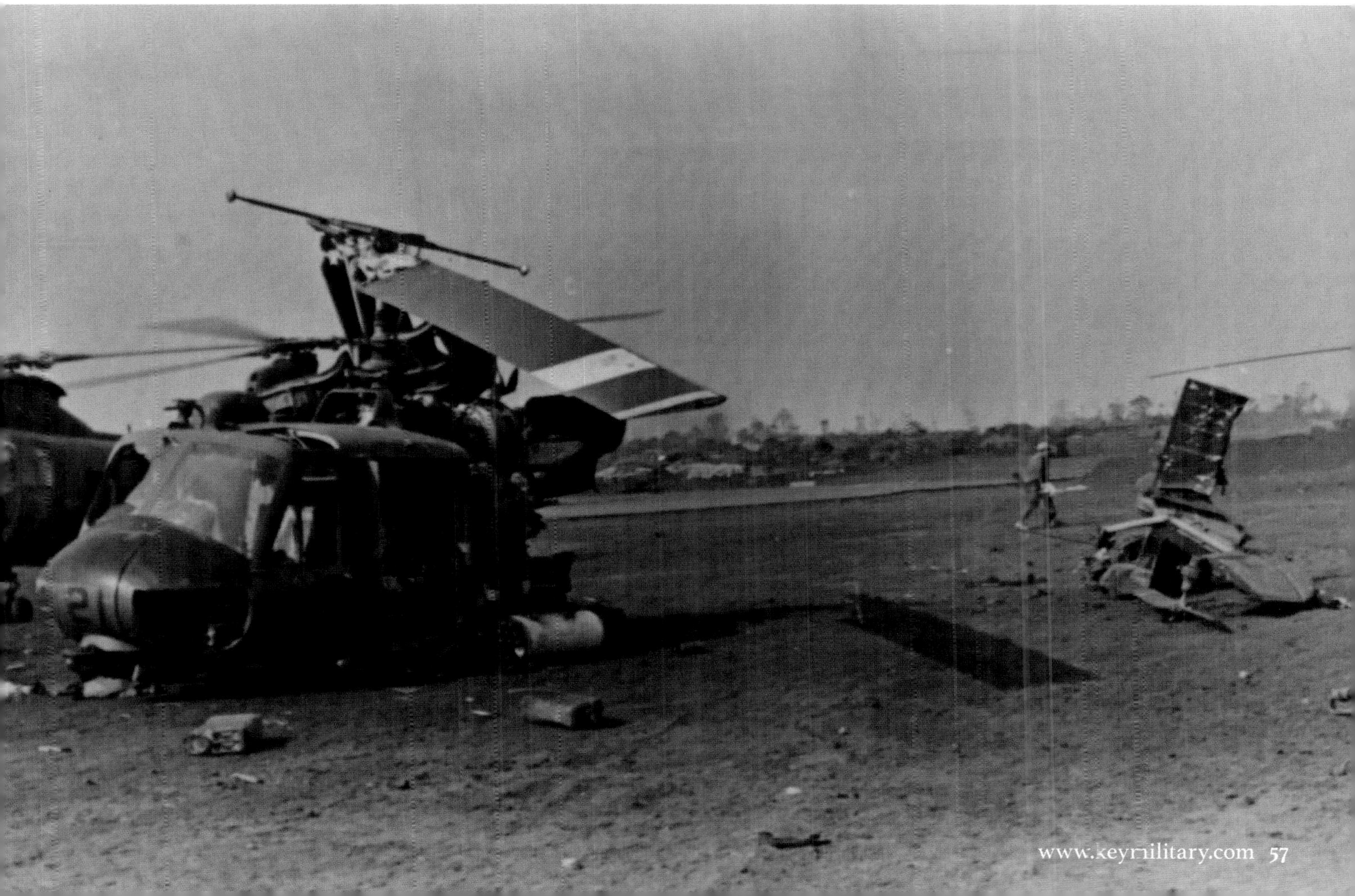

regime in the southern capital, Saigon (now Ho Chi Minh City).

By the end of 1967, the 6,000-strong Khe Sanh garrison was commanded by Colonel David E Lownds, a World War Two veteran. He set his troops to fortify the base after a steady stream of intelligence reports indicated that the NVA might be planning to try to overrun his command. Deep bunkers were dug to house the regimental command post, field hospital and troop shelters, which were strong enough to take a direct hit from an 82mm mortar. A series of revetments were built to protect the garrison's ammunition supply and fuel tanks. A steady stream of aircraft brought in extra ammunition and food to build up stocks in case the communists managed to close down the runway with artillery fire. A 25-metre-deep barbed-wire perimeter fence was laid and reinforced with tripwire-activated flares and Claymore mines to give the garrison warning of any attempts to infiltrate the garrison.

Westmoreland's decision to reinforce the Khe Sanh garrison brought him intense scrutiny from the sceptical US press corps in Saigon who immediately compared the base with the ill-fated French outpost at Dien Bien Phu, which was cut off and overrun by the communists in 1954. American commanders were convinced that Lownds' marines would not meet the same fate as the French Foreign Legion. A huge force of American air power was less than an hour's flying time away at Da Nang airbase. More importantly, the Americans built their base at the top of series of hills that dominated the surrounding terrain; this was unlike the French, who had built their base and airstrip in the bottom of valley. Once they lost control of the surrounding hills to the communists, the French could not use the air strip to bring in reinforcements and vital ammunition. US Marine commanders were confident they would defeat any attempt to overrun Khe Sanh. The intention was to use overwhelming US air power and artillery to kill as many NVA soldiers as possible if the base came under attack.

However, the North Vietnamese had other ideas. Unknown to the Americans, the communists were planning a country-wide offensive across South Vietnam during the Tet holiday (Vietnamese New Year) in January 1968. Vietcong insurgents and NVA divisions were simultaneously to attack towns and cities from the demilitarised zone (DMZ) in the north down to Saigon and the Mekong River Delta in the south. To distract US and ARVN combat troops from the populated coastal region, the communists was preparing to attack Khe Sanh to distract General Westmoreland from the upcoming Tet Offensive.

ABOVE: US President Lyndon B Johnson had a model of the Khe Sanh battlefield in the White House to allow him to follow every twist of the siege. (WHITE HOUSE)

Four NVA divisions were dispatched down the Ho Chi Minh Trail in December 1967, to be in position to attack Khe Sanh ahead of the Tet Offensive, which was due to kick off at the end of the following month. Its infiltration and deployment were undertaken under conditions of great secrecy and Lownds and his marines had little warning of what was coming.

It was only during January 20 that marine commanders at Khe Sanh started to pick up signs that an attack was imminent. A defector revealed the communist plans, but it was now too late to stop the attack that would come in a few hours' time.

Just after midnight, a flare was fired over the US base, to signal to the NVA assault force to attack. A NVA battalion had infiltrated to the edge of the US perimeter and detonated Bangalore torpedoes to clear safe routes through the minefields. Well-aimed mortar fire kept the marines inside their bunkers, as more than 300 communist troops charged forward. Within minutes, the NVA soldiers were fighting hand-to-hand with the marines defending the Hill 861 strong point. The only way to contain the attack was for the marines to call down mortar fire on their own positions. By dawn, the attack was contained, but the NVA was not finished.

At 0530 hours, a barrage of highly accurate communist artillery, mortars and rockets swept across the Khe Sanh base. The NVA's intelligence was excellent, and it knew exactly what to hit to cause maximum damage to the marines' defensive capability. During the morning of January 21, the main ammunition dump was targeted and 1,500 tons of ammunition started to explode. A cloud of CS riot-control gas was released across the base, and the ammo revetment containing them caught fire.

Battalion command posts were then hit and artillery rounds started to impact along the runway. Parking

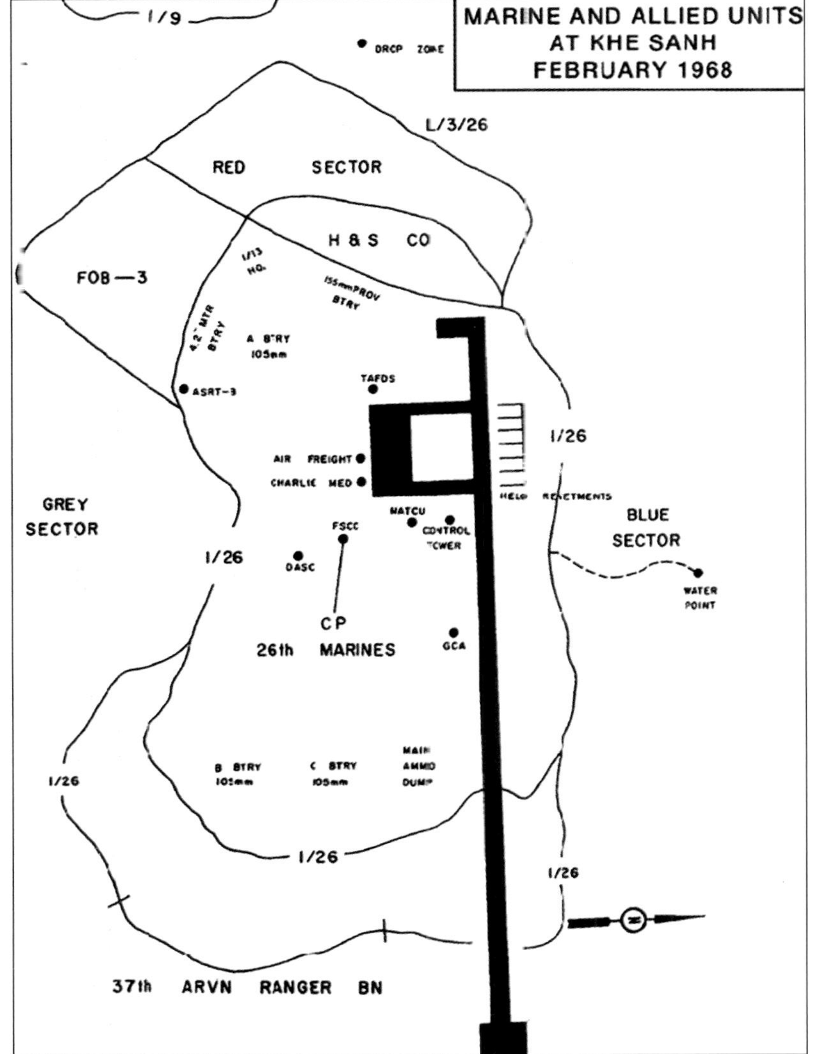

LEFT: (USMC HISTORY DIVISION)

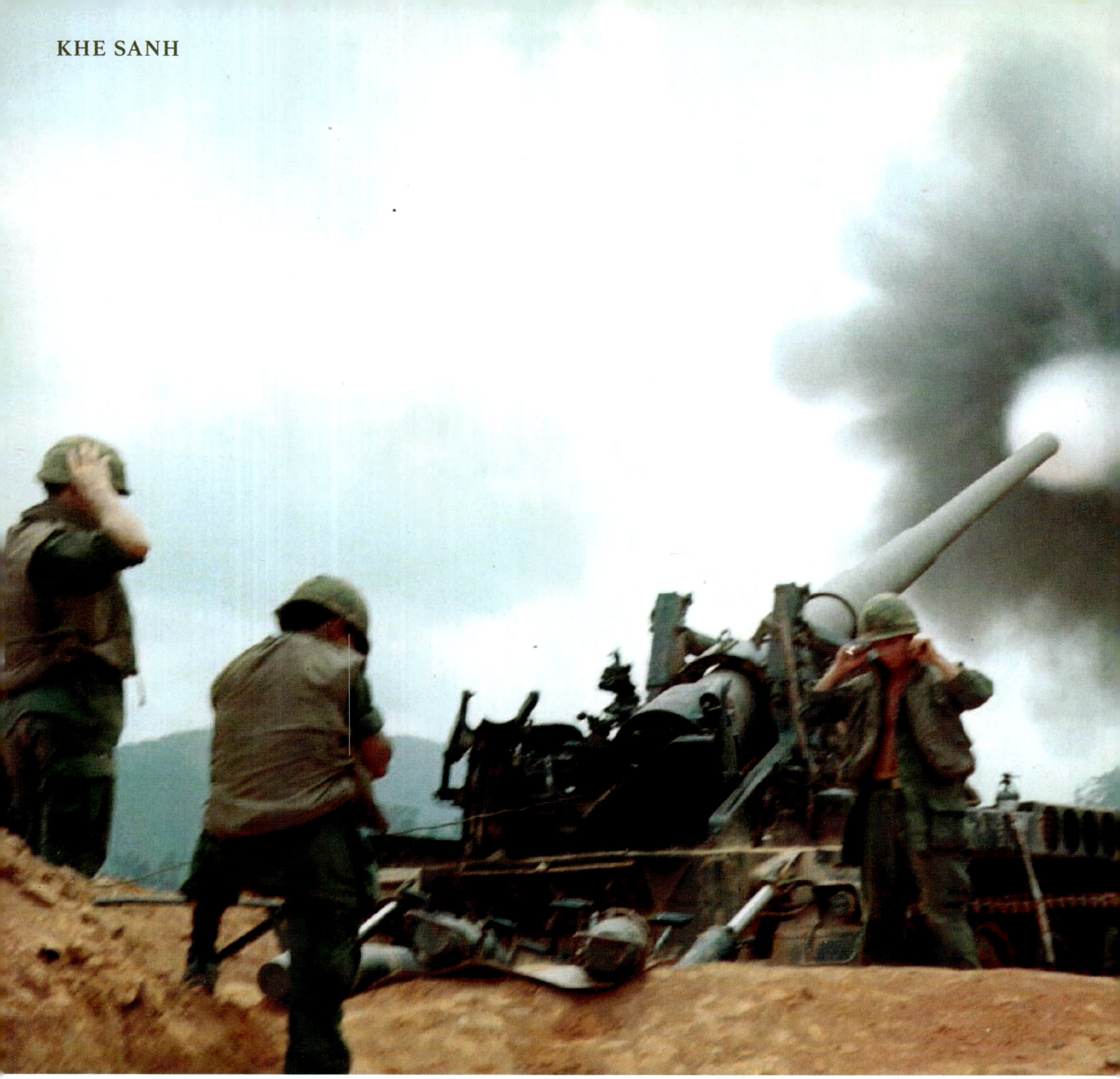

ABOVE: US Army M107 175mm heavy-artillery batteries fired in support of the marines at the Khe Sanh combat base throughout the siege. (US NATIONAL ARCHIVES)

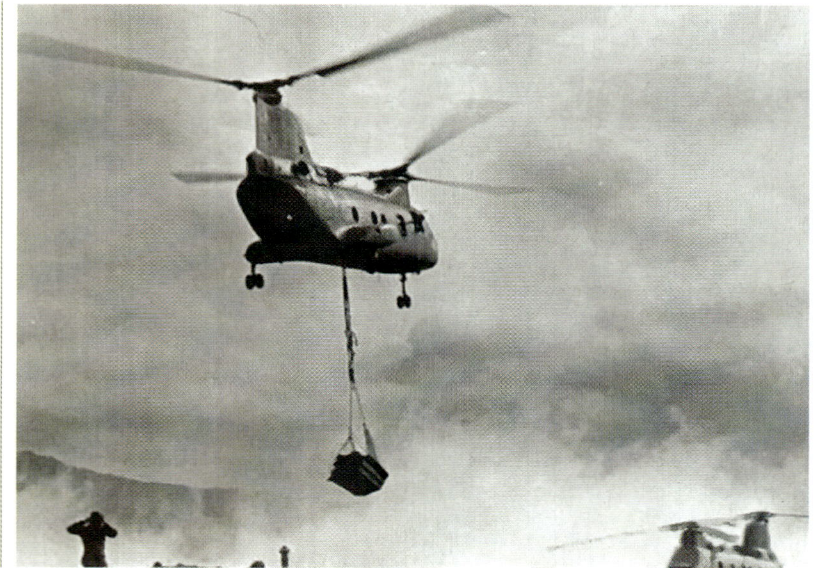

RIGHT: US Marine Corps CH-46 Sea Knight helicopters shuttled underslung loads of supplies and ammunition into Khe Sanh. (US NATIONAL ARCHIVES)

ramps for helicopters were swept by shrapnel, mess halls devastated, power generators knocked out and the artillery fire direction command post was also hit. By the end of the day, 14 marines were dead and 43 wounded. Crucially, almost all of the marines' ammunition reserves had been destroyed and more than half of the runway was chewed up by shell fire. Urgent action would have to be taken to restock the base with ammunition if the marines were to stay in the fight. The NVA's commanders certainly knew the weak points in US plans to defend Khe Sanh. If this bombardment was not enough, as darkness started to fall another contingent of NVA sappers tried to breach the barbed wire perimeter.

their offensive against the main US base at Khe Sanh. Eventually, the hard-pressed Green Berets and their local allies had to be evacuated by helicopters or make risky forced marches through the jungle back to the marine base. The heavy communist artillery and mortar fire made it too risky for Lownds' marines to foray out to rescue the Green Berets.

General Westmoreland now started to mobilise US airpower to help protect the beleaguered marines at Khe Sanh. The airlift was stepped up to begin to restock the base's ammunition reserve. This proved to be a continuous challenge, as repeated communist attacks meant the marine artillery battery and mortar teams were firing off ammunition just as fast as it arrived, preventing the building up of reserves. Priority was given to ammunition over food, water and even medical supplies. As a result, the marines in the foxholes around the base started to set up ponchos to collect water from the overnight rain. Food was always short, with the days of hot food in the base's mess hall a thing of the past.

The resupply effort was not helped by the communists positioning anti-aircraft guns under the runway's glide path leading to the loss of several aircraft and helicopters, so supply aircraft had to adopt a daring approach manoeuvre – corkscrewing down to the end of the runway then pilots would violently pull up the nose of their aircraft to land. This became known as the 'Khe Sanh approach'.

The US Air Force was ordered to step up its strikes on the Ho Chi Minh Trail to stop communist supplies and reinforcements reaching the Khe Sanh battle zone. Fields of sound sensors were dropped around the base to pick up the movement of troops and vehicles, to allow pre-emptive airstrikes to be ordered. The air offensive, dubbed Operation Niagara, was soon joined by

During the night, six US Air Force Fairchild C-123 Provider cargo aircraft were able to deliver 26 tons of ammunition, and a marine Sikorsky CH-53 Sea Stallion landed with a cargo of urgently needed blood supplies for the base's hospital. This set the scene for the next two months of the siege, with the marines hunkering down under communist bombardments, while at the same time fighting off occasional attempt to penetrate the perimeter. Keeping the airstrip open would be critical for the coming battle.

As the communist offensive unfolded, the two US Army Special Forces camps out in the jungle were first surrounded and then overrun. The communists brought up PT-76 tanks to help clear out the Americans from the border zone and ease

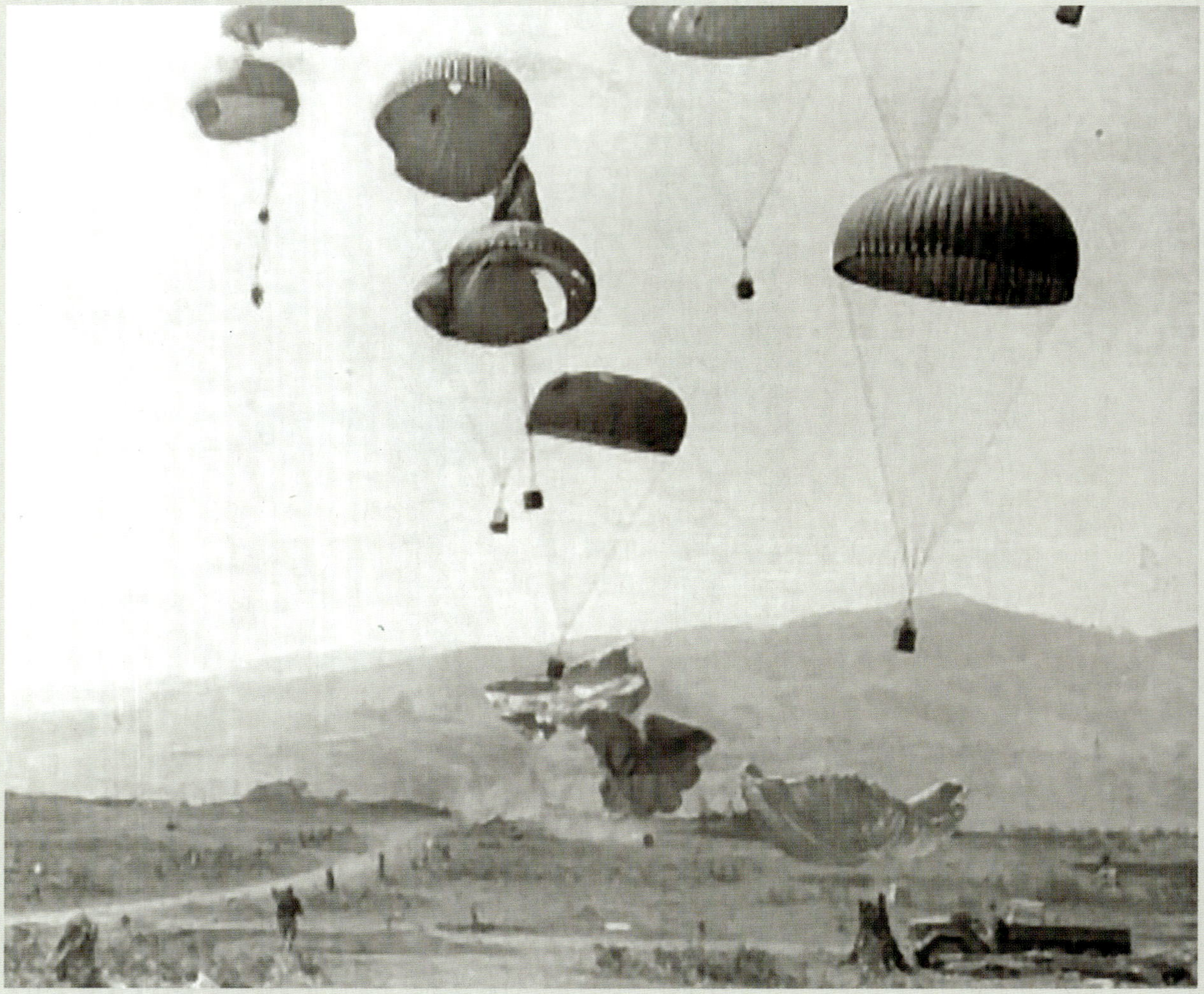

RIGHT: Parachute drops of supplies augmented the resupply efforts to keep the Khe Sanh combat base's ammunition dumps full throughout the siege. (US NATIONAL ARCHIVES)

waves of Boeing B-52 Stratofortress bombers. On January 30, the B-52s alone dropped 1,125 tons of bombs on targets around Khe Sanh.

On the night of February 3/4, the sound sensor field detected the movement of 1,500 to 2,000 communist troops towards Khe Sanh. An interdiction barrage by marine artillery, backed by US Army 175mm long-range howitzers outside Khe Sanh, was directed at the approaching column.

A few hours later, hundreds of NVA soldiers tried to storm Hill 861 again. More than 100 dead communist troops were discovered when the marines finally drove off the attack.

Through February, communist gunners kept up their bombardments of the base and made regular attempts to penetrate the perimeter wire. Heavy US artillery and air strikes forced the communists to stay under cover of the jungle canopy during daylight hours. In a bid to provide cover for their assault detachments, communist troops started to dig trenches from the edge of the jungle across the open ground to the American perimeter wire entanglement. These trenches were repeatedly hit by air strikes and artillery, prompting one American general to describe the land around the Khe Sanh base as looking "like pictures of the surface of the moon, in that it was cratered, pocked and blasted".

Even with the overwhelming American firepower, the communist gunners were striking Khe Sanh with more than 1,000 shells daily during February, killing and wounding dozens of marines each day. On February 23, the ammunition dump was hit again, detonating 1,600 American shells.

The launching of the Tet Offensive at the end of January put the US command in Vietnam under massive

BELOW: Almost non-stop close air support from US Marine and USAF aircraft was needed to keep communist troops at a distance from the Khe Sanh perimeter. (US NATIONAL ARCHIVES)

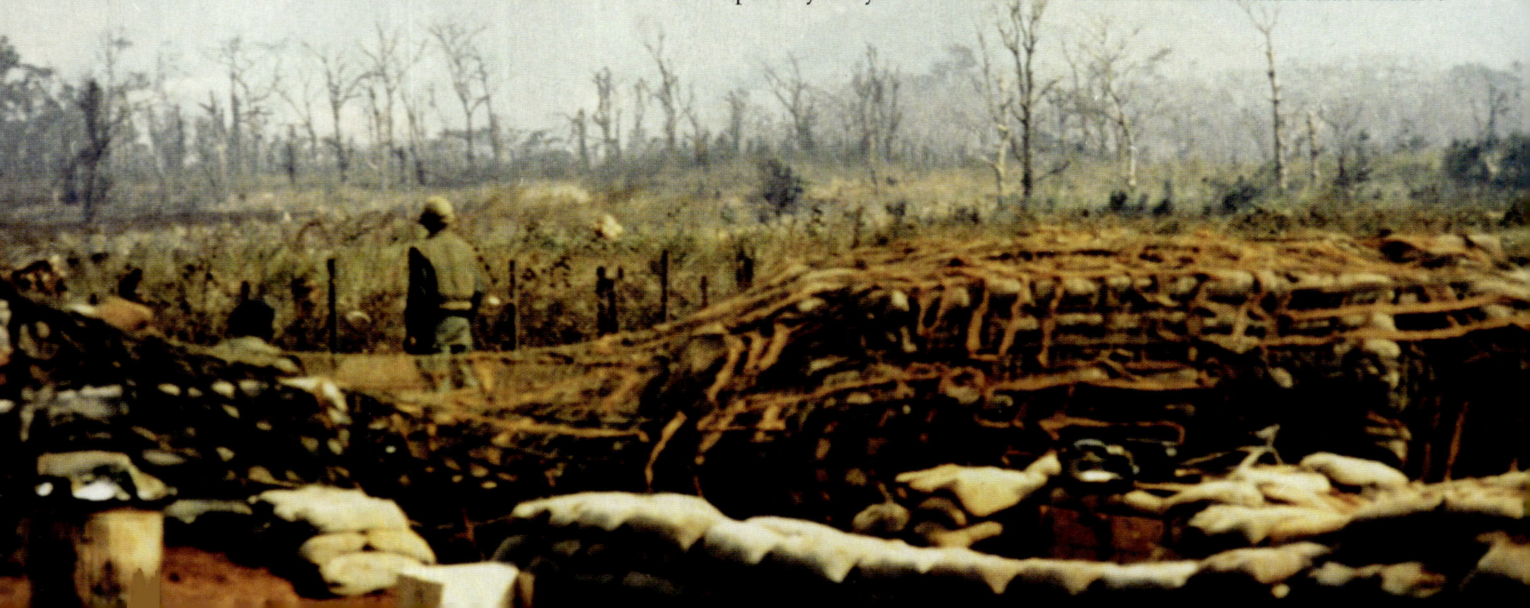

strain and there were few spare troops to ride to the rescue of Lownds' marines. By the last week of February, the Tet Offensive had been contained, and plans were under way to relieve Khe Sanh. But the marines there were not content to wait to be rescued and started a series of raids out of their base to drive back NVA positions from the perimeter. As the communist command started to pull back, the 26th Marine Regiment increased the size and duration of its 'search and destroy' missions into the jungle around the base.

On March 26, the US Army's 1st Cavalry Division (Airmobile) kicked off Operation Pegasus, to open a land corridor to Khe Sanh. By April 8, the Air Cav' arrived at Khe Sanh to end 77 days of siege.

Colonel Lownds and his marines held out against more than 40,000 NVA regulars; the communists were not able to repeat their victory at Dien Bien Phu.

The 26th Marine Regiment held its ground under relentless attack and bombardment with 10,908 communist artillery shells, rockets and mortar rounds being fired at the marine base. Between November 1967 and April 1968, 205 marines were killed and 1,668 wounded defending Khe Sanh. The intensity of the fight was illustrated by the body count of between 10,000 and 15,000 NVA killed during the battle. US aircraft dropped 103,500 tons of bombs in 24,449 missions defending Khe Sanh. US Marine and US Army gunners fired 102,660 rounds during the battle American firepower won the day.

The American public followed the battle daily on their television screens during the height of the battle and there was huge relief when the siege was lifted. US President Lyndon Johnson honoured the bravery of the 26th Regiment at a ceremony in the White House in May 1968, when he presented its commander and regimental sergeant major with its third Presidential Unit Citation. A new US Marine Corps legend was born.

Battle of Hue

Streetfighting Marines

ABOVE: In one of the iconic images of the Battle for Hue, 'Twentieth Century Angel of Mercy' US Navy Hospital Corpsman D R Howe treats the wounds of Private First Class D A Crum, of Company H, 2nd Battalion, 5th Marine Regiment. (USMC, SGT WILLIAM F DICKMAN)

In the early hours of January 31, 1968, communist troops launched a co-ordinated attack to seize the city of Hue. At 0233 hours, a red flare was fired over the city's historic citadel to signal the start of the attack. North Vietnamese Army (NVA) troops disguised as peasants and street traders, revealed themselves and started overrunning Army of Republic of Vietnam (ARVN) bases, government buildings and South Vietnamese police check points.

Taken by surprise on the Tet holiday (Vietnamese New Year), the ARVN defenders put up token resistance and were soon trapped in a handful of major bases around the city. With the roads into the city in communist hands, thousands of NVA troops poured in to begin setting up defensive positions. Vietcong political cadres joined them to seize government buildings and set a revolutionary

administration. Thousands of government officials, business leaders and others who were considered 'counter-revolutionaries' were rounded up by the Vietcong.

Many were later found dead in mass graves around the city.

The lightning assault on Hue was one of the few communist successes in the opening hours of the Tet

RIGHT: US Marines pushed forward into the centre of the city of Hue on February 2, with tank support to clear out determined communist defenders. (USMC ARCHIVE)

Columns of ARVN troops sent to help were ambushed and bogged down on the outskirts of the city. It was time to call for the US Marines.

The 1st Marine Regiment had been alerted for the mission early on January 31 and was soon heading towards the southern edge of Hue, which was separated from the rest of the city by Perfume River. This was the modern district of the city, containing several large concrete buildings including its university, hospitals and government administration.

The 5th Marine Regiment was close behind and both units were fully in position late on February 3,

➤

Offensive. Across South Vietnam more than 300,000 NVA troops and Vietcong fighters had attacked urban areas from the demilitarised zone (DMZ) in the north, down to Saigon (now Ho Chi Minh City) and the Mekong Delta. The declared aim was to seize urban areas and inspire the local population to rise up in revolution against the 'puppet regime' installed in South Vietnam by the Americans. Except in Hue, the offensive went badly wrong from the start. There was poor co-ordination. Soon the Americans and ARVN recovered from the surprise and staged violent counter-attacks. There was no uprising and vicious street fighting was taking place across the country as the surviving communist units were mopped up by US and ARVN troops.

The offensive looked better on television. When US news crews filmed a battle between the Vietcong sappers and US military policemen in the grounds of the US Embassy in the centre of Saigon, it sent shock waves across America. How could the enemy penetrate into the heart of the US presence in South Vietnam? The attack lasted less than seven hours and eventually all 19 Vietcong sappers were dead.

In the US Marine Corps sector, up in the north of the country, communist forces attacked in most towns and cities; air bases and camps came under artillery and rocket fire, forcing US personnel to dive for cover. The bombardment added to the confusion in the American command and for several vital hours the communists held the initiative, which enabled them to secure their hold on Hue.

The city was the former imperial capital of Vietnam and contained the historic citadel district, with its ancient palace, temples, theatres and other monuments. Today, it is a UNESCO world heritage site, but in 1968, the ancient city was surrounded by urban sprawl of a mix of French colonial buildings and 1950s-era modern structures.

Small ARVN and US military units had several compounds in the city. Those that held out against the initial communist strike were soon locked down and their defenders were trading fire with NVA sniper teams positioned around them. They started to radio for help to US units outside the city.

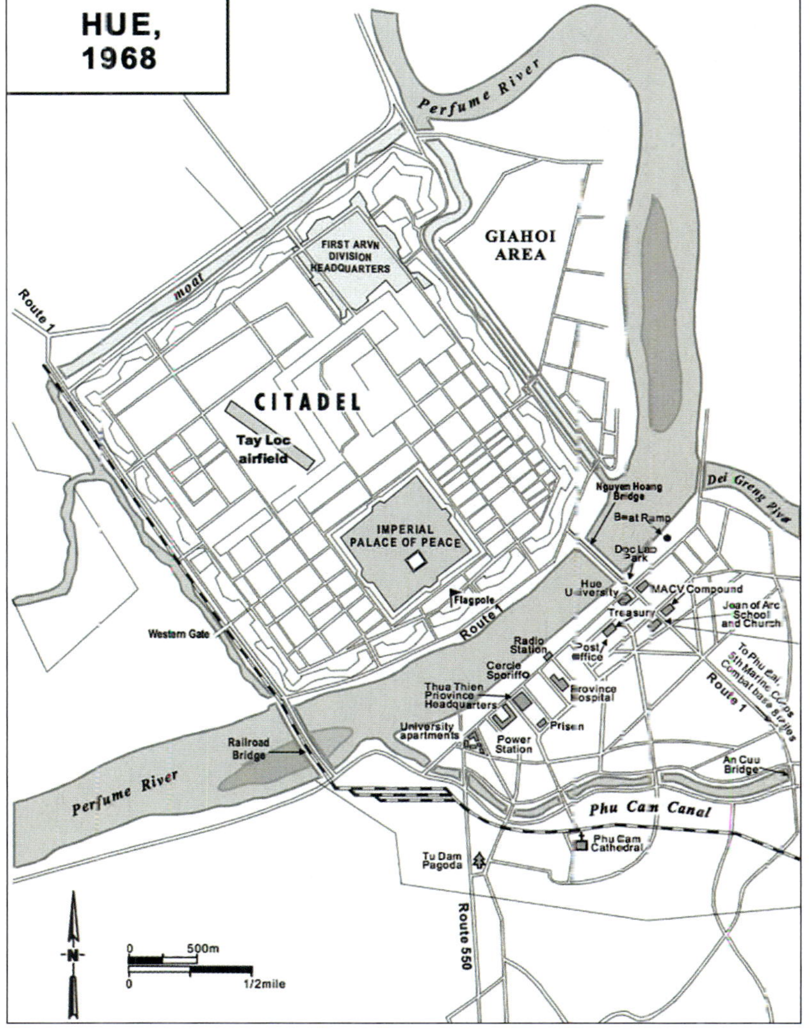

RIGHT: Marines trade fire with communist snipers in the street fighting in the modern district of Hue. (USMC ARCHIVE)

BELOW: Few parts of the city of Hue were not scarred by the intense fighting in February 1968. (USMC ARCHIVE)

to begin a determined drive to clear the southern district of communist forces. The following battle would be the most intense period of urban combat in the history of the US Marine Corps and would subsequently be immortalised in the Hollywood movie, *Full Metal Jacket*.

Two battalions of marines were committed to the operation, attacking in line abreast towards the Perfume River, which dissected the city from east to west. Communist troops had fortified almost every large building, barricaded the main roads and set up observation posts in high-rise buildings to call down mortar fire on any Americans who broke cover.

The battle broke down into a series of small running fire fights as US Marines worked their way northwards, clearing building after building. Demolition charges were used to blow holes in walls to allow the marines to enter buildings and gain a lodgement before the defenders could react. Defenders rolled hand grenades down stairwells or onto marines from upper-storey windows. This was nothing like the marines had experienced in Vietnam before. Company commanders and squad leaders had to improvise tactics to take on the defenders and maintain the momentum of the advance. Controlling high buildings was key, so once the marines had captured them, they sent sniper teams up onto their roofs to control the streets below. Anti-tank gunners carried 106mm recoilless rifles up stairwells to fire them from upper windows at NVA troops holding buildings across streets. Marine M48 tanks and Ontos anti-tank vehicles were pressed into service to blast communist strong points.

When marines stormed the provincial prison complex, NVA soldiers put up fierce resistance, ➤

LEFT: Marines had to fight house-to-house as they cleared every building in the modern district of Hue of regular North Vietnamese Army troops. (USMC ARCHIVE)

BELOW: A sniper from Company D, 1st Battalion, 5th Marine Regiment takes aim during the Battle of Hue. (USMC ARCHIVE)

so to try to flush them out of cellar bunkers the marines resorted to dropping canisters of CS riot-control gas into the enemy positions. Several communist soldiers were captured when they emerged into the light to avoid choking to death.

The marines then recaptured the provincial administration building and caused displeasure in the US high command when they were filmed by a CBS television news teams pulling down the Vietcong flag and raising the Stars and Stripes over the building, ignoring orders to only raise the South Vietnamese flag on captured positions.

By February 10, the communist defences in the south of the city had been broken. The NVA command ordered its troops to break contact and slip out of the Old City. As they exfiltrated their positions, NVA sappers blew up the Le Loi Bridge over the Perfume River, preventing the marines rolling north to join ARVN and US Army units fighting around the old citadel.

During the battle for the southern district, the marines claimed to have killed more than 1,000 NVA soldiers, as well as capturing six prisoners of war, and detaining 89 suspected Vietcong fighters. Marine casualties included 38 dead and around 320 wounded. In one marine company, every officer and NCO had sustained wounds, prompting one marine to comment: "We would start getting new guys and it just seemed that every time we got new guys, we would lose them just as fast as we got them."

North of the Perfume River, the ARVN and a small contingent from the 1st Cavalry were meeting heavy resistance. They had managed to punch a column through to open

a route to the besieged 1st ARVN Division compound on the northern edge of the citadel district, but then their advance stalled. Limits had been placed on the use of air strikes and artillery in the ancient city, making it even harder for ARVN to advance in the face of determined NVA resistance.

The 1st Battalion, 5th Marine Regiment was now brought into the city to bolster the drive in the citadel. After mustering in the marine-held southern district, they moved by US Navy landing craft up to the Perfume River to an assembly area to join the assault on the citadel. A battery of marine artillery moved close to the southern bank of the Perfume River so they could support their comrades as they cleared the last communist strong points.

The assault force advanced southwards and then hit strong resistance from NVA positions dug into the ancient city walls near the Dong Da Bridge Gate. Communist troops had buried themselves deep into the walls and could not be moved by small arms fire. Marine commanders set plans to blast a way through early on February 14. Naval gunfire from destroyers and cruisers offshore was laid on, backed up by heavy artillery fire and airstrikes. Marine aircraft made repeated runs, dropping high explosive bombs, fire rockets and then napalm. This appeared to have little effect, and the marines could not move forward. Reinforcements were called up and a repeat of the fire support was planned for the following morning.

After another bombardment, the tower above the gate collapsed creating a route forward for the

Once inside the citadel, the 5th Regiment found a completely different city scape. It comprised tightly packed streets of old buildings made from thick masonry walls, divided by narrow alleyways. The communist defenders had put up roadblocks and created firing points in walls to make it impossible for the attacks to move fast down the citadel's streets. Every building had to be systematically cleared by marines.

Heavy rain and cloud added to the marines' problems, making it very difficult for the pilots of strike aircraft to find any targets to attack or artillery observers to call down fire.

Once again, the marines turned to their M48 tanks and Ontos anti-tank vehicles to blast routes forward. Marine mortar teams were provided with CS gas rounds so they could drop gas shells through the roofs of buildings, flushing out communist defenders.

After four days of grinding fighting the high command ordered a temporary halt to allow the marines to rest and resupply.

On February 20, the marines were ready to attack again, but this time they came up with a daring tactic to break communist resistance. A platoon of marines found a gap in the communist defences and sneaked ●

marines who were now able to get inside the city walls and begin clearing out communist bunkers, firing positions with grenades and demolition charges. This battle cost the marines six dead and 50 wounded, against a position held by only 20 determined NVA soldiers.

ABOVE: Street fighting in Hue did not respect places of worship or ancient monuments. Every building had to be fought for by the US Marines. (USMC ARCHIVE)

LEFT: Hue burns after a heavy US air strike during the final push to capture the city's ancient Citadel. (USMC ARCHIVE)

marines were awarded the Medal of Honor for their bravery during fighting around Hue, illustrating the intensity of the fighting in the city.

During its battles in Hue, the marines suffered 142 killed and around 1,100 wounded. This was nearly a quarter of all allied casualties during the battle. The communist defenders suffered heavy losses, including between 2,500 and 5,000 dead, out of around 11,000 NVA and Vietcong committed to take Hue. The battle left 80% of the city's buildings destroyed and 116,000 of its 140,000 civilian population were made homeless. It took decades to restore many of the historic buildings devasted during the battle.

US Marine commanders described the fighting as a major success, devastating several NVA regiments and decimating the Vietcong insurgent organisation in the north of the country.

It did not look that way to the prestigious CBS News anchorman Walter Cronkite, who visited southern Hue on February 10 and viewed the fighting. He famously commented in a broadcast soon afterwards: "It seems now more certain than ever that the bloody experience of Vietnam is to end in a stalemate. It is increasingly clear to this reporter that the only rational way out then will be to negotiate, not as victors, but as an honourable people who lived up to their pledge to defend democracy and did the best they could."

US President Lyndon Johnson was dismayed at the report, saying: "If I've lost Cronkite, I've lost Middle America." Weeks later, Johnson announced he was stopping the bombing of North Vietnam and was opening peace talks with the communists. He also said he would not seek re-election in the coming presidential poll.

through it under cover of darkness to capture three strong points at the heart of the enemy defences. The rest of the 5th Regiment was now able to surge forward to clear the last communist positions in the southeast section of the citadel. By the end of February 21, the NVA defences had been broken and the communists decided to retreat from the citadel to fight another day.

After spending a couple of days clearing up the citadel and re-organising, the marine regiments were assigned new tasks to sweep the countryside around Hue city for any communist troops who had escaped from the previous battles.

Marine battalions formed up in classic 'search and destroy' mode to clear districts and villages of enemy troops. There was a series of sporadic engagements, in which the marines called down fixed-wing and helicopter gunship strikes to overcome resistance. As they swept around the city, they found mass graves containing the bodies of government supporters killed by the Vietcong after they captured Hue.

By March 2, the marine regiments were ordered to wrap up their operations in Hue and move to other tasks. This brought to an end nearly a month of high intensity urban combat, of a kind never experienced before by the US Marine Corps. Two

THE DESTINATION FOR
MILITARY ENTHUSIASTS

Visit us today and discover all our latest releases

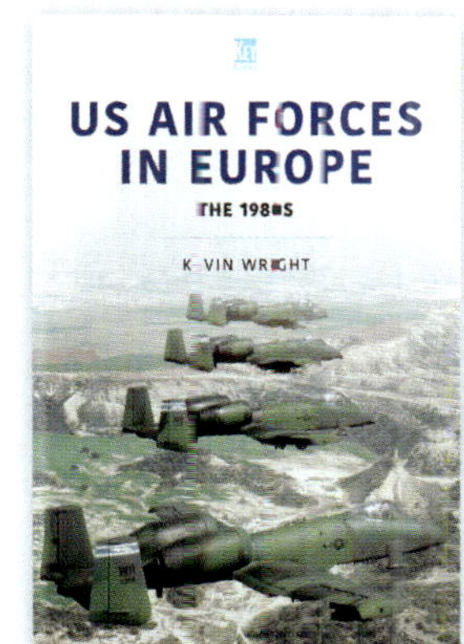

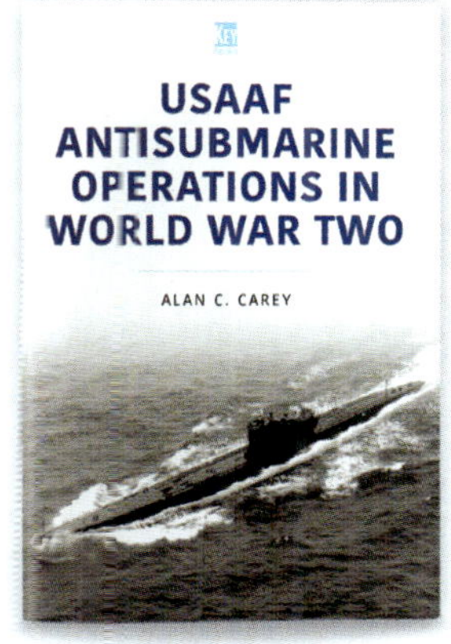

Order from our online shop...
keybooks.co.uk
Call +44 (0)1780 480404 *(Monday to Friday 9am - 5.30pm GMT)*
Free 2nd class P&P on BFPO orders. Overseas charges apply.

Operation Desert Storm

Marine air leads the way

ABOVE: US Marines pushed into Kuwait past hundreds of oil wells set ablaze by retreating Iraqi forces in their futile bid to thwart the coalition offensive. It took until November 1991 to put out the last of the fires. (US DOD/JOINT COMBAT CAMERA)

In response to the Iraqi invasion of the oil-rich Gulf state of Kuwait in August 1990, US President George H W Bush ordered more than 100,000 American soldiers to head to the Middle East to stop further advances by Saddam Hussein's troops.

The US Marine Corps was in the forefront of this response and the first Leathernecks of the 7th Marine Expeditionary Brigade touched down in Saudia Arabia on August 14, 1990 less than two weeks after the Iraqi invasion. These marines were the first wave of the build-up of the I Marine Expeditionary Force (I MEF), under the command of Lieutenant General Walter Boomer, which by February 1991 would reach 85,000 personnel. This was the first time since the Vietnam war that a full MEF-sized contingent of marines had been deployed into a combat zone.

The main components of I MEF, would be the ground units of the 1st and 2nd Marine Divisions, the strike aircraft and helicopters of the 3rd Marine Aircraft Wing (3 MAW) and the logistic experts of the 1st Force Service Support Group. This build-up included more than 220 fixed-wing aircraft and 170 helicopters under the command of 3 MAW, which were based in Saudi Arabia, Bahrain or on US Navy ships in the Northern Arabian Gulf.

RIGHT: The 2nd Marine Division staged Exercise Imminent Thunder in December 1990 in eastern Saudi Arabia to deceive the Iraqis into believing that the US Marines would launch an amphibious assault on the Kuwait coast. (US DOD/ JOINT COMBAT CAMERA)

By the end of 1990, more than 500,000 US troops were in the Middle East preparing to attack under the command of US Army General Norman Schwarzkopf. He was keen to use the massive airpower under his command to pummel Iraqi defences to minimise US casualties and speed up the expulsion of Saddam Hussein's troops from Kuwait. He set his air commander the challenge of reducing the strength of Iraqi troops in Kuwait by 50%. They were to be relentlessly bombed for more than a month to knock out their tanks, artillery and bunkers before the first coalition

ground troops crossed into Kuwait. Coalition artillery would then join in the relentless bombardment, causing Iraqi conscripts to flee their positions or put their hands up in surrender.

In the coalition war plan, I MEF was assigned the task of capturing Kuwait City and providing support to allied Arab armies, positioned on the left and right flanks of the marines. D-Day for the air campaign was set for January 17, 1991. The bulk of I MEF was still in its assembly areas as the air assault started, and the aviators of 3 MAW would be the first marines to see action in Operation Desert Storm.

For the first time, marine aviators would lead the charge in a US Marine Corps battle.

Just before 0230 hours on January 17, the first wave of 46 marine McDonnell Douglas F/A-18 Hornets, Grumman A-6E Intruders and EA-B Prowlers were airborne from Shaikh Isa Air Base to join a massive armada of coalition aircraft heading to strikes on key Iraqi command and control facilities across Iraq and Kuwait. Targets included Shaibah, Tallil, Qurnah and Al Rumaylah airfields, as well as Al Amarah and targets around Basra. Four A-6s were tasked to destroy Scud ballistic missile maintenance buildings at the Qurnah Airfield 30 miles north of Basra.

After dawn on January 17, the 3 MAW's aircraft shifted their attention to targets in northern Kuwait and Iraq. Despite poor weather across the region, McDonnell Douglas AV-8B Harrier II jump jets started to bomb Iraqi artillery positions just across the border from the Saudi town of al-Khafji. The 1st Marine Division had sent its reconnaissance battalions forward to set up observation posts along the Kuwait-Saudi border to monitor Iraqi troop movements and provide early warning to Arab battalions deployed to defend Saudi Arabia.

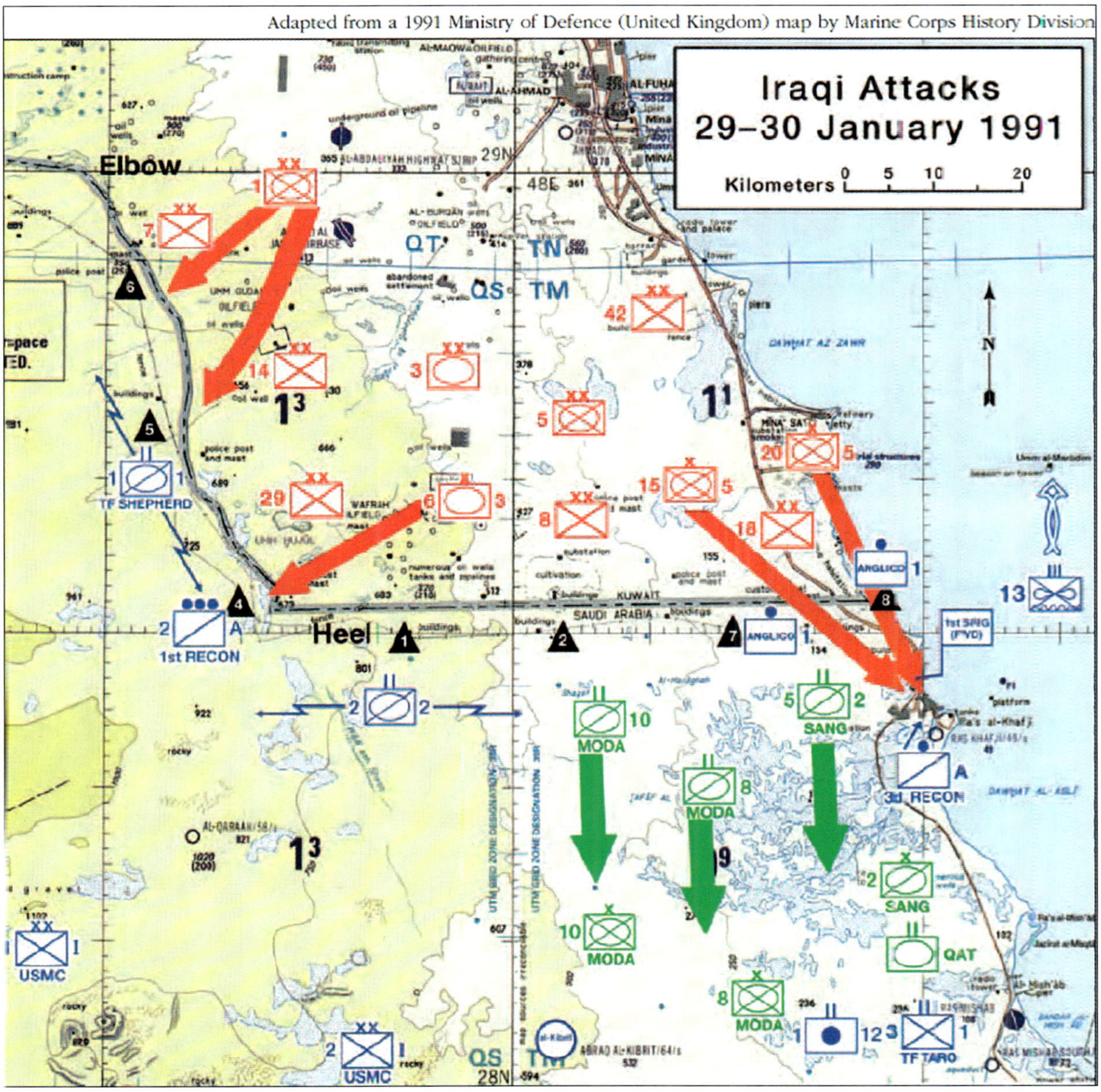

ABOVE LEFT: Lieutenant General Walter Boomer commanded the I Marine Expeditionary Force during Operations Desert Shield/Storm, which proved to be the largest US Marine Corps deployment since the Vietnam war. (US DOD/JOINT COMBAT CAMERA)

ABOVE RIGHT: US Marine reconnaissance units roll into Kuwait International Airport in light armoured vehicles after the retreat of Iraqi forces from Kuwait on February 27, 1992. (US DOD/JOINT COMBAT CAMERA)

LEFT: (USMC HISTORY DIVISION)

RIGHT: Marine artillerymen from the 2nd Marine Division fire their M-198 155mm howitzer in support of the opening of the ground offensive to free Kuwait during Operation Desert Storm. (US DOD/JOINT COMBAT CAMERA)

Other marine ground reconnaissance units in light armoured vehicles (LAVs) patrolled out in the desert along the border with Kuwait. Marine air-naval gunfire liaison teams were sent to observation posts to co-ordinate the provision of artillery and air support in case the Iraqis moved south.

Four days after the start of the air campaign, marine artillery joined the battle by launching a series of 'raids', in which gun batteries moved at night close to the border, bombarded targets and then retreated south at daybreak. Battery F, 2nd Battalion, 12th Marine Regiment, conducted the first such artillery raid against Iraqi rocket positions at

BELOW: Flight deck crews aboard the amphibious assault ship USS *Nassau*, sailing in the Northern Arabia Gulf, refuel two AV-8B Harrier jump jets as a third Harrier comes into land during Operation Desert Storm. (US DOD/JOINT COMBAT CAMERA)

0315 hours on January 21. Over the coming weeks, the relentless coalition bombardment began to have an impact and the marine observation posts along the border started to receive the surrender of defecting Iraqi troops. By February 1, I MEF had gathered 137 enemy prisoners of war and over the next fortnight another 101 Iraqis had surrendered to the marines.

The first ground battle of the war began on January 29 when an Iraqi mechanised battalion advanced into al-Khafji and met no organised resistance from Arab troops. The I MEF sent its reconnaissance marines to find out what was happening in the border town. In the early hours of January 30, the reconnaissance teams started to call in marine Bell AH-1W Cobra gunships to engage the Iraqi armour, with TOW missile systems, 20mm cannon fire and 2.75mm rockets, destroying several tanks and armoured vehicles.

Nine Iraqi soldiers waved white flags at the helicopters to surrender. The battle raged through the southern half of al-Khafji on January 31 as Saudi troops backed by US airpower launched a counter-attack. Marine Harriers and AH-1Ws provided direct

support to the Saudi and Qatari troops, with the air-naval gunfire teams directing the Cobras in a strafing run against the town's water tower, and Harriers destroyed Iraqi vehicles at the major road intersection in that quarter of the city.

Over the next three weeks, the 3 MAW stepped up its bombing campaign against Iraq troops dug in along the Kuwait-Saudi border. I MEF had moved its two divisions up to assembly areas just south of the border, where they waited to begin the attack. The plan was for the marines to open four breaches through the Iraqi minefields and bunker lines, to allow I MEF columns to push north towards Kuwait City. Tanks fitted with mine ploughs would clear safe routes for following vehicles and, once on top of the Iraqi bunkers, marines would jump down to round up the demoralised defenders. At this point, the marines were at their most vulnerable to attack by Iraq's stocks of chemical weapons, potentially inflicting thousands of casualties and stalling the coalition advance.

To neutralise this threat on the day before 'Ground-Day', February 24, 3 MAW's strike aircraft flew 450 missions against targets across Kuwait. As the I MEF crossed the border, 3 MAW launched a maximum effort to ensure its Hornets, Intruders and Harriers were airborne constantly

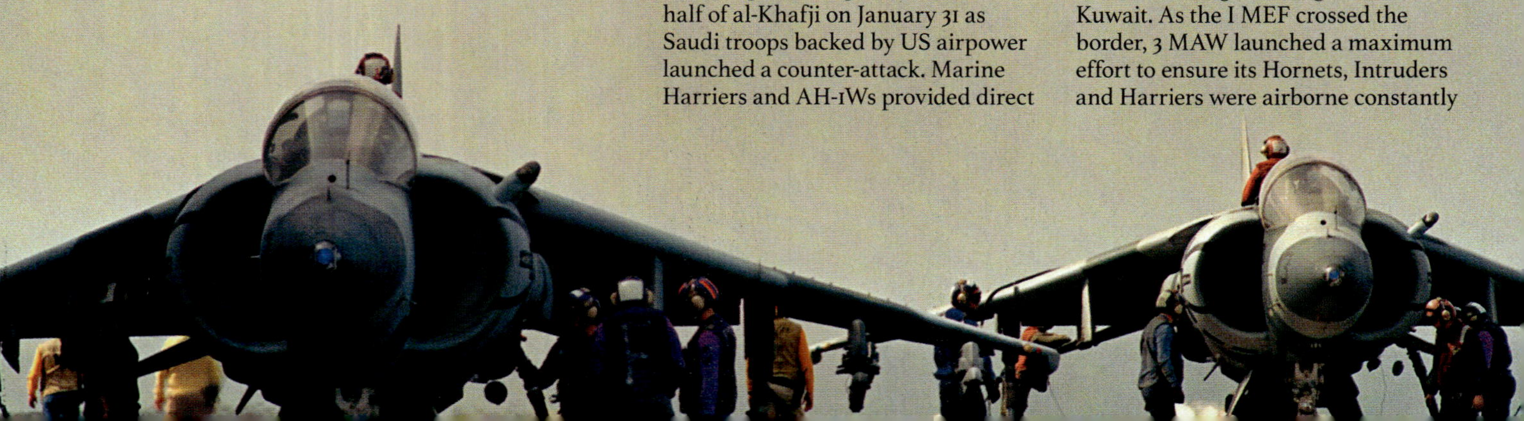

above the I MEF columns, ready to strike at any Iraqi gun batteries opening fire on the marines as they moved forward.

The marine columns quickly penetrated the first and then the second Iraqi defence lines, without encountering any serious resistance, and thousands of Iraqi prisoners were rounded up. Fog and smoke from oil wells set on fire by the Iraqis shrouded the battlefield and made it difficult for marine pilots to find targets, but by mid-morning, this started to clear, allowing Cobras to begin flying top cover for the advancing US Marines. This was just in time for them to engage two Iraqi armoured brigades that tried to stage a counter-attack. The marine gunships soon knocked out several tanks, sending the Iraqis reeling.

During February 25, the Iraqi army was ordered to retreat from Kuwait and soon thousands of troops and hundreds of vehicles were fleeing up the main road to the border from Kuwait City. Coalition intelligence spotted the convoy and US air commanders were ordered to attack and destroy it. Marine A-6Es were the first to attack, hitting the front and rear of the convoy with CBU-78 Gator mine-dispensing cluster bombs. Soon the Iraq column was trapped, then 3 MAW dispatched nearly 300 Harrier and Hornet sorties to attack it. During the attack that lasted into daylight hours, more than 1,400 vehicles were destroyed and several thousand Iraqi soldiers were killed. The remainder of the Iraqi soldiers fled the scene on foot, heading out of Kuwait across the desert.

With the Iraqi army on the run, I MEF was able to advance unopposed to the edge of Kuwait City on February 27. America's Arab allies were given the honour of being the ➤

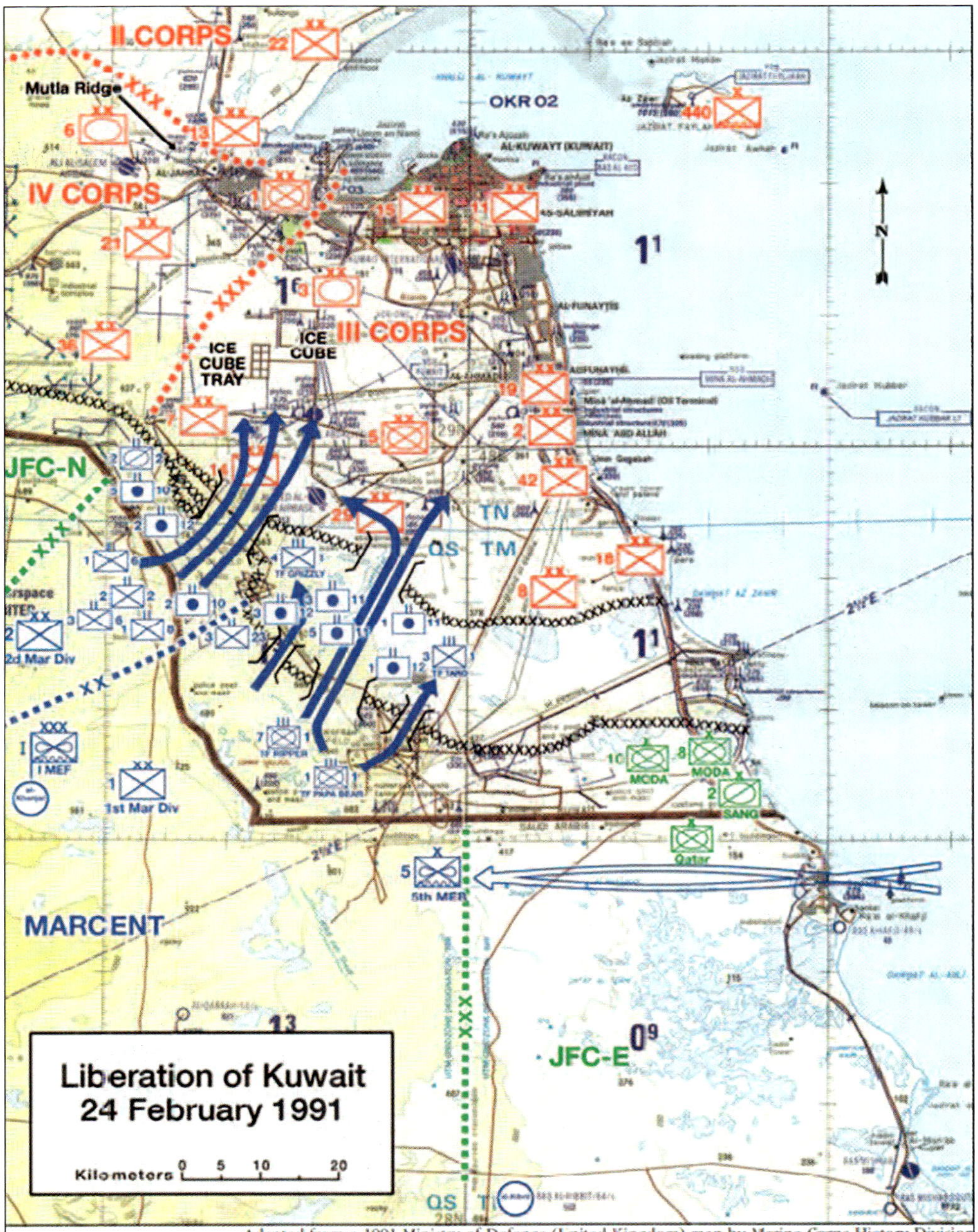

Adapted from a 1991 Ministry of Defence (United Kingdom) map by Marine Corps History Division

ABOVE: (USMC HISTORY DIVISION)

LEFT: An M-60A1 main battle tank equipped with reactive armour and mine-clearing rollers and ploughs stands by at the head of a column of AAVP-7A1 amphibious assault vehicles as the 2nd Marine Division prepares to enter Kuwait at the start of the ground phase of Operation Desert Storm. (US DOD/JOINT COMBAT CAMERA)

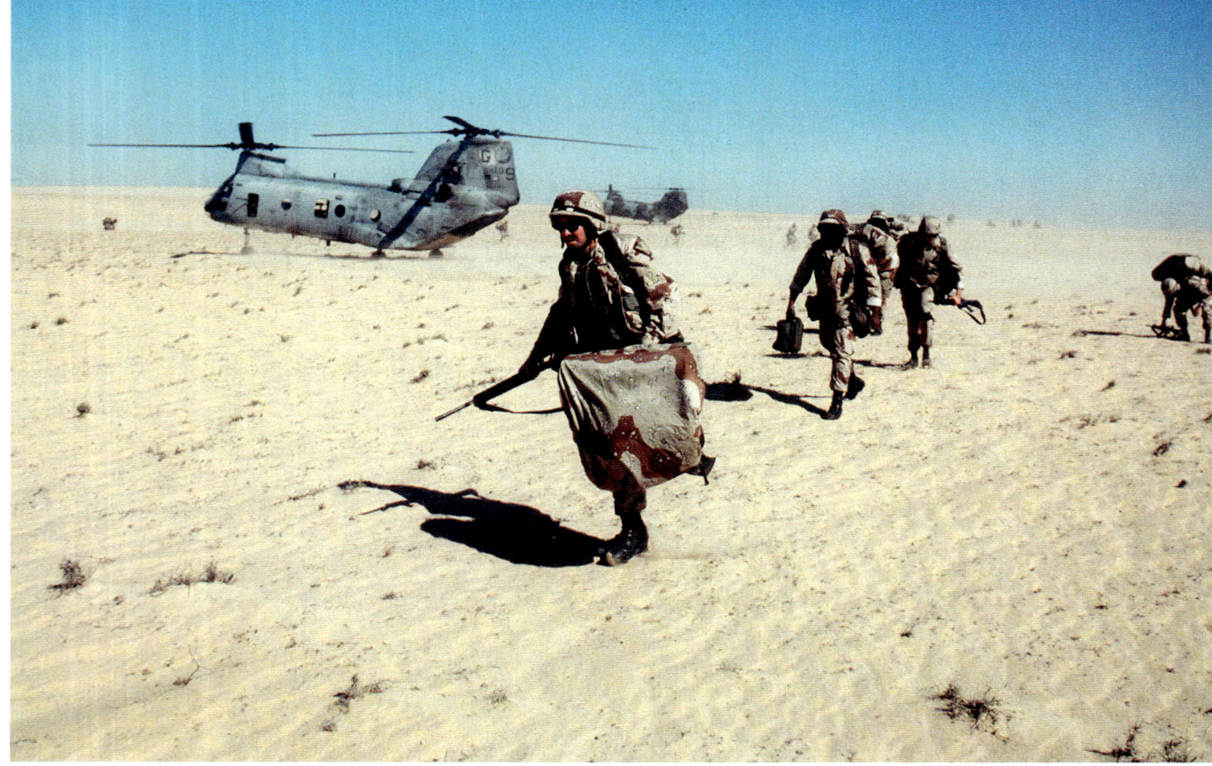

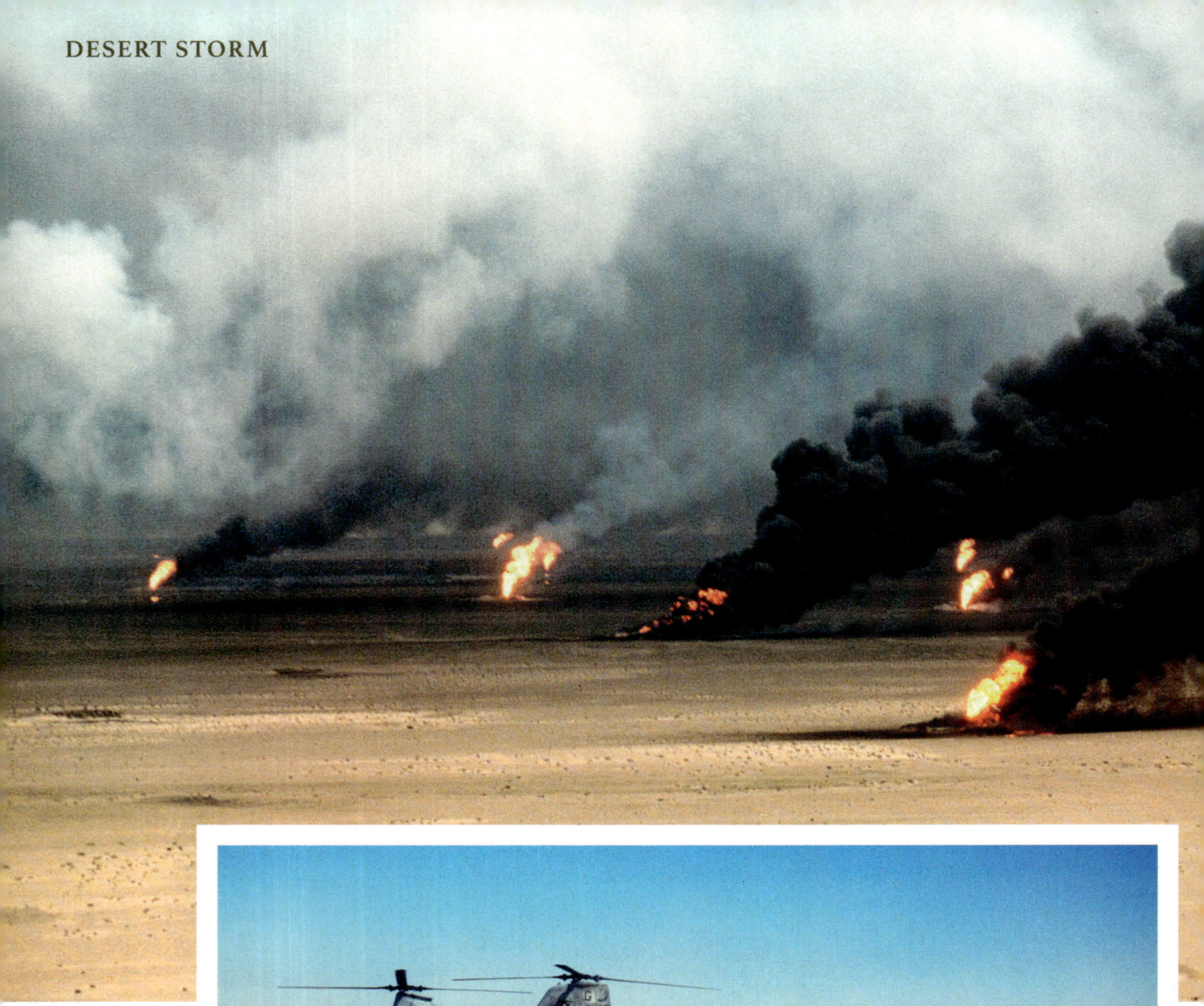

ABOVE: Kuwait's oil fields were set alight by the retreating Iraqis, creating an apocalyptic environment of huge smoke plumes, covering much of the emirate with choking, acrid fumes. (US DOD/JOINT COMBAT CAMERA)

RIGHT: Marines of the 2nd Marine Division disembarking from a CH-46E Sea Knight helicopter of Marine Medium Helicopter Squadron 263 (HMM-263) during a rehearsal for the invasion of Kuwait. (US DOD/JOINT COMBAT CAMERA)

first coalition troop to enter the city, allowing the marines of I MEF to stop and rest around Kuwait City. The scene was apocalyptic: more than 700 oil wells were on fire; thousands of abandoned Iraqi vehicles littered the battlefield; devastated bunkers and artillery batteries were everywhere; dazed and traumatised Iraqi soldiers were wandering around offering to surrender to any American they could find.

For many of the marines of I MEF, the ground war was an anti-climax. Few fired their rifles and the first Iraqis they encountered only wanted to surrender. General Schwarzkopf's air campaign had proved remarkably successful.

In 18,000 sorties, 3 MAW inflicted huge damage on the Iraqi army. Marine AH-1Ws were credited with destroying 97 tanks, 104 armoured personnel carriers and other vehicles and two anti-aircraft artillery positions.

US Marine fixed-wing aircraft dropped 16,742 high-explosive bombs and 15,889 cluster bombs, as well as 4,202 laser-guided bombs and 41 AGM-45 Maverick guided missiles during Operation Desert Storm.

By the time the ceasefire was called on February 28, I MEF had suffered only 24 killed in action and 92 wounded in action to liberate Kuwait. Senior US Marine commanders largely attributed this to the superlative air support they received by 3 MAW. The Iraqi army had been defeated from the air before I MEF had even crossed its start line. The marine aviators of 3 MAW had been instrumental in this aerial victory, smashing apart the Iraqi divisions in the path of I MEF.

Five marine aviators were captured during Operation Desert Storm and were released in the days following the ceasefire, after four Harrier and two Rockwell OV-10 Bronco observation aircraft were shot down. The prisoners received two of America's most prestigious awards, which no US serviceman ever aspires to attain, the Purple Heart and the Prisoner of War Medals. One marine Harrier pilot was rescued after being shot down and two were killed in action.

The liberation of Kuwait was a very one-sided victory. The Iraqis did not put up much resistance and they could not cope with the overwhelming firepower of I MEF and 3 MAW

General Schwarzkopf spoke to General Boomer on the tactical radio net shortly after Kuwait International Airport had been secured, summing up the drive that I MEF had made to reach its objectives: "It was another glorious chapter in the history of the Marine Corps."

ABOVE: Kuwaiti citizens turned out in their thousands to celebrate the retreat of Iraqi forces from Kuwait and to greet the advancing US Marines. (US DOD/JOINT COMBAT CAMERA)

LEFT: Demolished vehicles line Highway 8 to the north of Kuwait City, after being relentlessly pounded by US Marine Corps strike jets. Thousands of Iraqis died in the carnage, leading to the scene being dubbed the 'Highway of Death'. (US DOD/JOINT COMBAT CAMERA)

In the aftermath of the 9/11 attacks on New York and Washington DC, the United States unleashed its military power on Afghanistan to hunt down the mastermind of the atrocities, Osama bin Laden and his al Qaeda organisation.

Before the man-hunt could begin in earnest, the US military had to defeat Afghanistan's Taliban regime that was giving the terrorist leader sanctuary. By November 2001, after several weeks of air and cruise missiles strikes, the US military was poised to put boots on the ground in the central Asian country to establish the first American base on Afghan soil. Small groups of US Army Special Forces had already entered Afghanistan to mobilise rebel fighters against the Taliban, but it was only a matter of time before large combat forces were needed to complete the victory.

US Central Command chief, General Tommy Franks, had massed a contingent of US Marines, dubbed Naval Expeditionary Task Force 58 (TF 58), off the coast of Pakistan on board the amphibious warships USS *Peleliu* and USS *Bataan,* to be ready to pounce should an opportunity arise.

There were more than 2,000 marines of the 15th Marine Expeditionary Units (MEU) embarked on the USS *Peleliu*, along with 25 helicopters and a detachment of six McDonnell Douglas AV-8B Harrier IIs. The Harriers of VMA-311 did not immediately join the US-led air offensive but were held back to provide combat search and rescue coverage if any of the US Air Force heavy bombers and US Navy carrier-borne aircraft went down over enemy territory. In November 2001, this changed and VMA-311's jets started flying bombing missions from the USS *Peleliu*, using air-to-air refuelling from Royal Air Force Vickers VC10 and Lockheed Tristar tanker aircraft. They hit targets identified by US Special Forces air controllers working with tribes fighting the Taliban. The USS *Peleliu* was joined by the USS *Bataan*, with the 26th MEU and six more AV-8Bs of VMA-223 embarked.

One of the most famous modern marine commanders, Brigadier General James Mattis headed the TF 58. He was a well-read military historian who also had a reputation for looking after his marines. US President

Objective Rhino

Hunting al Qaeda

ABOVE: An AH-1W flies top cover for a USMC vehicle convoy heading out of FOB Rhino. (US DOD/JOINT COMBAT CAMERA)

RIGHT: US Marines escorted by AH-1Ws arrived at FOB Rhino to establish the first US base in Afghanistan. (US DOD/ JOINT COMBAT CAMERA)

Donald Trump later appointed Mattis as his defence secretary because of the general's reported nickname, 'Mad Dog'. Mattis later disowned this, saying his callsign as a regimental commander was 'Chaos', which reportedly stood for 'Colonel Has Another Outstanding Solution'.

The USS *Peleliu* had been off the Pakistani coast since early October, and it sent detachments of marines ashore to set up refuelling points in Pakistan to support US combat search and rescue helicopters. By early November, Franks gave Mattis his orders for the coming operation.

The objective of the marines was to "make sure that the enemy didn't feel like they had any safe haven, to destroy their sense of security in southern Afghanistan, to isolate Kandahar from its lines of communication and to move against Kandahar". It was hoped that the Taliban would mass its forces against Mattis and his marines, so they could be destroyed by US firepower.

US Special Forces commanders were initially sceptical and feared the marines would never be able to find any Taliban targets. Mattis told them this would not be problem, as the Taliban would come to him, adding: "I'm just going to go in and stick a Marine battle colour [flag or standard] out in the sand and say, 'bring it on'."

With the military situation in southern Afghanistan appearing to ➤

ABOVE: The devastating 9/11 attacks on New York and Washington DC prompted President George W Bush to order US troops to strike Afghanistan to hunt down the al Qaeda network's bases. (US DOD/ JOINT COMBAT CAMERA)

LEFT: Osama bin Laden and his al Qaeda network was the target for Task Force 58. (US DOD/JOINT COMBAT CAMERA)

The USS *Bataan* with the 26th Marine Expeditionary Unit embarked joined the USS *Peleliu* off the coast of Pakistan to form Task Force 58. (US DOD/JOINT COMBAT CAMERA)

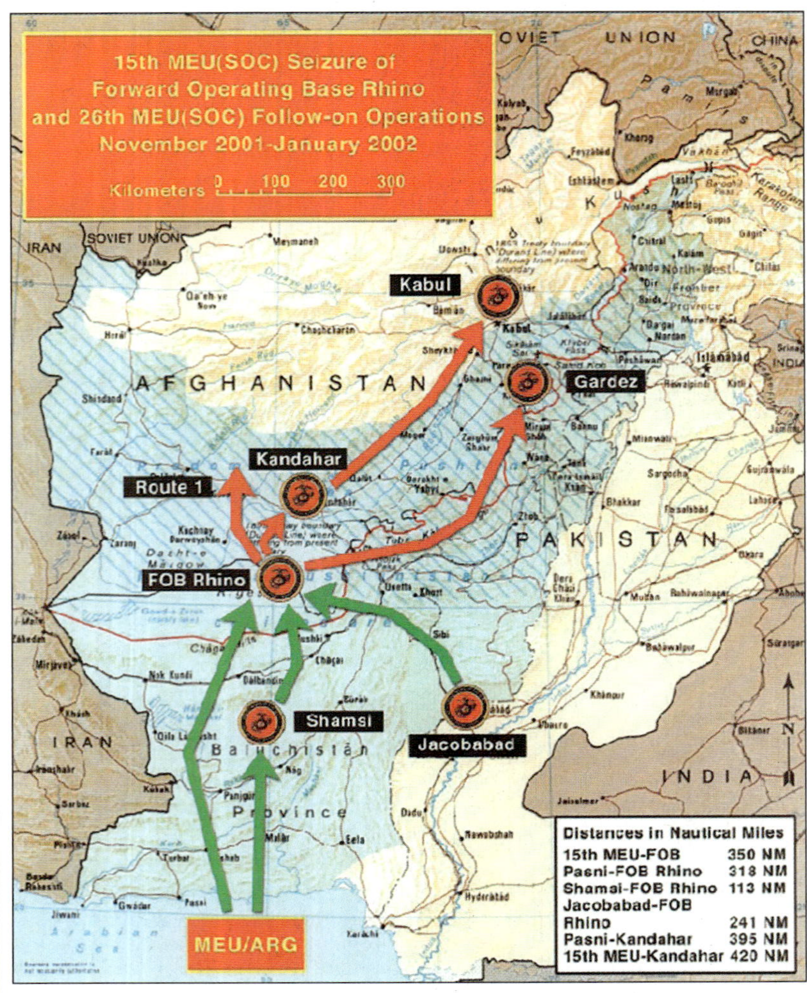

RIGHT: (USMC HISTORY DIVISION)

at a US-controlled airstrip, operated by marine detachments. At the same time, the assault force headed towards a 57-mile-long helicopter aerial refuelling track established just south of the Afghan border to take on fuel from the KC-130K tankers.

As the assault division was exiting its refuelling track, just five miles south of the border, the escort force rejoined the formation and began to cross into Afghanistan. A pair of AH-1Ws flew point for the formation to watch out for hostile forces, while commanders in the UH-1Ns monitored radio nets for reports of emerging threats.

As the assault force crossed the border behind the Cobras, the moonlit terrain shifted from flat desert to low mountains, and the speeding aircraft rose from 75ft to 200ft above sea level to compensate for the decrease in visual contrast. The crews also conducted penetration checks, switching off unnecessary devices that produced illumination or emitted an electronic signature, to decrease the likelihood of premature detection during the final leg of their journey. As the assault element approached the abandoned airfield, visible two miles in the distance, the escort flight leader relayed confirmation that the runway remained clear of hostile forces by transmitting the radio code word: "Winter."

RIGHT: AH-1Ws launched from the USS *Peleliu* were the first US attack helicopters to operate over Afghanistan. (US DOD/ JOINT COMBAT CAMERA)

be moving more favourably in the last week of November, Franks decided the time was ripe to introduce US combat forces into the region. TF 58's mission began with operations to seize Objective Rhino, an old dirt airstrip in the desert to the west of the Taliban capital, Kandahar. Six US Marine Corps Sikorsky CH-53E Sea Stallions – three each from the 15th and 26th MEUs – carrying more than 200 marines were launched from the USS *Peleliu*. The first three helicopters conducted night aerial refuelling with marine Lockheed KC-130R Hercules tankers en route to the objective, 350 nautical miles away from the ships in the northern Arabian Sea. The three helicopters in the second wave had difficulty conducting aerial refuelling but pressed on. The first CH-53Es were flown by crews from Marine Medium Helicopter Squadron (HMM) 163 and had the distinction of delivering the first US conventional troops safely onto Afghan soil.

The first flight of aircraft lifted off from the USS *Peleliu* around 1615 hours on November 25 and headed inland, with an escort force of four Bell AH-1W Cobra and three Bell UH-1N Huey helicopters.

The escort force first headed towards Shamsi in Pakistan to refuel

RIGHT: CH-53E Sea Stallions were refuelled in mid-air as they transported the first wave of US Marines to Objective Rhino. (US DOD/ JOINT COMBAT CAMERA)

LEFT: Brigadier General Jim Mattis (centre in green flak jacket) commanded Task Force 58 for the insertion operation into southern Afghanistan. (US DOD/JOINT COMBAT CAMERA))

After more than four hours in the air, the first flight of CH-53 helicopters and their Cobra escorts began to descend toward the landing zone at ten-minute intervals, guided towards their destination by flashing infrared strobe lights that the US Navy SEALs had placed in the middle of the dirt runway. Due to severe brownout conditions – thick, towering dust clouds stirred up by the aircraft's spinning rotor blades – several of the pilots were forced to approach the runway on a number of occasions before successfully landing. The Huey and Cobra helicopters began to land, taking up positions along the airfield where they remained on a 15-minute strip alert. In a classic case of military understatement, one Cobra pilot later remarked: "It was a fairly busy 30, 40 minutes until the second wave hit the deck."

The marines had been met by a SEAL reconnaissance team that had been inserted on November 21 to keep the airstrip under surveillance. A US Navy Lockheed P-3C Orion AIP aircraft provided continuous intelligence, surveillance and reconnaissance (ISR) coverage around the marines throughout the night and on all subsequent nights. At the same time, a US Air Force Northrop Grumman E-8C Joint STARS surveillance aircraft provided wide-area coverage with its radars, which could detect vehicle movement over hundreds of square miles of desert.

The operation was a tour de force of power-projection operations. Once US Air Force Special Tactics Squadron (STS) personnel inspected the dirt strip and declared it to be KC-130-capable, additional marines flew in on KC-130s from the US airbase at Jaccbabad in Pakistan, where they had been pre-positioned. The first KC-130 to land on the dirt airstrip was flown by a VMGR-352 detachment aircrew, landing an hour-and-a-half after the insertion of the heli-borne assault force.

The marine security force now spread out around the airstrip to set up a perimeter and secure the site ❯

BELOW: Waves of US Marines arrived on CH-46E Sea Knights in the days following the establishment of FOB Rhino. (US DOD/JOINT COMBAT CAMERA)

for more aircraft and helicopters to follow. Each of them had little more than the kit and ammunition they could carry in a rucksack. Once in position, they started digging foxholes to be ready to repel the expected Taliban counter-attack. General Mattis's marines spent a cold night standing sentry in the foxholes, not knowing what would happen when the sun came up.

The following day, an E-8A Joint STARS radar surveillance aircraft detected several Taliban armoured vehicles to the northwest of the marine outpost. After US Navy Grumman F-14 Tomcat fighter jets confirmed their identity, more F-14s from the USS *Theodore Roosevelt* and AH-1Ws, flying from the newly renamed Forward Operating Base (FOB) Rhino, were called to attack the column.

The marine Cobras, which had the callsign Evil Eye 34 and 35, headed towards the convoy and – at the E-8A's request – helped co-ordinate the attack, watching as the Tomcats engaged the armoured personnel carriers. After the US Navy fighters had completed their bombing run, striking just in front of the lead armoured personnel carrier and disabling it, the marine gunships took their turn. Emerging from behind a nearby ridge, the Cobras used their 20mm cannon and rockets to engage the two armoured vehicles and eight to ten dismounted personnel.

One of the Cobra pilots later described the attack, saying: "At least some of the Taliban were out of the vehicles. I'm guessing they thought they hit a mine since the F-14s were so high. They heard us and some of them started firing

wildly in the air toward the sound of the Cobras – the rest started running. We made several passes destroying the vehicles and killing the squad. Passing back over the convoy, the pilots used their night-vision goggles and infrared sensors to assess the battle damage, but determined that nothing of military value was left."

Once American boots were on the ground in Afghanistan, the Taliban started to mobilise attacks against FOB Rhino. At this point, the two AV-8B squadrons stepped up their patrols around the desert outpost, hitting convoys of armed Taliban pick-up trucks with bombs or shooting them in strafing runs.

The first wave of USAF Boeing C-17 Globemaster aircraft arrived at FOB Rhino on November 28, transporting 'Seabee' personnel from Naval Mobile Construction Battalion 133 to begin improving the conditions of the airstrip to allow it to take sustained air operations. By this point, more than 1,000 US Marines were ashore in Afghanistan, backed by artillery and wheeled light

ABOVE: After Task Force 58 took control of Kandahar International Airport on December 14, reinforcements started to surge into Afghanistan to turn the site into a major US base. (US DOD/JOINT COMBAT CAMERA)

LEFT: Establishing their first base at Objective Rhino in November 2001, US troops remained in Afghanistan until August 2021. (US DOD/JOINT COMBAT CAMERA)

ABOVE: In the early months of 2002, marine units of Task Force 58 spread out around Afghanistan searching for former al Qaeda bases to collect intelligence to try to prevent future attacks by Osama bin Laden's acolytes. (US DOD/JOINT COMBAT CAMERA)

armoured vehicles (LAVs) and were ready to start offensive operations.

The marine base was rapidly expanding into a hub to support US operations across Afghanistan. On December 6, John Walker Lindh, the so-called 'American Taliban', who had been captured by US Special Forces in northern Afghanistan, arrived at FOB Rhino, earning the notorious distinction of being the first of many detainees eventually held by TF 58.

It was now time for TF 58 to strike out from FOB Rhino, with vehicle convoys of LAVs and Humvees heading out to the north and east to interdict main roads to interrupt Taliban supply lines. The P-3s provided overwatch and a pair of

Cobras scouted ahead to look for Taliban traffic.

The marines set up a series of roadblocks and engaged Taliban fighters who attempted to bypass them. By December 9, Kandahar had fallen to anti-Taliban fighters and three days later Mattis flew by helicopter to meet the leaders of the new rulers of Kandahar, which included the future president of Afghanistan, Hamid Karzai. It was agreed that the marines would move to take possession of Kandahar International Airport on December 14 to establish a large base to support US operations across southern Afghanistan. A vehicle convoy was greeted by a US Army Special Forces team that had helped Karzai's militia capture the airfield a few days earlier.

Marine CH-53s then started to arrive from FOB Rhino carrying a security force to establish a perimeter around the airfield.

By early January 2002, TF 58 closed down FOB Rhino and the marines had relocated to the Kandahar airport to begin helping allied special forces hunt down the remnants of the Taliban and al Qaeda. US Army troops now started to arrive to take over the security of the airport, to allow the marines to head for home.

The US Marine Corp official history of the opening months of Operation Enduring Freedom describes the activities of TF 58 as a major success: "From a strategic perspective, the arrival of a sizable conventional force

Staff in 2001, later observed: "The insertion of Task Force 58 had a deep psychological impact on the Taliban and al Qaeda – they were confronted with a military situation which now unhinged any hope they had for a gradual pullback from the north and a chance to hold from their area of greatest strength... The insertion of Task Force 58 fundamentally changed the equation for the enemy from one of grim hope to hopelessness."

LEFT: America's Afghan allies helped defeat the Taliban and al Qaeda in 2001, but subsequently they proved to be unreliable partners. (US DOD/JOINT COMBAT CAMERA)

BELOW: Once Task Force 58 was firmly established at Kandahar International Airport, FOB Rhino was closed down. It had served its purpose. (US DOD/JOINT COMBAT CAMERA)

demonstrated America's resolve to confront the sponsors of terrorism directly and signalled an end to Taliban rule. From an operational perspective, Task Force 58 successfully blocked the western escape route from Kandahar and threatened the enemy's last remaining urban stronghold. The strategic agility and operational reach showcased by the US Navy amphibious squadrons and US Marine Corps expeditionary units validated the utility of task-organised expeditionary forces, particularly in respect to the effectiveness of long-range, ship-to-objective manoeuvre."

Marine General Lieutenant General Gregory S Newbold, director of operations for the Joint Chiefs of

Drive on Baghdad

Toppling Saddam Hussein

RIGHT: Dealing with unrest across Iraq in the wake of the collapse of Saddam Hussein's regime proved a major challenge to the US military. (DOD, SGT JEREMIAH LANCASTER)

For the US Marines who fought in the southern Iraqi city of Nasiriyah, the road from the Euphrates River to the Saddam Canal was called 'Ambush Alley'. During most of March 23, 2003, the marines of Task Force Tarawa battled with Iraqi troops and irregulars along the 4km length of road, trading small arms, anti-tank rockets and tank fire.

Then at the height of the battle two US Air Force Fairchild A-10A Warthog ground attack jet mistook the leading marine units for enemy troops and started to strafe them. By the end of the day 18 marines were dead and dozens injured in the bloodiest battle of the opening phase of Operation Iraqi Freedom.

Despite this setback, just over two weeks later the advance guard of the 1st Marine Division had entered the Iraqi capital Baghdad and the country's infamous dictator, Saddam Hussein, had fled his opulent presidential palace.

The full-on invasion of Iraq to overthrow Saddam Hussein and his regime, was ordered by US President George W Bush after he received intelligence indicating – later found to be erroneous - that the Iraqi leaders were developing nerve gas and other weapons of mass destruction.

The US Marine Corps contributed the I Marine Expeditionary Force (I MEF), under the command of Lieutenant General James Conway, to the invasion force and its 81,500 marines started gathering in Kuwait during the first two months of 2003.

Conway and his command team worked with their US Army counterparts to develop a plan for a blitzkrieg-style advance on Baghdad to defeat the Iraqi army in less than a month. Fast moving US columns would by-pass Iraqi towns and cities along the Euphrates and Tigris valleys, as coalition air power pounded Iraqi Republican Guard divisions positioned south of Baghdad. Once US forces were massed outside the Iraqi capital, they would surround the city before striking at the heart

BELOW: Marines from the 15th Marine Expeditionary Unit cross into Iraq at Az Zubayr, Iraq, in the early hours of March 23, 2003. (USMC, LCPL BRIAN L WICKLIFFE)

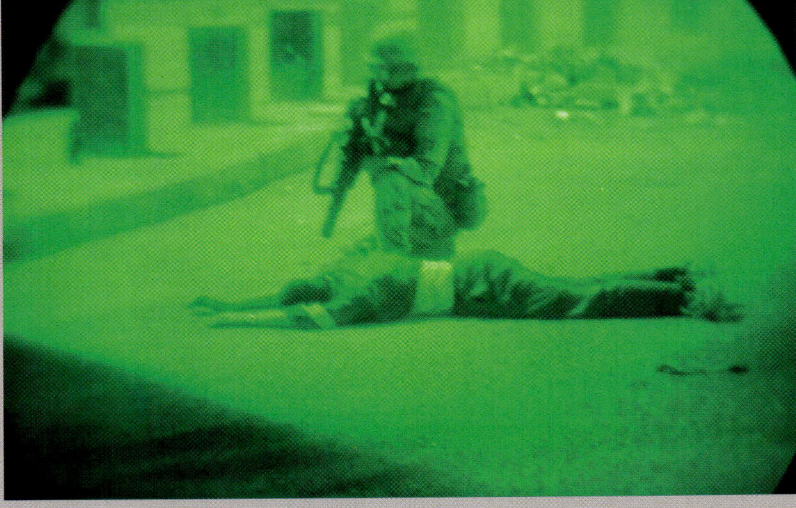

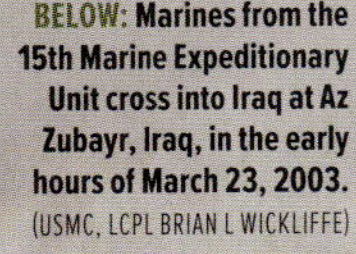

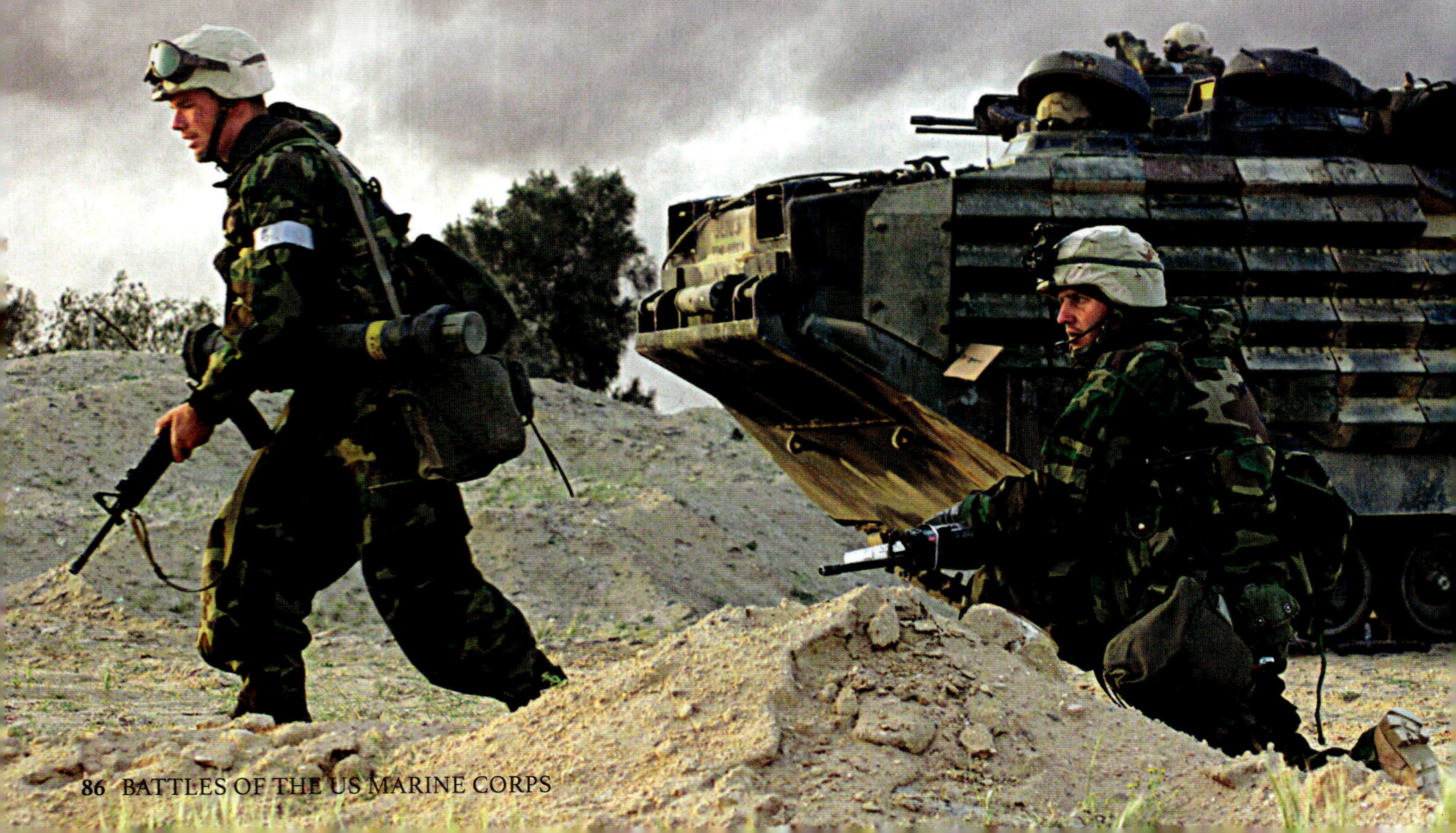

LEFT: Marines of Charlie Company, 1st Battalion, 5th Marine Regiment return fire against an Iraqi army ambush. (USMC, SGT KEVIN R REED)

BELOW: (USMC HISTORICAL DIVISION)

of the regime's power. The idea was to use 'shock and awe' to break open the Iraqi defences, leading to rapid regime collapse.

For marines of I MEF, this would be unlike any other battle fought by the US Marine Corps. Marine units were grouped into mechanised columns to advance at speed across Iraq, with minimal logistic support. Each of the 1st Division's four regimental combat teams (RCT) had M1A1 Abrams tanks to take on and defeat Iraqi tanks. Wheeled Light Armoured Vehicles (LAVs) were assigned to reconnaissance battalions to scout ahead looking for Iraqi troops. The bulk of I MEF's infantry rode northwards in LVTP-7 (Landing Vehicle, Tracked, Personnel-7) troop carriers, nicknamed 'Amtracks', and Humvee wheeled utility vehicles.

Moving behind the combat units were convoys of hundreds of trucks of the 1st Force Service Support Group, carrying the I MEF's supplies of ammunition, food and fuel. Overhead, the strike jets and attack helicopters of the 3rd Marine Air Wing (3 MAW) were to patrol ahead of the 1st Division's column to find and neutralise pockets of Iraqi resistance.

After President Bush issued an ultimatum on March 17, demanding Saddam Hussein stand down from power within 48 hours, US and coalition troops began to move out of their desert camps into dispersal areas in Northern Kuwait. Within hours, 20,000 Marines and more than 5,000 vehicles of the 1st Division were within striking distance of the Iraqi border posts.

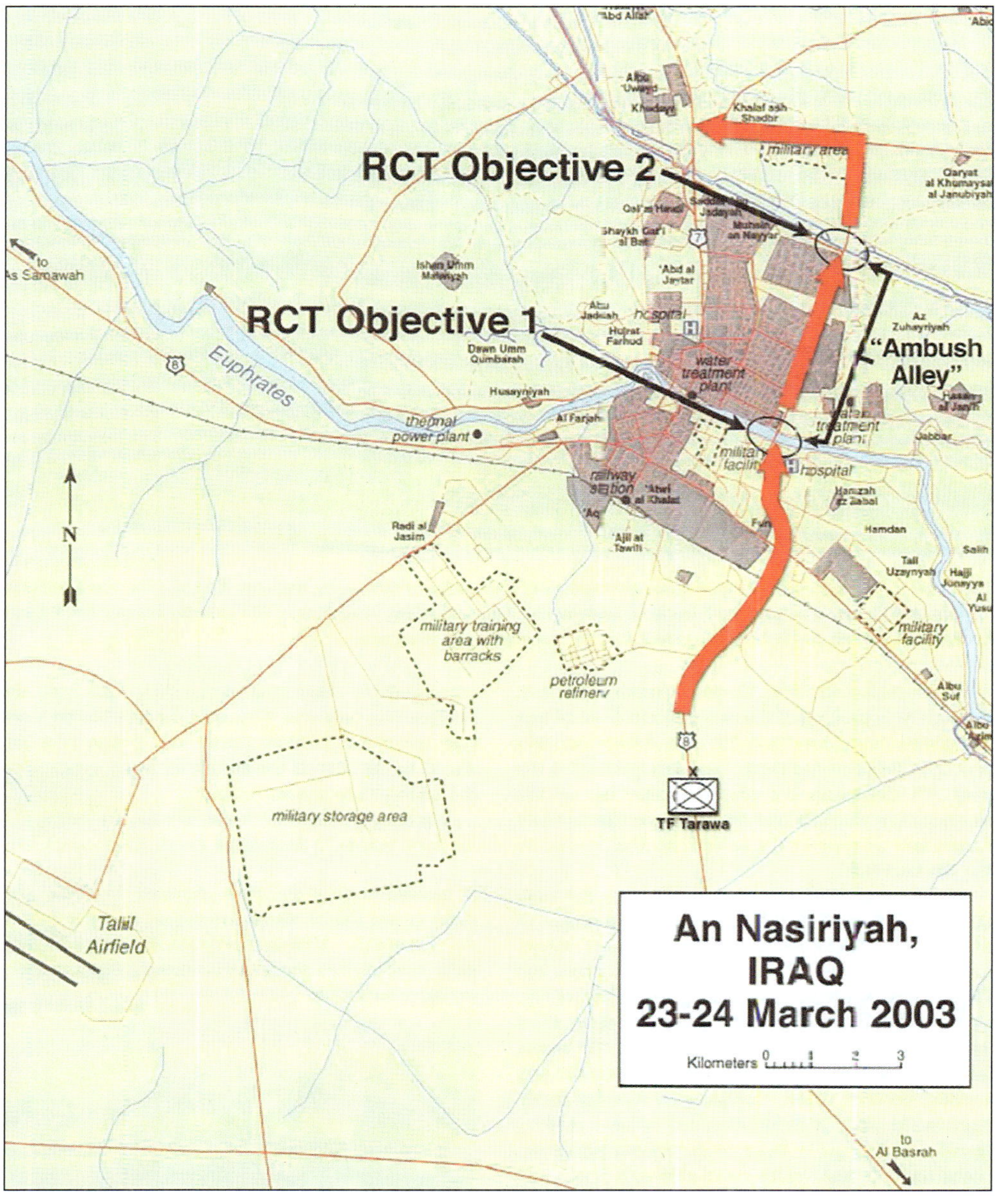

RIGHT: US Marines assigned to Combat Services Support Battalion 18 work to retrieve a destroyed USMC Amphibious Assault Vehicle, (AAV7A1) lost on 'ambush alley' during the Battle for Nasiriyah. (US DOD/JOINT COMBAT CAMERA)

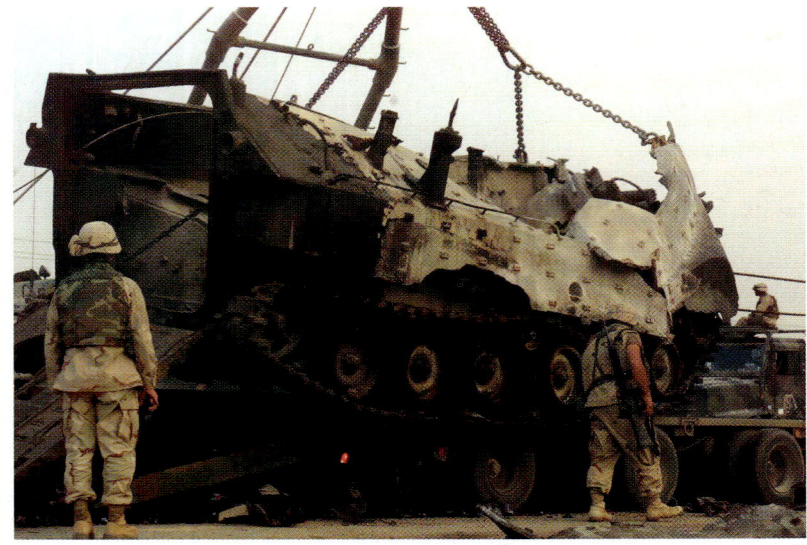

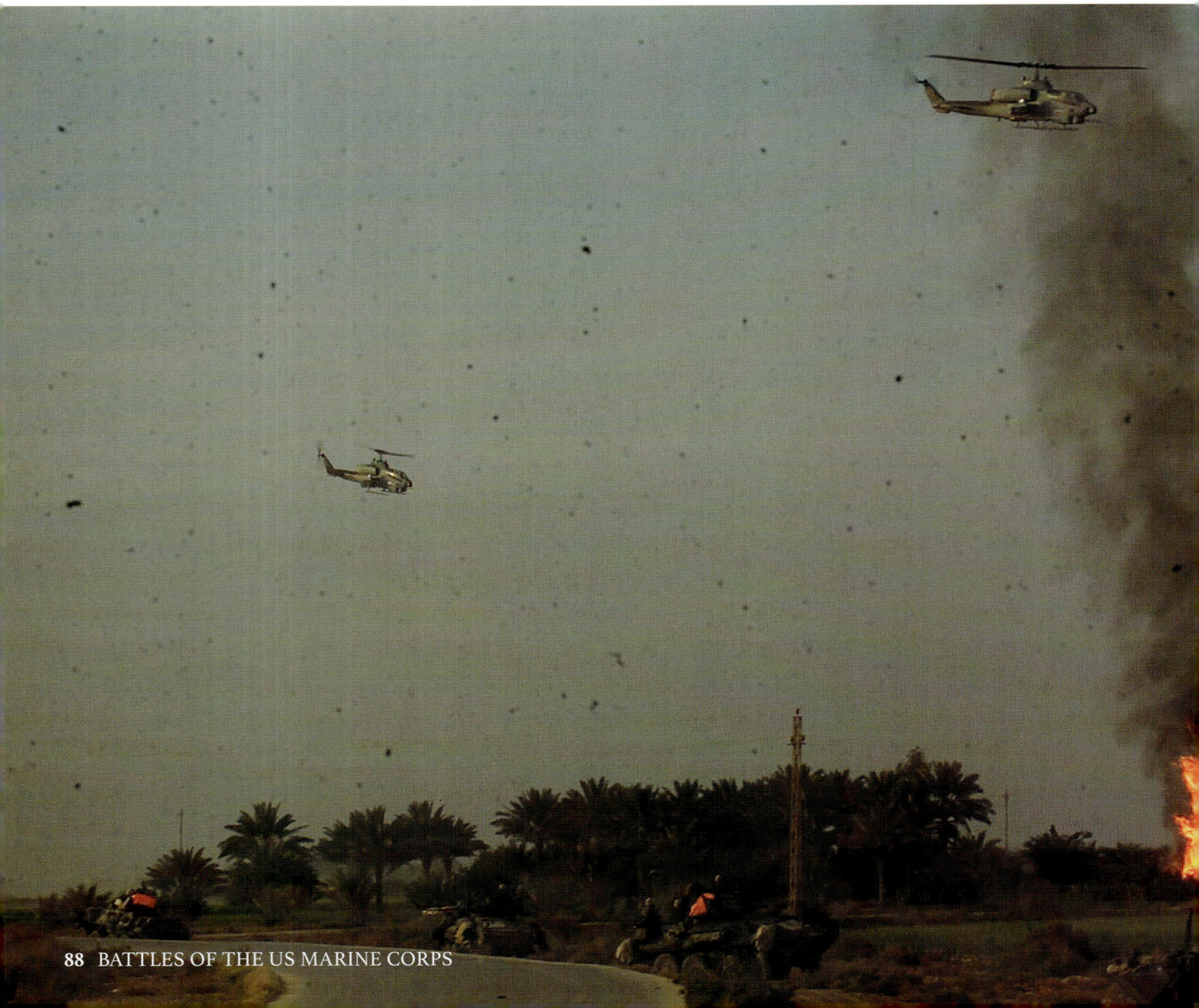

BELOW: US Marine Cobra helicopters provide close air support during a firefight between Iraqi soldiers and Delta Company 1st Light Armored Reconnaissance Battalion in an ambush by Iraqi soldiers. (USMC, LCPL ANDREW P ROUFS)

On the night of March 20/21, the 5th Marine Regimental Combat Team opened the drive on Baghdad by overrunning several Iraq border posts defended by the demoralised and poorly armed troops of the 51st Mechanised Brigade. An artillery bombardment hit multiple Iraqi positions, prompting the survivors to flee so when the marine columns rolled forward, there was hardly any resistance. After seizing oil wells around the southern city of Basra, the 1st Division columns turned northwest and headed towards the city of Nasiriyah. Task Force Tarawa was leading the advance, with the mission of securing strategic bridges in the city to allow the rest of I MEF to cross and head for Al Kut, which lay on the River Tigris and would allow the marines to advance into the eastern suburbs of Baghdad. The US Army's 3rd Infantry Division was advancing in parallel with I MEF and would drive up the Euphrates valley into the western districts of Baghdad.

On the morning of March 23, US Army columns were skirting through the desert to the south of Nasiriyah, when a convoy of trucks from a 507th Maintenance took a wrong turn and ended up inside the city. It was ambushed, leaving 11 GIs dead and six as prisoners of war.

Soon afterwards, Task Force Tarawa approached Nasiriyah and ran into the remnants of the ambushed US Army column. US Marine commanders decided to press on

to their objectives inside the city. It was hoped the sudden arrival of the heavily armed marines would force the Iraqis to retreat without putting up a fight, as had happened on the border.

The lead marine company crossed over the large Euphrates River bridge and then pressed onto the Saddam Canal bridge, 4km to the north along a wide main road. It soon reached its objective and stopped to defend the bridge, to allow the rest of I MEF to cross. The bridge ends and the road were raised above the flat desert, which left the marine company and its vehicles exposed with little cover. Iraqi machine guns, snipers and mortars now opened fire from buildings close to the northern end of the bridge.

Along the road between the two bridges, the rest of Task Force Tarawa's six infantry companies also came under fire. This road subsequently became known as 'Ambush Alley'. The marines started to call down artillery fire and air strikes to neutralise the Iraqi fire positions. Just as this battle was unfolding, two A-10As appeared over the lead company on the Saddam Canal bridge, hitting an Amtrack. A second A-10A then continued to attack the marines, in what would become the worse incident of friendly fire of the 2003 invasion. Eight marines were killed by A-10As.

Amphibious Assault Vehicles of Regimental Combat Team 5, move along in column up an Iraqi highway during the sandstorm that engulfed Iraq on March 24. (USMC, SERGEANT KEVIN R. REED)

US Army engineers built a bridge across a river on the outskirts of Baghdad to allow Delta Company of the 1st Marine Light Armored Reconnaissance Battalion to push on into northern Iraq. (USMC, LANCE CORPORAL ANDREW P. ROUFS)

LEFT: Displaced Iraqi civilians caught in a firefight north of Nasiriyah are taken to the medical triage area of Regimental Combat Team 1 to receive treatment for injuries on March 26. (JSMC, CPL MACE M. GRATZ)

For the rest of the day, Task Force Tarawa was stuck on the road trading fire with the Iraqis, who were well-armed and well-motivated. It took a while for M1A1 tanks to be moved forward to provide the marines with the firepower they needed to drive back the Iraqi fighters. By the end of the day, ten more marines had died and eight LVTP-7s knocked out.

While Task Force Tarawa battled to control 'Ambush Alley', the rest of I MEF had wait out in the desert. It was not until the evening of March 24 that the chaos was cleared up and the 1st Marine RCT could start moving north. Even before it had got going, a huge sandstorm engulfed southern Iraq, bringing the advance on Bagdad to a halt for another two days. ➔

BELOW: (USMC HISTORICAL DIVISION)

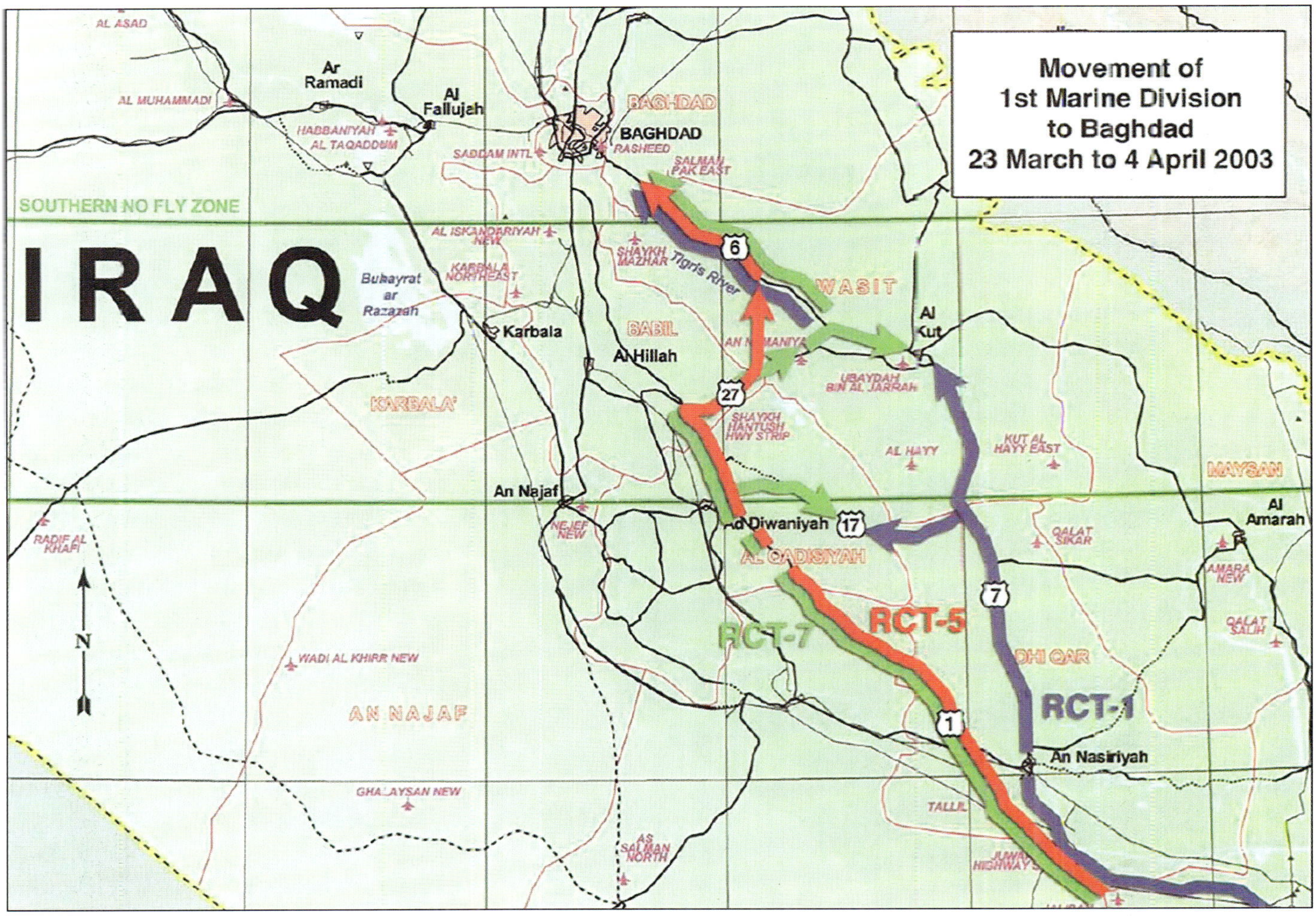

With the situation in Nasiriyah under control and the weather clearing, I MEF now headed for Baghdad at a rapid pace on April 1. Iraqi resistance was starting to crumble but the 1st Division's commander, Major General James Mattis, was determined to maintain the tempo of the advance so decided to by-pass Al-Kut, rather than attempt to seize it.

By now all of I MEF's marines were exhausted by lack of sleep. They were still having to wear heavy and uncomfortable chemical protection suits out of fear that Saddam Hussein would now unleash his feared arsenal of weapons of mass destruction. Mattis took drastic action to keep his troops advancing, including relieving the commanding officer of the 1st RCT, who was considered not to be advancing aggressively enough.

The attention of 3 MAW was now switched to striking at the reserve armoured divisions of the Iraqi Republican Guard. This was a classic battlefield air interdiction mission, striking at the enemy second and third echelon reserves. Hundreds of Republican Guard tanks were knocked out to open the way for the marines to continue driving north.

Supply convoys were struggling to keep up with the marine columns, so the 3 MAW was drafted to begin flying food, ammunition and fuel bladders forward. Sikorsky CH-53E heavy lift helicopters dropped cargo pallets off next to marine columns.

A stretch of highway was converted into an improvised airstrip for 3 MAW Lockheed KC-130T Hercules airlifters. Then I MEF captured An Numaniyah airfield and turned it into a forward airhead to step-up the re-supply effort.

As I MEF columns reached the outskirts of Baghdad, Mattis split his force to ensure the city was surrounded. The 5th Marine RCT swung north to compete the encirclement of the city, while the 1st and 7th Marine RCTs drove straight into the eastern suburbs. There was a tough fight to cross the Diyala River, but once marine engineers built a pontoon bridge, the advance continued.

US Army columns had now captured Baghdad International Airport and were sending raiding parties of tanks into the centre of the city. Known as 'Thunder Runs', these missions involved dozens of tanks driving through the city and opening fire against pockets of resistance. This display of overwhelming firepower broke the will of the last Iraqi troops defending their capital.

By April 9, I MEF units were in position to begin their final assault and early in the morning launched a series of 'armed reconnaissance in force' missions to probe Iraqi defences. Instead of having to fight street by street with diehard regime remnants, the marine columns were greeted by crowds of civilians cheering the marines as liberators. Occasionally, Iraqi snipers opened fire on the marine columns, but they were soon neutralised by tank fire or air strikes, allowing the marines to continue advancing.

A marine column reached Firdos Square in downtown Baghdad late in the afternoon to be greeted by a huge crowd of happy residents. International news crews arrived to film the celebrations. The marines told the Iraqis that they were going to pull down a huge statue of Saddam Hussein. Cable was wrapped around the statue and attached to a M88 recovery vehicle of the 1st Tank Battalion. Video footage of the statue being pulled down by the marines was broadcast live around the world to graphically symbolise the end of Iraqi dictator's rule.

By April 10, Saddam Hussein had fled, and resistance collapsed. A column of marines was dispatched to capture the Iraqi leader's home city, Tikrit, with 3 MAW aircraft flying top cover. The convoy was supplied from the air as it moved at speed towards Tikrit. As it approached the city, they received intelligence that American prisoners of war were being held near the city, a detachment of the 3rd Light Armored Reconnaissance Battalion was dispatched to rescue the seven US Army soldiers, including five survivors from the 507th Maintenance Company. Tikrit was captured on April 14, signalling the end of the combat phase of Operation Iraqi Freedom.

Across southern Iraq, Task Force Tarawa, which had been protecting I MEF's line of communication, started to move to take control Al Kut and Al Amarah, only to find that their citizens had already driven out the Iraqi troops and established their own local administrations.

I MEF was now re-positioned from around Baghdad to take control of southern Iraq to maintain law and order to allow the restoration of public utilities and other services to the civilian population.

In May, the first I MEF units started to be withdrawn from Iraq and return to the home garrisons, but this turned into a long-drawn-out process. Looting and lawlessness gripped much of Iraq, requiring marine units to remain on duty. The last marine units handed over their sector to replacements at the start of September 2003 and it took another two months to complete the withdraw all its marines and equipment from Iraq.

Operation Iraqi Freedom had been a stunning victory for I MEF. In less than a month, Conway's marines had advanced more than 600km from Kuwait to Tikrit, defeated several Iraqi divisions and pulled down a statue of the Iraqi dictator in his capital. The speed and violence of I MEF's advance had completely overwhelmed the Iraqis, proving the success of the 'shock and awe' strategy. The low level of I MEF's casualties – 75 killed in action and 300 wounded – is testimony to its success. While Saddam Hussein's army had been easily defeated, the subsequent American occupation of Iraq was soon descending into chaos. US military personnel and civilian administrators struggled to get the power and water supplies working again. Law and order broke down in many places. Within months insurgent groups linked to pro-regime factions and Iranian backed political parties were openly attacking US troops. US Marines would soon have to return to Iraq.

LEFT: Marines from the 1st Battalion, 7th Marines cover each other as they prepare to enter one of Saddam Hussein's palaces in Baghdad in the final days of the operation to capture the Iraqi capital. This was the peak of US military success in Iraq and American soldiers were soon locked in bitter battle with insurgents across the country. (US DOD/JOINT COMBAT CAMERA)

BELOW: A M88 recovery vehicle of the 1st Marine Tank Battalion famously pulled down the statue of Saddam in Firdos Square in the centre of Baghdad, live on global television. (US DOD/JOINT COMBAT CAMERA)

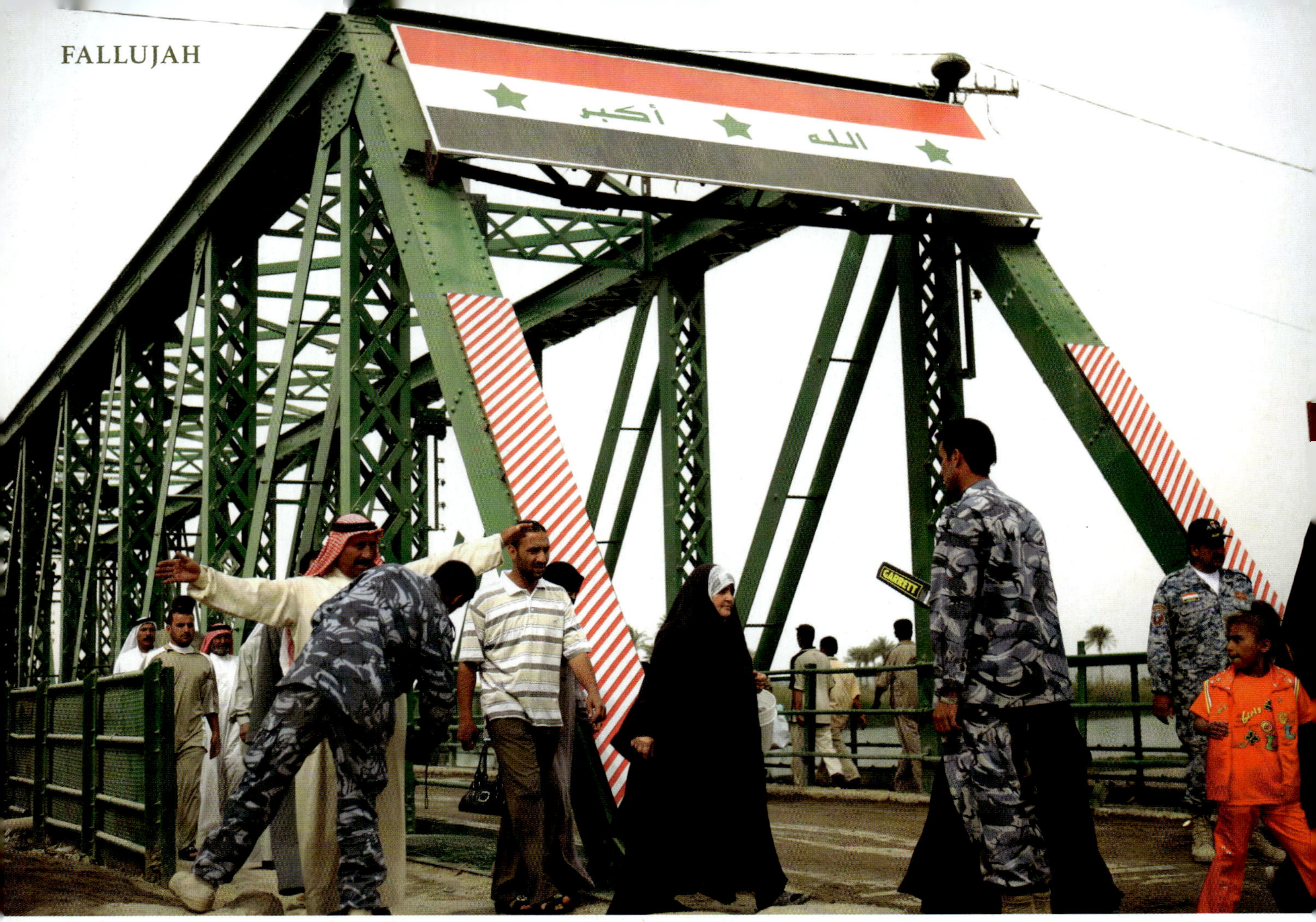

Battle for Fallujah

Phantom Fury unleashed

ABOVE: A frenzied attack on private security operatives of the Blackwater company at Fallujah's Old Bridge set off a chain of events that led to an all-out attack on the Iraqi city by the 1st Marine Division. (US DOD/JOINT COMBAT CAMERA)

By the spring of 2004, Iraq was engulfed in violence as insurgents fought running battles with US and coalition troops. Hundreds of American troops had been killed in ambushes and roadside bomb attacks.

The insurgency was two pronged. In the centre of the country, in a region known as the 'Sunni Triangle', a mix of old regime supporters and Al-Qaeda supporting Jihadis were operating. To the south, Shia insurgents backed by Iran were trying to capture and control towns and cities. The US Army occupation force was outnumbered and under pressure.

When the time came to rotate the US units in the Sunni Triangle, the I Marine Expeditionary Force (I MEF) was earmarked to replace the paratroopers of the famous 82nd Airborne Division. Less than a year after fighting their way to Baghdad, the I MEF's marines and attached US Navy sailors would be returning to the fight.

The commander of the 1st Marine Division, Major General James Mattis, issued a motivational instruction as it prepared to deploy. "This is our test, our Guadalcanal, our Chosin Reservoir, our Hue City. Fight with a happy heart and keep faith in your comrades and your unit. We must be under no illusions about the nature of the enemy and the dangers that lie ahead. Stay alert, take it all in stride, remain sturdy, and share your

RIGHT: Operation Phantom Fury culminated in American marines and soldiers sweeping into Fallujah, and going house-to-house to clear insurgents from the city. (USMC, LCPL JAMES J. VOORIS)

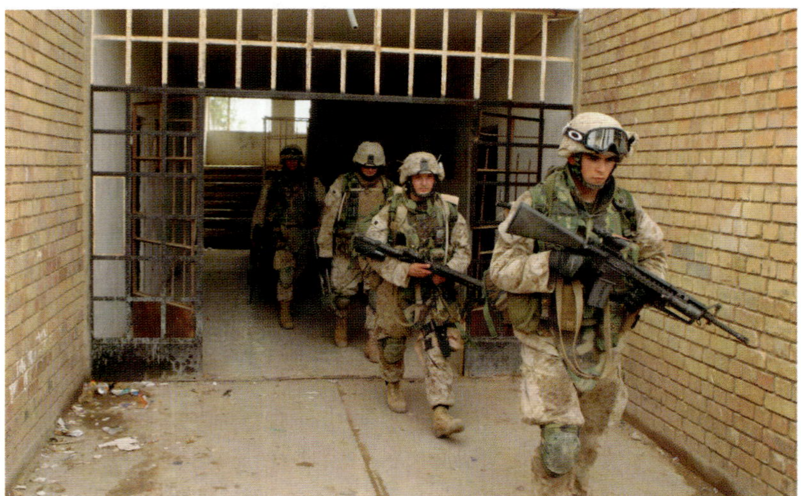

courage with each other and the world. You are going to write history, my fine young sailors and marines, so write it well. Semper Fidelis."

Little did he know that in a few weeks' time his marines would be locked into the most intense urban battle since the fight of Hue City in Vietnam in 1968.

I MEF had barely taken over their posts from the 82nd Airborne when four civilian security contractors from the US company Blackwater drove into the city of Fallujah, 50km to the west of Baghdad. The city was under the control of the Sunni insurgents. The American's SUV was ambushed, and they were killed. Their bodies were then set on fire and finally hung from the side of the Old Bridge over the Euphrates River, in the centre of the city, as local people danced and cheered. When video footage of the gruesome incident was broadcast, US President George W Bush was outraged. He demanded that the US military take Fallujah and avenge the deaths of the Americans.

Lieutenant General James Conway, who was still in command of I MEF, was ordered to rapidly mobilise his troops to clear Fallujah of insurgents.

Five days later, Mattis launched Operation Vigilant Resolve with four battalions of marines, backed by locally recruited Iraqi army and para-military battalions. The 1st Division had little time to prepare for the operation and most of its units were still engaged in controlling increasing insurgent activity in their local areas. A multi-pronged assault started on April 5, but it soon ran into heavy resistance from well-armed insurgents. In a major blow, the Iraqi units either refused to fight or in some cases deserted en mass to the insurgents. Iraq's newly installed government refused to support the US offensive and by the end of April it had to be called off. In a face-saving compromise, a locally recruited unit, dubbed the 'Fallujah Brigade' was supposed to take control of the city from the insurgents. No one was fooled. Fallujah remained under insurgent control.

American commanders were determined to take the city, which was now seen as the centre of the wider insurgency across the Sunni Triangle, allowing insurgents groups a safe haven where they could re-group and re-arm. Generals Conway and Mattis began working on more deliberate plans to capture the city. It would require far more force and a systemic approach to clearing and holding every building and street. The marine generals would not get to execute their plans, as they handed over their post in the summer of 2004 after completing their command ➔

ABOVE: In the immediate response to the deaths of the Blackwater operatives in April 2004, the 1st Battalion, 5th Marine Regiment, were deployed to seal off Fallujah. (US DOD/JOINT COMBAT CAMERA)

LEFT: Checkpoints set up by the 1st Marine Division attempted to seal off the insurgent stronghold of Fallujah from reinforcements. (US DOD/JOINT COMBAT CAMERA)

A US Marine Corps M-1A1 tank blocked access along a main route leading into Fallujah on April 5, 2004, as part of a bid to seal the city off from the rest of Iraq. (USMC, MSGT HOWARD J FARRELL)

assignments. Mattis was replaced as commander of 1st Division by Major General Richard Natonski, who had led Task Force Tarawa during the Battle for Nasiriyah in March 2003, and Lieutenant General John Sattler relieved Conway as head of the I MEF.

Over the summer of 2004, between 3,000 to 4,000 insurgents had gathered inside Fallujah. As well as launching daily forays out of the city to strike at marine bases, they set to work to fortify their positions in case the Americans decided to strike again. Fortified lines of resistance were built to block routes into the city and turn almost every building into a strong point, with sniper holes opened in walls and deep bunkers in cellars so insurgents could take cover during artillery bombardments. Earth berms were used to block every road and check points were set-up around the city's boundary to control the movement of civilians. Weapons, ammunition and food were stockpiled

A M-198 155mm howitzer crew of 4th Battalion, 14th Marine Regiment engages enemy targets in support of the November 2004 assault on Fallujah. (US DOD/JOINT COMBAT CAMERA)

to allow the fight to go on for several months. Tunnels and covered walkways were built between strong points, so the insurgents could avoid US aerial surveillance.

The insurgents were not planning a static defence. They were prepared to allow the Americans to overrun parts of the city and then use their tunnels to disappear from view, before re-emerging in districts US troops had considered cleared. The idea was to keep the battle going for weeks or even months and inflict heavy casualties on the attackers.

From May to October, I MEF closed the noose around Fallujah in the build up to a major ground assault to clear the city of insurgents. The attack was scheduled for November 2004 in the days following the US Presidential Election. Drones were used to monitor the city 24/7 to build up a detailed intelligence picture of the insurgent defence lines. Electronic eavesdropping was used to monitor enemy radio communications. US and Iraqi units progressively closed down road access to the city to cut off their flow of supplies and new recruits to the insurgents, then a firm siege line was established around the city's perimeter.

ABOVE: US Army and coalition forces were deployed to hold the outer cordon around Fallujah during October and November 2004, to give the 1st Marine Division a freehand to clear the city. (USMC, STAFF SGT AARON ALLMON I)

LEFT: US Marines and soldiers conducted their break-in operation under the cover of darkness to give them a tactical advantage over the insurgents' hold on Fallujah. (US ARMY, SPC AARON RITTER)

By the end of October, the assault force was in place. Two marine regimental combat teams (RCT), supported by a US Army brigade from the 1st Cavalry Division were massed for the attack. This time six battalion-sized Iraqi units were attached to the division for the assault, now called Operation Phantom Fury. They had been specially trained for the mission and had US Army Special Forces advisors attached to ensure their loyalty.

Once President Bush was re-elected, the final go-ahead was given for the attack to begin. The bulk of the assault force, 1st and 7th RCTs, was massed on the northern edge of the city, with the rest, including the bulk of the Iraqi units, in blocking positions to stop any insurgents escaping from the American attack.

A massive artillery barrage opened on the evening of November 8 against the northern suburbs of the city. All around the perimeter, US units staged diversionary activity to keep the insurgents guessing as to where the main assault would come.

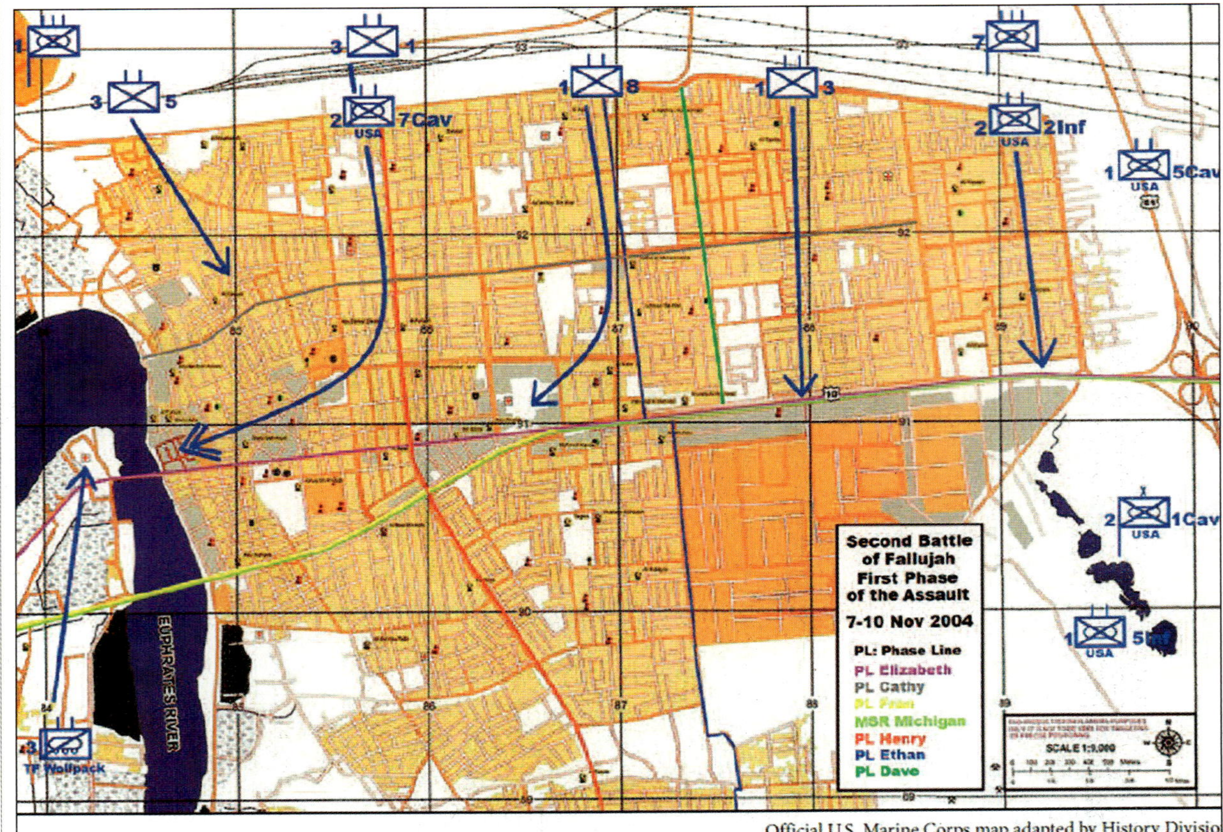

RIGHT: (USMC HISTORY DIVISION)

Official U.S. Marine Corps map adapted by History Division

ABOVE: M1A1 tanks advanced deep into the heart of Fallujah to spearhead the advance of the 1st Marine Division, firing at point blank range into insurgent strong points. (US DOD/JOINT COMBAT CAMERA)

The first breaches were then made in the outer defence line by M1A1 Abrams tanks fitted with mine ploughs and engineers followed behind to clear away any surviving mines and improvised explosive devises. Metal roadways were positioned by the engineers to allow follow-on columns of wheeled vehicles to pass into the city.

The American tanks provided overwatch for the nighttime breaching operation, engaging insurgent snipers and anti-tank missile teams that tried to fire on the assault force.

Once the first marine infantry units were in the city, they moved to capture specific buildings that had been identified as insurgent strong points. Tank fire or air strikes with satellite-guided Joint Attack Munitions (JDAMs), were used to neutralise any resistance. Once their objectives were secured, the marines started to spread out to clear each neighbouring building. This was a very methodical and deliberate tactic. Each marine unit was assigned a specific district to capture, hold and clear. Only once a district was declared cleared, it would be handed over to the Iraqis, so they could try to re-establish government control and begin providing humanitarian assistance to any surviving civilians. In fact, there were few civilians left in the city by the time the Americans attacked.

The objective for the first day was the main east to west road that divided the city centre, which the marines designated Phase Line Fran. It was two kilometres from the northern edge of the urban area.

For most of November 9, the marines and the 1st Cavalry units cleared up to PL Fran. On the next day, the 1st Cavalry's tanks swung west to link up with Iraqi Commando units attacking across the main road bridge into the city. This opened the way for the capture of the city centre, along with the main local government buildings.

This was by no means the end of the battle. All across the city the insurgents were putting up furious resistance to the marines. The battle now broke down into a series of running firefights across the city as the marines systematically engaged and then captured the insurgent strong points, one-by-one, and then cleared all the buildings around them. This was slow and dangerous work, as the marines had to first suppress insurgent fire with tanks, artillery or air strikes. Then they used demolition charges to break into the enemy strong points, before going room to room to clear them of enemy fighters. The marines took casualties from enemy fire and improvised explosive devices planted around the insurgent strong points. This fight went on until November 20 and concluded with the final sweeps in Fallujah's southern suburbs. There was no obvious end to the fighting, just a gradual reduction in fighting as insurgent resistance faltered. By the last week of November, Iraq troops and police were operating in every district of the city. Civilians were starting to return. Reconstruction was soon underway. It was urgently needed, as almost every building in the city had been damaged to some degree.

The fighting in Fallujah was on a scale not seen before in the Iraq war. For six months, I MEF and the Iraqi insurgents had battled for

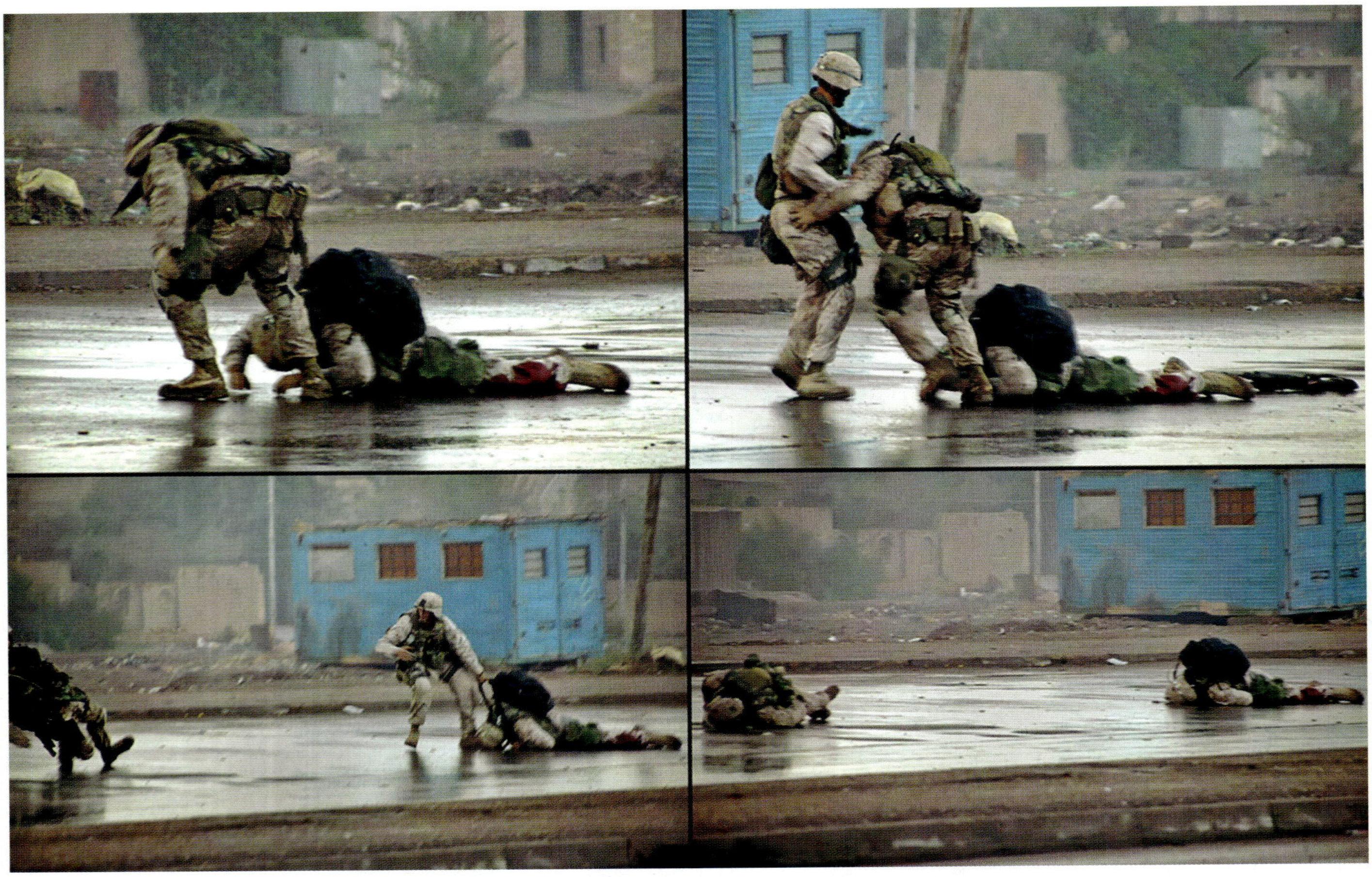

ABOVE: US Marine Platoon Gunnery Sergeant Ryan P Shane and another marine from the 1st Battalion of the 8th Marine Regiment pull a fatally wounded comrade to safety while under fire during the Battle for Fallujah. (USMC, CPL JOEL A. CHAVERRI)

RIGHT: Naval Mobile Construction Battalion 4's Chief Engineering Aide Ardell Ball (centre) studies an aerial photograph of Fallujah streets during a survey of the battle-scarred city, as the 'Seabee' unit prepared to move into the city to restore utilities to allow the civilian population to return. (US NAVY, JOC(AW) SUZANNE M. SPEIGHT)

RIGHT: Iraqi soldiers and police followed the 1st Marine Division into Fallujah to begin the return of the city to the control of the Baghdad government. (US ARMY, SFC JOHANCHARLES VAN BOERS)

control of the city. This culminated in the final US clear operation in November 2004.

US commanders employed unprecedented levels of fire power to ensure the safety of the marines who spent more than a week clearing Fallujah, building by building. The assault force had to repeatedly call for air support and by the time the battle was over, 318 precision bombs, 391 rockets and missiles, as well as 93,000 cannon rounds, had been used by US Marine Corps strike jets. During the final assault, McDonnell Douglas AV-8B Harrier IIs were constantly overhead providing close air support to the marines. The Harrier pilots were now expert at using their Litening II targeting pods to find and hit targets in narrow Iraqi back streets, leading the technique to be dubbed 'keyhole CAS' after the surgical procedure.

I MEF lost 70 marines killed in action and 651 were wounded in action, with 394 eventually returning to duty. Supporting US Army units lost six killed and 36 wounded.

US intelligence estimated between 1,200 and 2,000 insurgents were killed and a further 1,500 men were captured by the marines, but these were never all confirmed as insurgents. Around 600 to 800 Iraqi civilians were reported killed during the battle, according to local health agencies.

The Battle of Fallujah is credited with being one of the US Marine

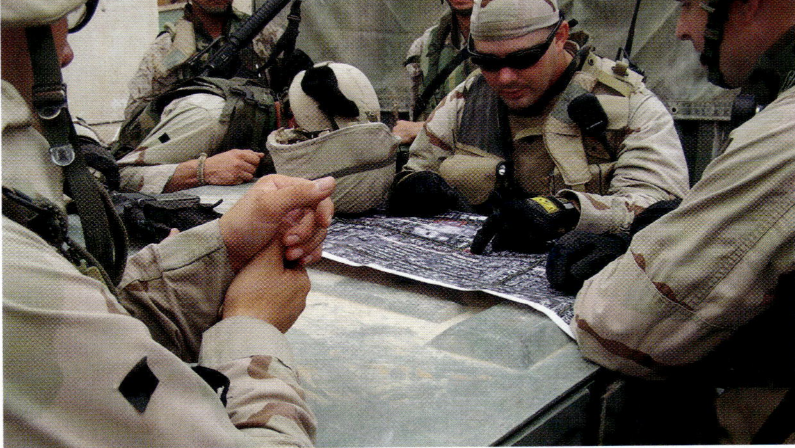

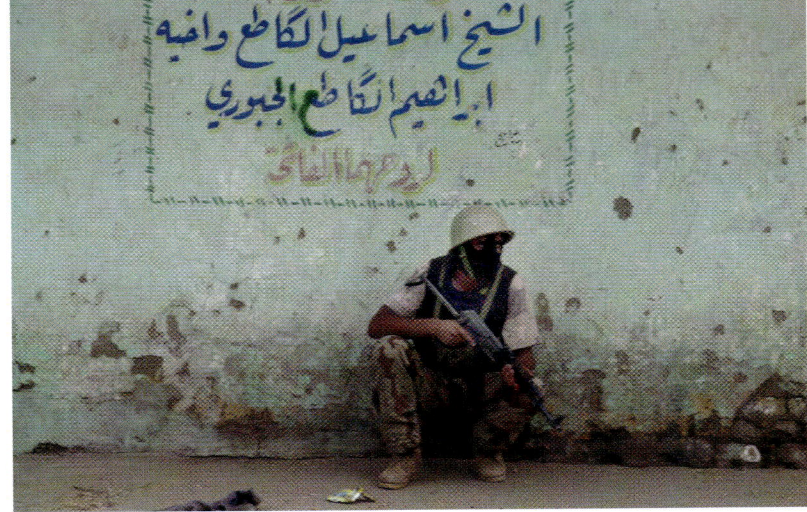

Corps' most intense battles since the Vietnam War. It is seen as a textbook operation, which will be taught in the military academies, as 'how to capture enemy held cities'.

American commanders claimed the capture of Fallujah dealt a decision blow to the insurgency in the Sunni Triangle, denying the insurgents in the region their last safe base of operations. In January 2005, elections were held for the new Iraqi government, which the Americans hoped would allow them to begin withdrawing their troops The recapture of Fallujah dealt a heavy blow to the insurgents, but they soon bounced back and upped the intensity of their revolt against the US occupation. It would be six more years until the last US troops left Iraq.

LEFT: Few buildings in Fallujah were undamaged in the US assault and it took years to rebuild the city. (US NAVY, PH2(AW) PHILIP FORREST)

BELOW: Once Fallujah was declared cleared of insurgents, the 1st Marine Division ordered its units to fall back and hand security inside the city to the Iraq military and police. (USMC, LANCE CORPORAL JAMES J VOORIS)

By air, land and sea

US Marine Corps in the 21st Century

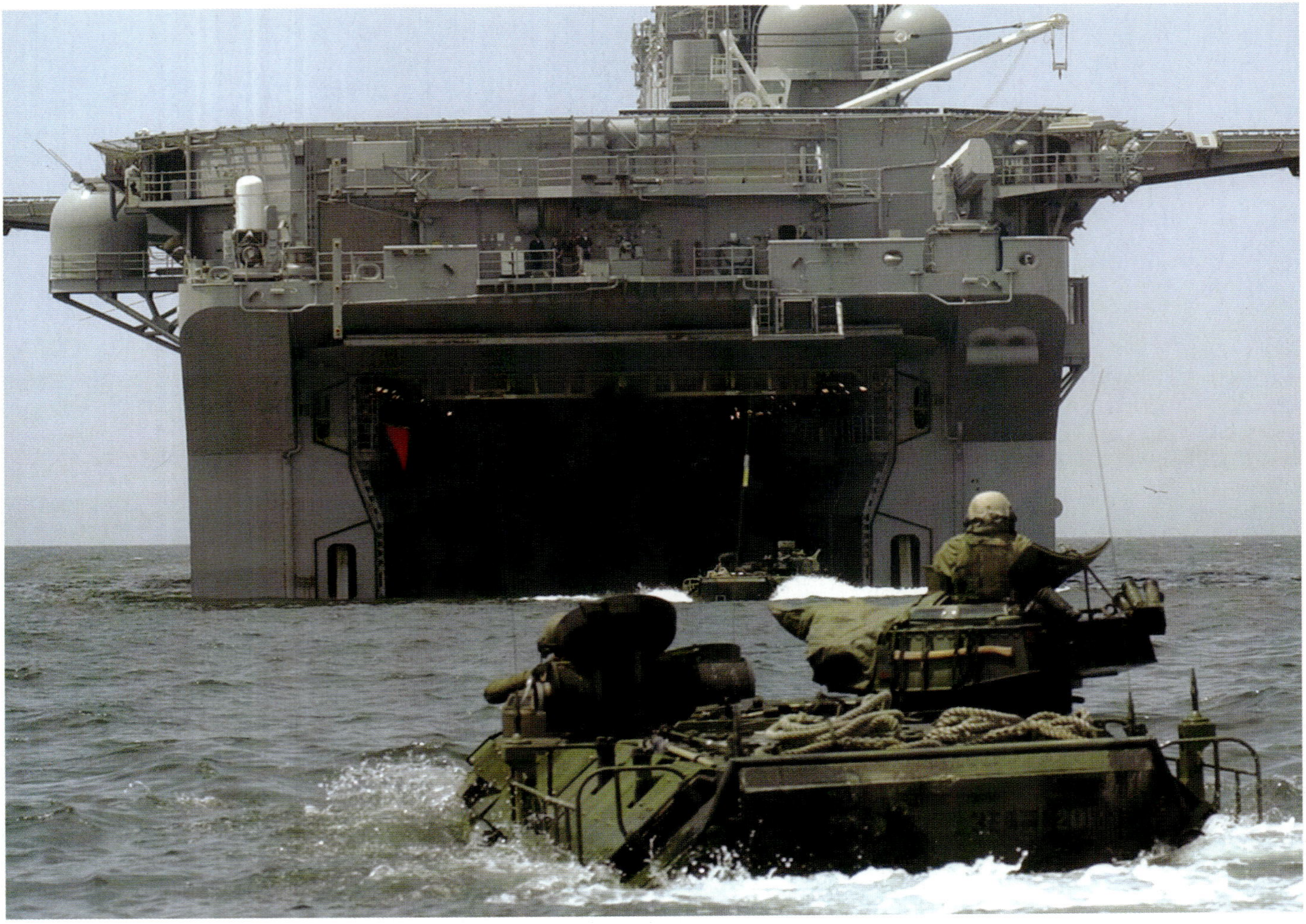

ABOVE: Landing on enemy controlled shores is the primary mission of the United States Marine Corps, and it has developed specialist tactics and equipment to be America's amphibious warfare. (USMC)

The United States Marine Corps is the world's largest amphibious force. Its 168,000 active-duty personnel dwarf many other military services, and it is bigger than almost all European armed forces.

It is currently one of the five US armed services, and the Marine Corps Commandant sits as a member of the US Joint Chiefs of Staff. For administrative purposes it is part of the Department of Navy. Its sister service, the US Navy, has an important role to play in delivering marine units to operational theatres on board amphibious shipping.

The modern US Marine Corps operates as a combined arms force, bringing together air, land, and sea forces under a single commander to achieve their objectives.

This is the modern-day successor of the Fleet Marine Force that allowed the marines to achieve victory in World War Two. The corps uses the Marine Air-Ground Task Force (MAGTF) concept to organise its units at every level of operations.

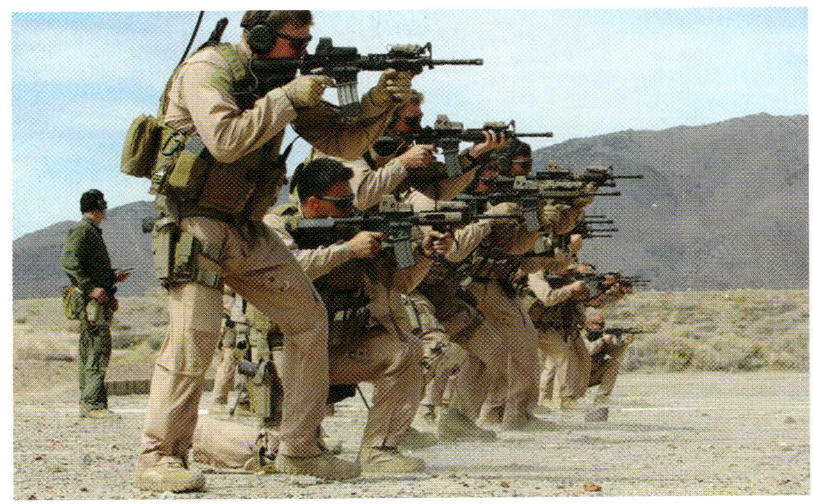

A MAGTF is composed of four elements: the command element (CE), the ground combat element (GCE), the aviation combat element (ACE) and the logistics combat element

RIGHT: Marksmanship has always been a core skill of US Marines and today's marines continue that tradition by maintaining their expertise in infantry combat skills. (USMC)

LEFT: Amphibious Assault Vehicles deliver marine infantry onto defended beaches. (USMC)

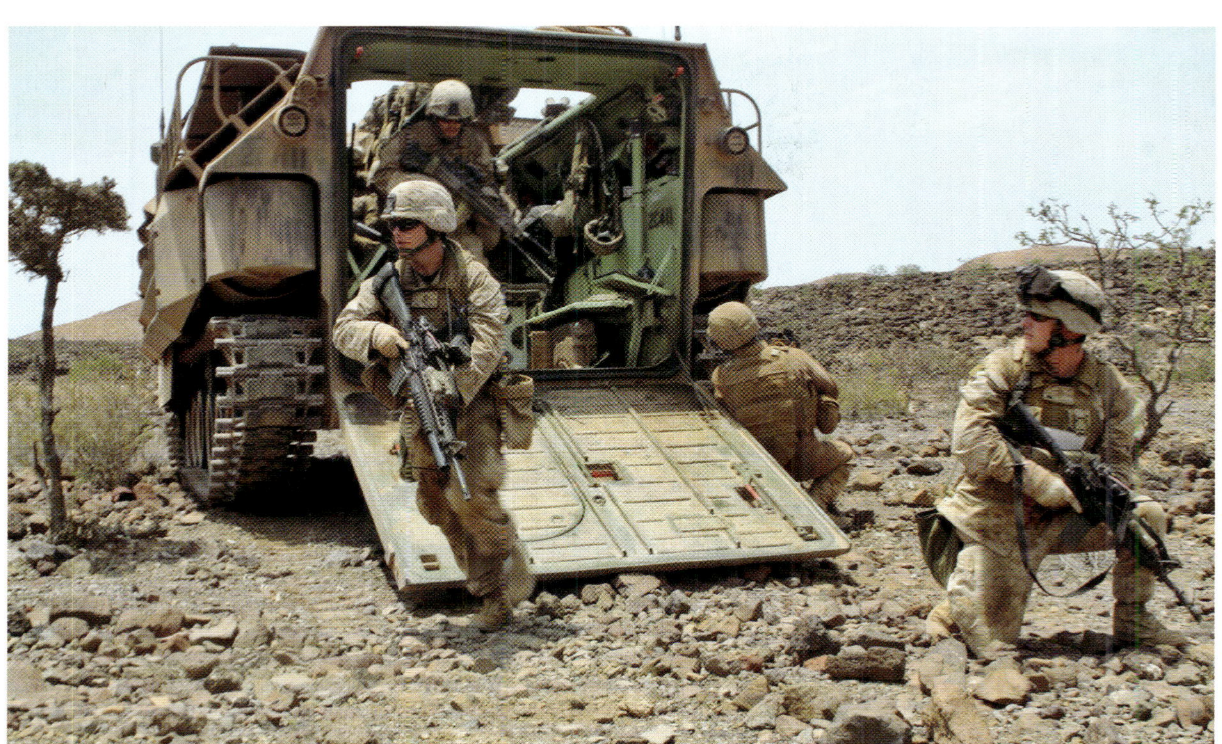

(LCE). Each MAGTF can operate independently or as part of a large US or coalition force. They are temporary commands that are formed for a specific mission and dissolved after the completion of their mission.

A MAGTF varies in size from the smallest, a Marine Expeditionary Unit (MEU), based around a reinforced infantry battalion, and a composite aviation squadron, up to the largest, a Marine Expeditionary Force (MEF). A MEF is equivalent to an army corps-sized formation, which brings together a marine ground division, an air wing, and a logistics group under a USMC lieutenant general.

The modern USMC is structured as a force generation organisation to provide deployable units to theatre or regional combatant commanders for training exercises, routine deployment, or combat operations.

The two peacetime MEFs are based in the continental United States and a third is forward

BELOW: For more than 100 years US Marine Corps aviators have provided their infantry comrades with close air support. (US NAVY)

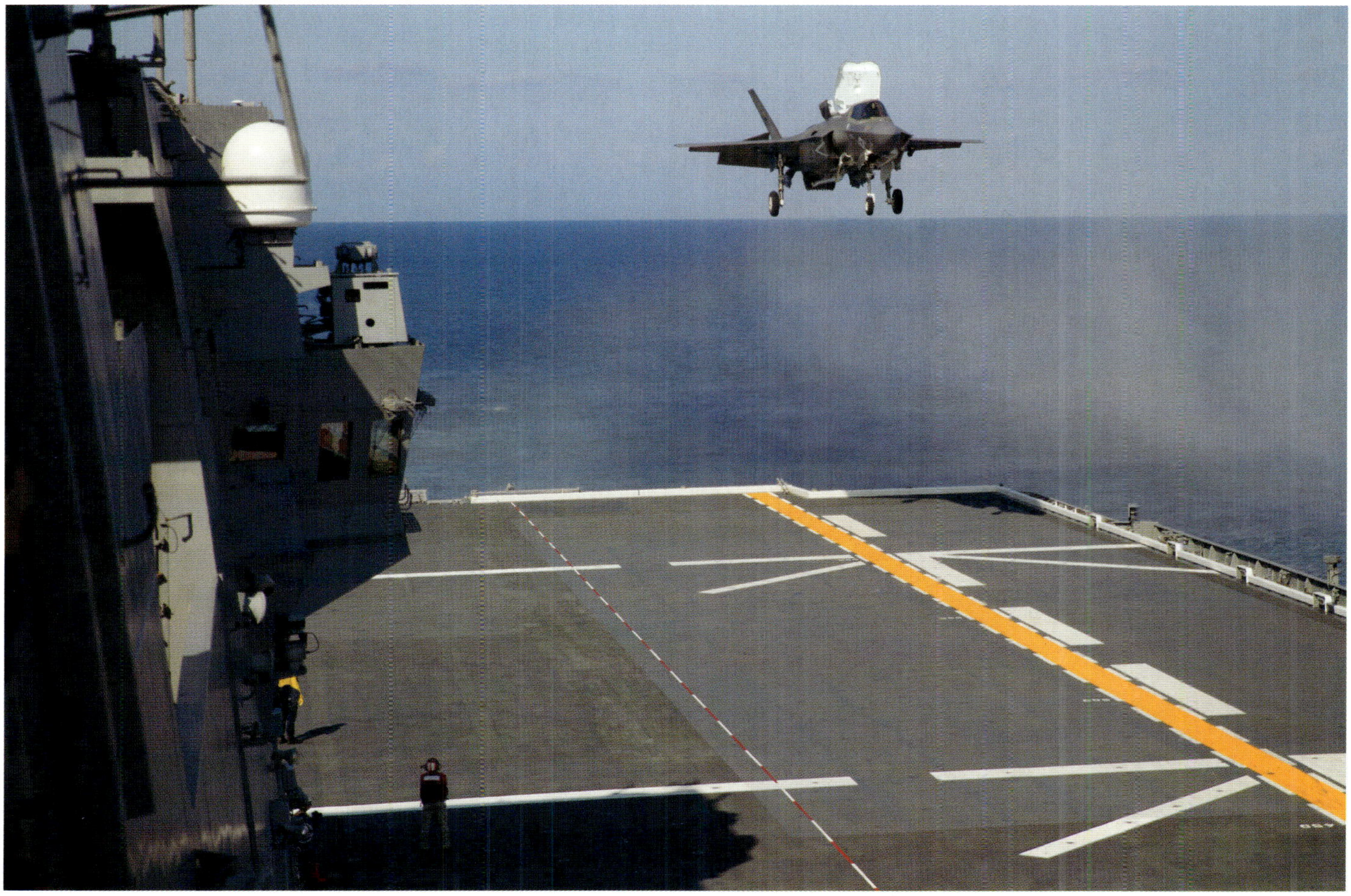

deployed in Japan. Each MEF operates on a readiness cycle to generate forces that are trained and equipped for overseas operations to specific timelines.

Currently each year, one or two MEUs are generated to serve aboard Amphibious Ready Groups (ARG) that forward deploy to Europe, the Middle East, and Far East. These serve six months at a time and stand ready to conduct a range of missions, including non-combatant evacuation operations (NEOs).

To provide more crisis coverage, over the past decade, Special Purpose Marine Air-Ground Task Forces, Crisis Response (SPMAGTF-CR) have been formed at land bases in the Middle East and in the Mediterranean to deploy by helicopter and aircraft to incidents, such as the NEO mission to Kabul in Afghanistan in August 2021.

For major crises, such as the 1991 and 2003 Iraq wars, full MEF-sized formations of marines have been deployed. These operate as corps-sized manoeuvre formations, fighting alongside the US Army.

ABOVE: For 20 years, the US Marines fought in Afghanistan and played a prominent role in the final withdrawal from Kabul airport in August 2021. (USMC)

BELOW: Since the 1960s, the US Navy has operated a fleet of amphibious assault ships which combine docks for landing craft and 'flat top' flight decks for helicopters. (US NAVY)

US MARINE CORPS – MAJOR UNITS 2025

I Marine Expeditionary Force (Camp Pendleton, California)
  1st Marine Division (Camp Pendleton, California)
  3rd Marine Aircraft Wing (MCAS Miramar, California)
  1st Marine Logistics Group (Camp Pendleton, California)

II Marine Expeditionary Force (Camp Lejeune, North Carolina)
  2nd Marine Division (Camp Lejeune, North Carolina)
  2nd Marine Aircraft Wing (MCAS Cherry Point, North Carolina)
  2nd Marine Logistics Group (Camp Lejeune, North Carolina)
  2nd Marine Expeditionary Brigade (Camp Lejeune, North Carolina)

III Marine Expeditionary Force (Camp Butler, Okinawa, Japan)
  3rd Marine Division (Camp Courtney, Okinawa)
  1st Marine Aircraft Wing (Camp Foster, Okinawa)
  3rd Marine Logistics Group (Camp Kinser, Okinawa)
  3rd Marine Expeditionary Brigade (Camp Butler, Okinawa)

Marine Forces Reserve
  4th Marine Division (New Orleans, Louisiana)
  4th Marine Aircraft Wing (New Orleans, Louisiana)
  4th Marine Logistics Group (New Orleans, Louisiana)

US Central Command
  5th Marine Expeditionary Brigade (Bahrain)

the top US commander in the Middle East and Secretary of Defense from 2017 to 2019 under President Donald Trump. He reputedly selected Mattis to head the Pentagon after hearing he was nicknamed 'Mad Dog', on account of his aggressive battlefield tactics.

When a crisis erupts anywhere in the world, the President of the United States first dispatches an aircraft carrier and then his next move is to order a MEU, to sail to the sound of battle. It is not surprising that MEUs are often nicknamed "America's 911 Force", after the telephone number for American police and other emergency services.

The full title of these units is Marine Expeditionary Unit (Special Operations Capable), or MEU (SOC), and they are some of the most high-profile parts of the US military.

A MEU (SOC) is a self-contained intervention force of 2,200 Marines, who are embarked on a small ARG. When combined with

In 2003, the I Marine Expeditionary Force led the US advance on Baghdad.

For the counter insurgency campaign in Afghanistan, a divisional-sized MAGTF operated alongside British forces to control Helmand Province from 2010 to 2014. Units from across the US Marine Corps rotated into Afghanistan to sustain the fight against the Taliban.

The corps has long been a professional service, and it has a formidable reputation as a fighting force. This is due, in part, to the tough training regime that its recruits undergo and the professionalism of its officers. Perhaps the most famous modern USMC officer is General Jim Mattis, who rose to be

LEFT: The MV-22 Osprey tiltrotor, which can land and take off like a helicopter but has the level flight performance of fixed wing aircraft, has transformed US Marine Corps air assault operations. (US NAVY)

BELOW: US Marine Corps Amphibious Assault Vehicles emerge from the surf onto the sand of Freshwater Beach in Australia, during the landing phase of Exercise Crocodile '99 in October 1999. (DOD, PO 1C DANIEL E SMITH)

RIGHT: Contingents of marines on US Navy warships must maintain their weapons proficiency to ensure they are ready for action, every day of the year. (US NAVY)

escorting warships, submarines and patrol aircraft they are known as an Expeditionary Strike Group, or ESG.

Each MEU (SOC) is a self-contained amphibious force that is able to deploy by ship, landing craft, or aircraft to a crisis zone. It has its own integral ground combat units, aviation support, and landing crafts.

The USMC elements normally comprise:

- reinforced infantry battalion, designated as a battalion landing team or ground combat element.
- composite aviation squadron, of Bell MV-22B Osprey tiltrotors, Sikorsky CH-53E Sea Stallion heavy lift helicopters, Bell AH-1Z Cobra helicopter gunships, Bell UH-1Y Huey utility helicopters, McDonnell Douglas AV-8B Harrier or Lockheed Marin F-35B

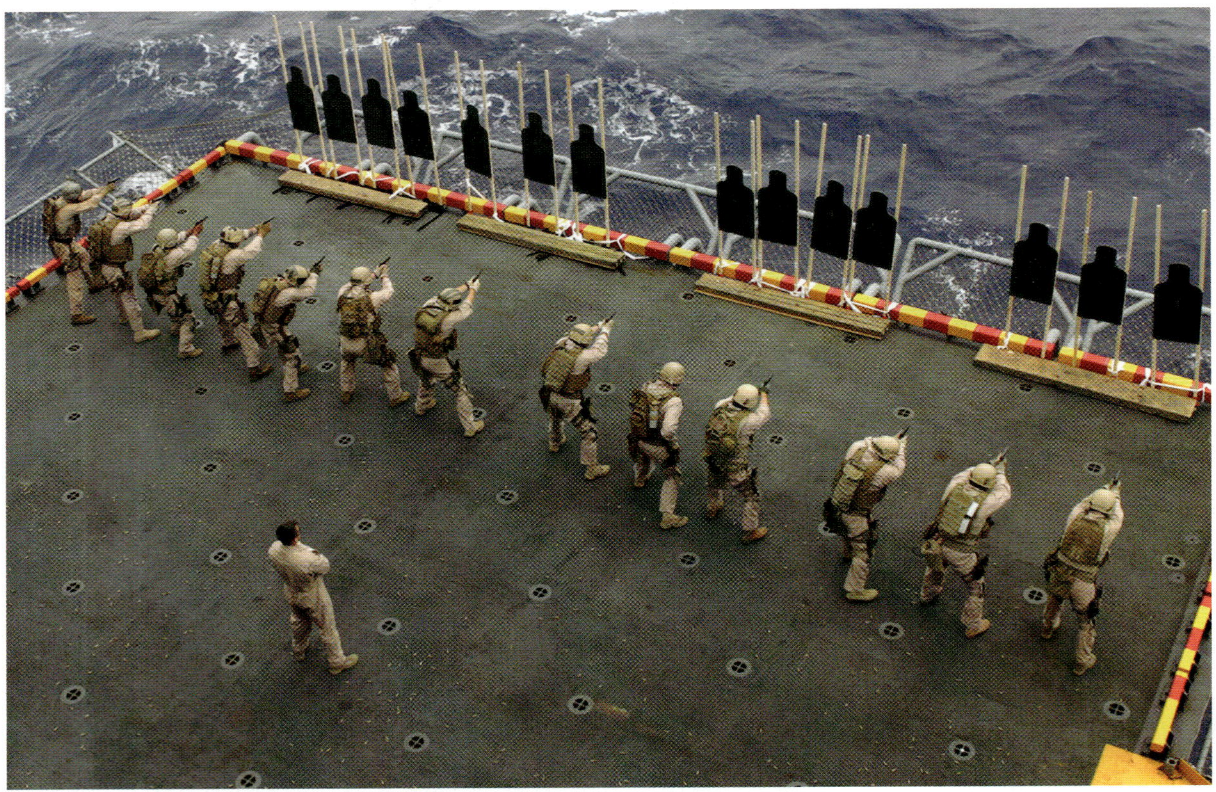

BELOW: The USS *Boxer* was the fourth of the eight Wasp-class landing helicopter dock (LHD) ships built between 1989 and 2009. She was commissioned into the US Navy in 1995. (US NAVY)

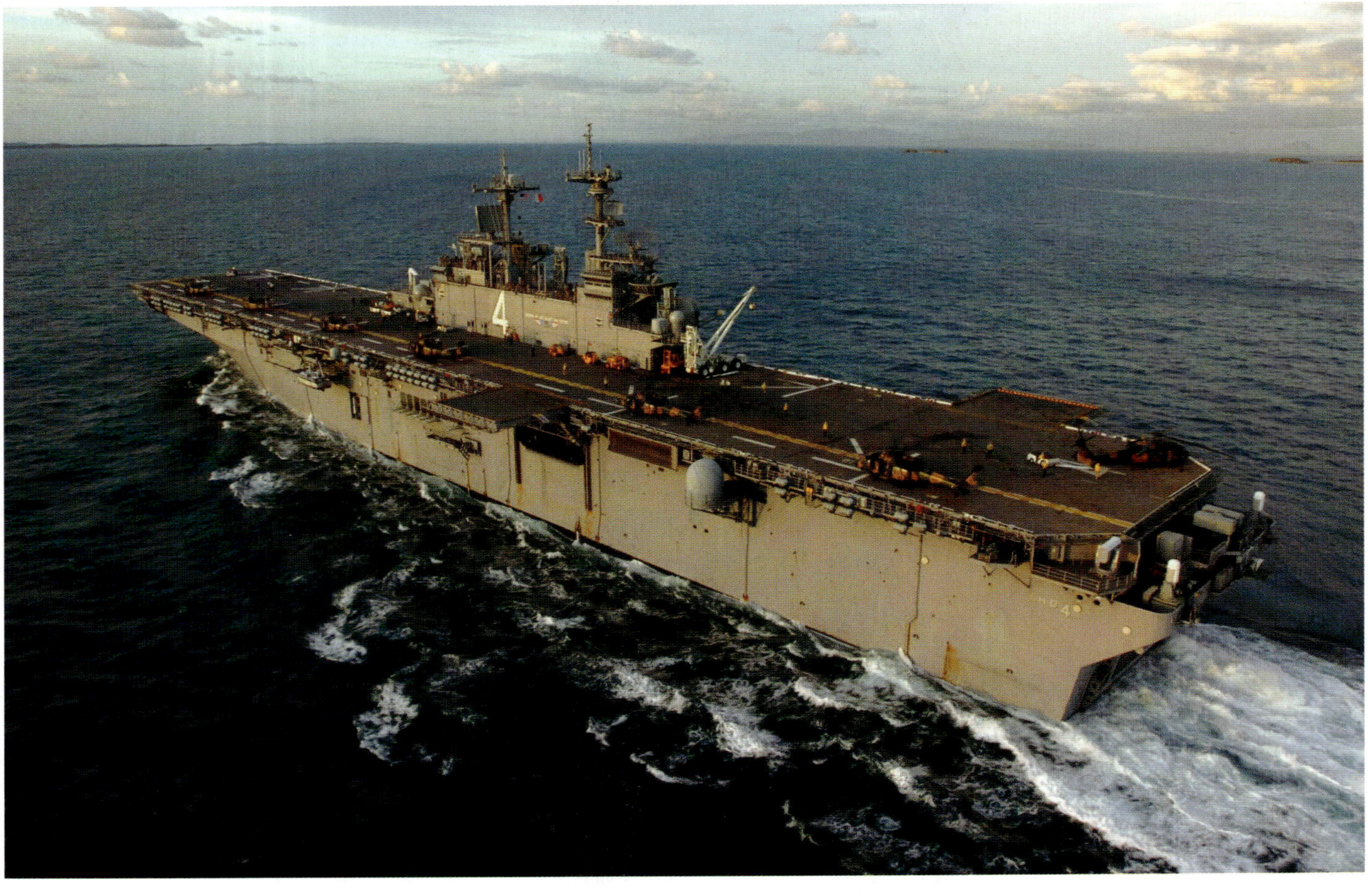

LEFT: Today's US Marines are trained at the recruit depots at Parris Island and San Diego. (USMC)

Lightning II jump jets, forming the aviation combat element.

- combat logistics battalion providing the logistics element.

A MEU (SOC) is usually commanded by a USMC colonel, but the ARG and ESG are led by US Navy admirals. The elements of the MEU(SOC) are embarked across the three ships of the ARG, which usually comprise a flat top amphibious assault ship, a transport dock ship and a landing dock ship. These ships usually act as the home base for the ARG's landing craft and hovercraft, which are dubbed landing craft air cushions, or LCACs.

The US Marine Corps must generate fully trained and equipped MEU (SOC) to meet the requirements set by the Joint Chiefs of Staff and regional combatant commanders around the world. For most of 2024 and 2025, the US Marine Corps and US Navy was required to have one MEU(SOC) at sea in the Pacific or Indian Ocean regions and another carrying out training close to its home port. Two other MEU(SOC)s were held at readiness to sail within a week or so of getting a call to arms.

A decade ago, at the height of the 'Global War on Terrorism', the USMC generated three or four MEU(SOC)s at a time with two usually deployed in the Middle East or Mediterranean, as well as one being at sea in the Pacific region.

The composition and high readiness of MEU(SOC) means they are often called upon to react to situations were US citizens need to be evacuated from crisis or conflict zones. These non-combatant evacuation operations, or NEOs, are often high profile and show off the capabilities of the modern US Marine Corps in a very positive light. These capabilities are also very welcome if a MEU (SOC) is called to provide humanitarian assistance after natural disasters. ❯

MARINE EXPEDITIONARY UNITS (SPECIAL OPERATIONS CAPABLE)

I Marine Expeditionary Force (Camp Pendleton, California)
- 11th MEU(SOC)
- 13th MEU(SOC)
- 15th MEU (SOC)

II Marine Expeditionary Force (Camp Lejeune, North Carolina)
- 22nd MEU(SOC)
- 24th MEU (SOC)
- 26th MEU (SOC)

III Marine Expeditionary Force (Camp Smedley D. Butler, Okinawa, Japan)
- 31st MEU (SOC)

BELOW: US Navy amphibious readiness group (ARGs) bring together a marine landing force, marine aviation, and naval ships. (US NAVY)

RIGHT: The US Navy has a fleet of Landing Craft Air Cushion (LCAC) hovercraft to move vehicles, cargo and personnel ashore from the well decks of landing dock ships. (US NAVY)

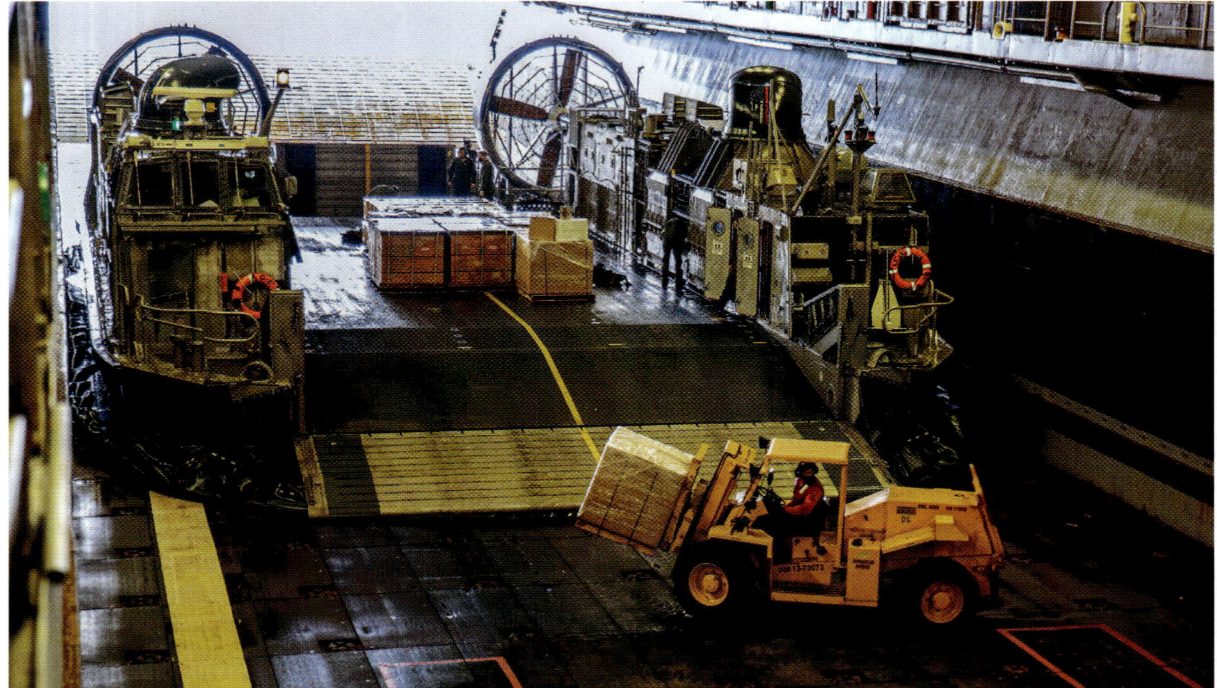

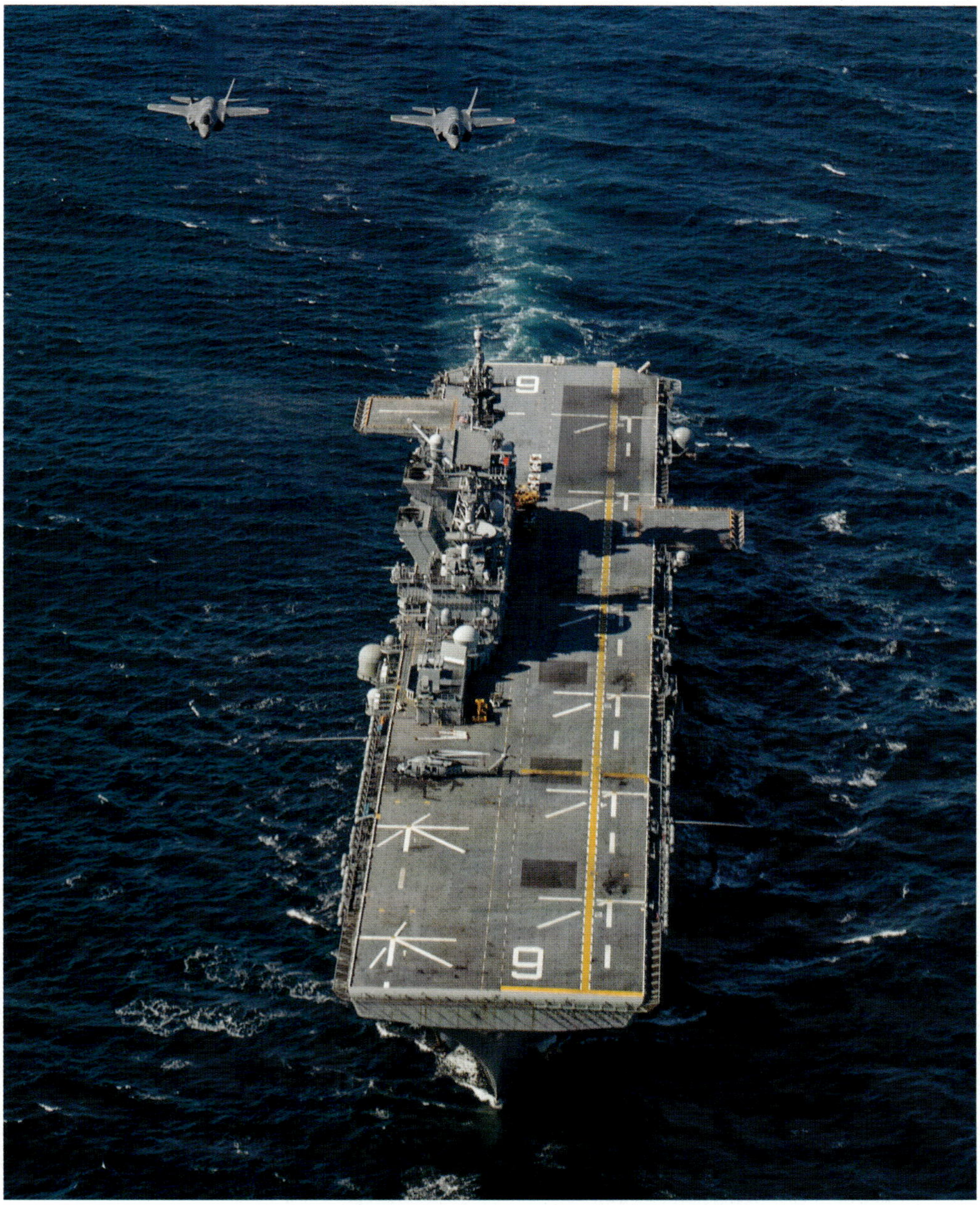

BELOW: US Marine aviators now fly the fifth generation F-35B Lightning II jump jet from US Navy landing ships. (US NAVY)

US Marine Corps – Aviation

The US Marine Corps is unique among the world's amphibious forces in having its own integral aviation branch. It currently boasts more than 300 fast jet combat aircraft and more than 800 helicopters. This is bigger than many air forces and means US Marines never have to want for air support when they go into battle.

The first USMC aviation units were formed before World War One and a little over 20 years later there were 145 squadrons supporting marines in the battles of the Pacific campaign.

Although USMC aviators are trained at US Navy flight schools, they must first pass the marines' basic officer or recruit training. They are marines first, aviators second. This ethos is the key to ensuring marine aviation is always overhead when marines are fighting on the ground.

USMC aviation units are configured to operate across a spectrum of tactical scenarios as amphibious operations unfold. In the first phase, USMC units must be able to operate from a range of US Navy warships. The Boeing F/A-18E/F Super Hornet squadrons are trained to fly off US Navy aircraft carriers to strike at targets far behind enemy lines. Close air support is the job of the AV-8Bs, F-35Bs and AH-1Zs embarked on assault ships.

Moving the landing force ashore is the task of the MV-22B, CH-53s and UH-1Ys. They also help in moving supplies into beachheads and evacuating wounded personnel. The MV-22B is unique to the USMC and it can carry marines on long distance

LEFT: A new generation of US Marine graduate from basic training at Parris Island. (USMC)

missions, with their range being extended by air-to-air refuelling from land-based USMC Lockheed Martin KC-130J Hercules tanker aircraft.

When the amphibious force lands ashore, the aviation support moves ashore to operate from forward airfields. Naval Construction Battalions, or Seabee, are trained and equipped to work with USMC combat engineers to rapidly build airfields, fuel tanks and ammunition dumps in combat zones. The USMC has air traffic control teams, aircraft technicians, logistic support, and security teams to ensure flight operations can continue at a high tempo.

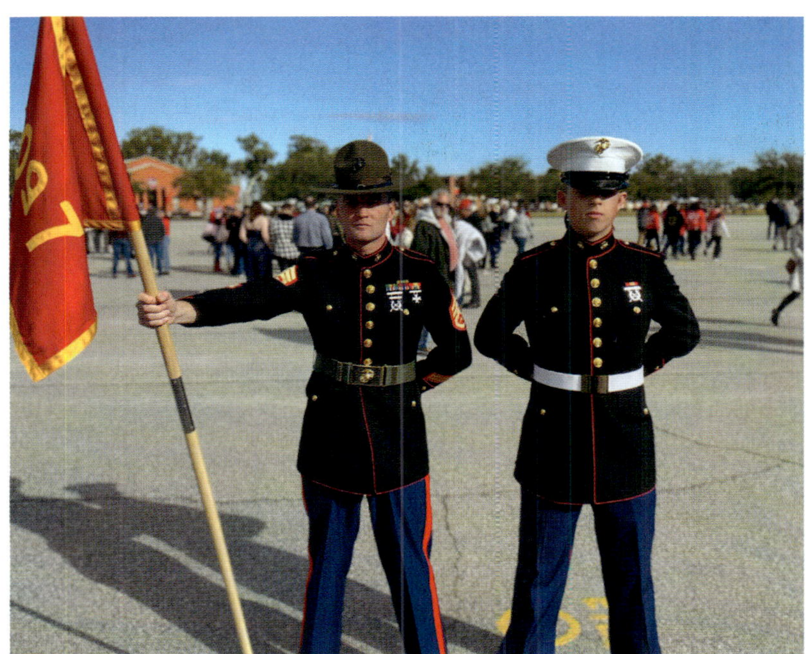

USMC aviation units are also trained to operate in a range of configurations, from small independent squadrons assigned to a MEU (SOC). This later kind of unit combines several types of aircraft and helicopters under a single commander, and they are usually embarked on amphibious assault ship or helicopter carrier.

During a large-scale operation, several squadrons can be combined into marine air groups that deploy to overseas theatres of operations. In the 1991 and 2003 Gulf Wars, full Marine Expeditionary Forces were deployed to the Middle East and their aviation element comprised a full marine air wing, with the complete spectrum of combat aviation units.

In these big wars, the US military has tried to centralise control of all US air units in an operational theatre under a single air component headquarters to direct air power for strategic effect. To ensure USMC doctrine of marine airpower being directed by USMC commanders is applied successfully, the USMC assigns officers to the centralised air headquarters to co-ordinate air operations and ensure marine aviation is allocated to support sectors of the battlefield where marine ground units are fighting.

BELOW: A squadron of US Marine Corps VM-22 Osprey prepare to launch an air assault operation from the USS *Wasp*. 'Putting marines over the beach' remains the core mission of the US Marine Corps. (US NAVY)

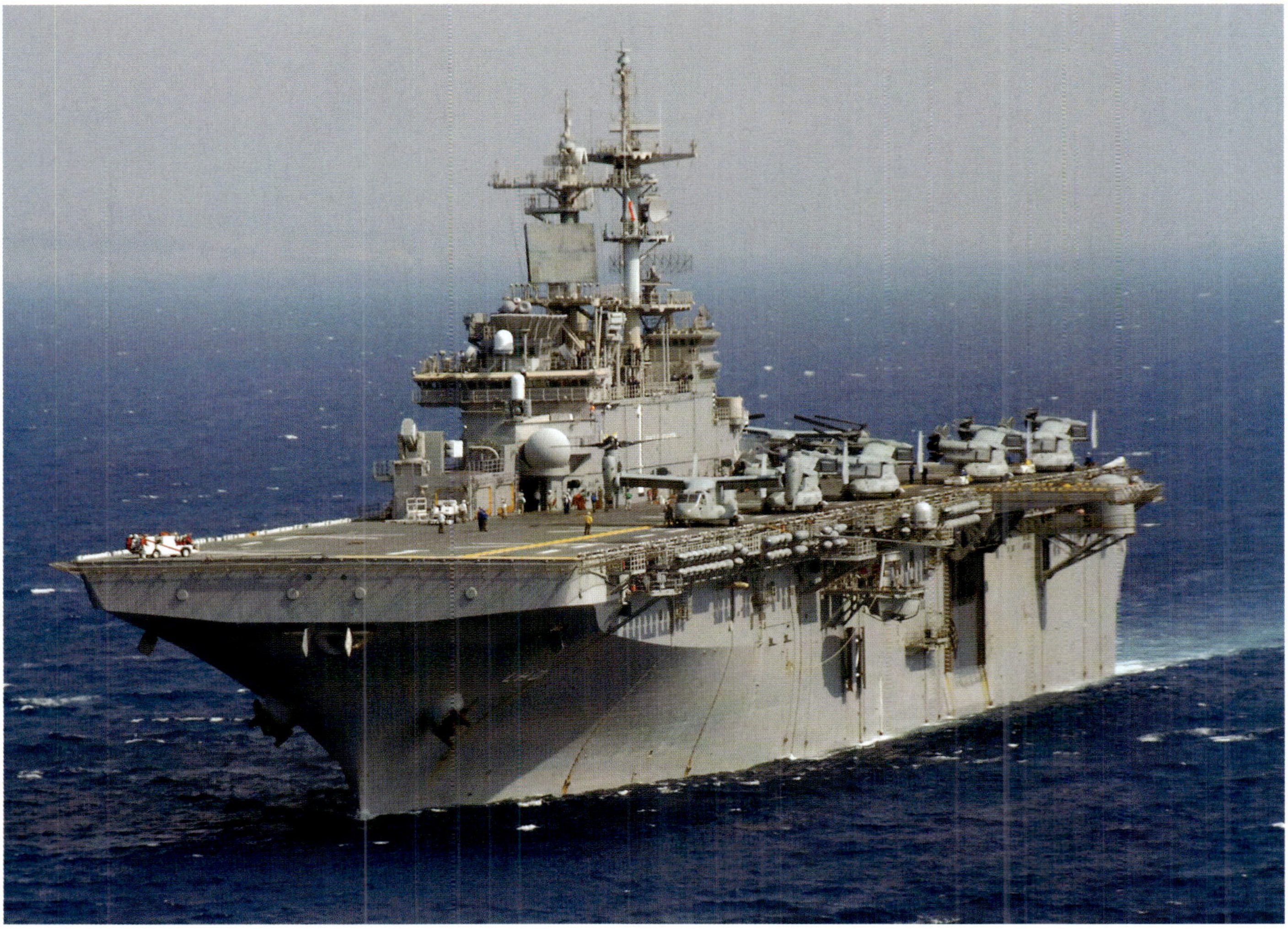

Future Marines

A new Pacific strategy?

ABOVE: The Pacific is now a key operational theatre for the US Marine Corps as tension rise with China. (USMC)

As the US Marine Corps approaches its 250th anniversary, its leadership is looking to the future and adapting to fight the conflicts of tomorrow.

For a decade, the US Navy and US Marine Corps have been re-orienting and restructuring for a potential conflict with China. The growth of Chinese air, naval and amphibious power is seen as threating US interests and allies in the Pacific, prompting a re-imaging of how US forces will try to contain and ultimately defeat any aggression by Beijing's military. Under the 2018 US National Defence Strategy, this future conflict was envisaged as being fought in 'layers'.

This strategic rivalry is now setting new challenges for the leadership of the corps, as they try to keep it relevant in this new era. Under the new US naval concept of operations, US forces will firstly be involved in confrontations short of war with

RIGHT: Dispersed operations across island chains in the Pacific is an important new development for the US Marine Corps as it looks to position long-range weapon systems to dominate vital waterways and naval 'choke points'. (USMC)

Chinese forces as they try to encroach in the territorial waters of US allies, seizing disputed islands, violating fishing agreements and interfering with the free passage of US warships through international water ways. This is sometimes called the 'contact layer'.

If Beijing should try to escalate its competition with the US, it could dispatch its air, naval and amphibious forces to capture Taiwan or islands across what is called the First Island Chain. This is a string of major Pacific archipelagos that stretches from Japan down through the Ryukyu Islands, Taiwan, the northern Philippines, and Borneo, down to the Malay Peninsula. The fight to contain these attacks is called the 'blunt layer'.

To support its offensive, Chinese air and long-range missile strikes are expected to hit US airbases in South Korea, Japan, Okinawa and Guam, as well as US aircraft carrier battlegroups operating in the region. In response, the US aims to mobilise its military might to drive back any incursions the Chinese might have been able to make along the First Island Chain. This is called the 'surge layer'.

In this scenario, the US Marine Corps leadership thinks it will not be possible to repeat the strategy from World War Two and massing naval and amphibious power to launch

landings with large formations of troops to recapture territory.

The era of marines winning a close quarter battle with their tactical skills and fighting spirit could be over. In future battles across the Pacific, the Chinese missile and air threat will mean US forces will not be able to mass or operate from fixed bases. Any future battle will be fought with long-range stand-off weapons.

This has led the US Marine Corps to look again at how they could fight in the First Island Chain in all phases of any conflict with China.

It is having to learn how to operate in a dispersed way, both in defence and offensive. This will make it more difficult for hostile satellites and drones to track marine units. By rapidly moving around and not staying in a fixed position for any length of time, Chinese surveillance and targeting will be massively complicated.

In this scenario, anti-ship missiles and air defence systems will play a critical role, allowing Chinese ships and aircraft to be taken out at long range and missiles to be knocked down before they hit their targets.

LEFT: The US Marine Corps is learning how to rapidly move its HIMARS launchers by air, land and sea to confuse enemy surveillance. (USMC)

The Chinese missile and air threats will make it very difficult for US ships and aircraft to safely penetrate into the First Island Chain to recapture land, meaning that US forces will have to operate in small groups to reduce the risk of catastrophic casualties.

In 2022, the US Marine Corps formed its first unit configured to fight in this new strategic environment. The 3rd Marine Littoral Regiment (MLR) was stood up in Hawaii to operate across the Pacific in a range of scenarios. Its 3rd Littoral Combat Team – formerly 1st Battalion, 3rd Marines – has traded in much of its infantry combat equipment for the NMESIS (Navy Marine Expeditionary Ship Interdiction System) which combines the Norwegian designed Naval Strike Missile (NSM) with an unmanned JLTV-based mobile launch platform to enable the marines to fire anti-ship missiles from land. The weapon has a range of up to 300km,

RIGHT: Covert reconnaissance of enemy coastlines by divers still has a place in the modern US Marine Corps as it looks to operate in diverse environments. (USMC)

BELOW: US Marine riflemen are now training to hold beach defences to deter Chinese and North Korean amphibious forces seizing the territory of American allies in the Pacific region. (USMC)

LEFT: Marine Littoral Regiments are equipped with the MADIS air defence system to defeat enemy drone swarms. (USMC)

so is well placed to dominate key shipping choke points in the First Island Chain.

Ground-Based Air Defense (GBAD) Battery of the 3rd Littoral Anti-Air Battalion (3d LAAB) operates within the regiment to protect key assets from air and missile attack with the Marine Air Defense Integrated System (MADIS), which integrates Stinger heat-seeking missiles onto a Joint Light Tactical Vehicle (JLTV).

To allow its assets to operate in a dispersed way, its communications and logistics units have been expanded and reconfigured to support small contingents of marines. A second littoral unit, the 12th MLR, was formed on Okinawa in 2023.

The 3rd MLR was put to the test in March and April 2025, when it deployed with its NEMISIS and MADIS systems to the Philippines for Exercise Balikatan 25 to practice

defending the island nation from a simulated Chinese amphibious attack.

US Marine aviation units have also been working to develop ways of working in the new environment. They have been carrying out experiments, to operate in small groups of up to six Lockheed Martin F-35B Lighting II stealth aircraft from improvised air strips on Pacific Islands, to launch simulated raids on Chinese forces. These exercises

BELOW: Air defence systems, such as the vehicle mounted MADIS, were deployed to the Philippines for Exercise Balikatan 25 in March and April 2025. (USMC)

RIGHT: The Norwegian designed Naval Strike Missile has been adopted by the US Marine Corps as part of the NMESIS weapon system to allow enemy warships to be engaged at ranges out to 300km. (DOD)

involved marine Bell-Boeing MV-22B Osprey tiltrotors and Lockheed Martin KC-130J Hercules airlifters to rapidly deploy to set up airstrips to re-arm and refuel F-35Bs. Once their mission is accomplished, the aviation group will rapidly re-locate before the Chinese would have time to find and attack them.

The re-orientation of the corps to this new style of warfare was controversial at the time, because it involved the disbanding of all its tank battalions and reduced its conventional artillery batteries in favour of long-range missiles and rockets. The then Marine Corps Commandant, General David Berger, took a lot of criticism for abandoning its heavy combat power but he pushed through with his radical plans.

As US Marines celebrate the corps' birthday, they will realise that they face a different challenge to that faced by their forefathers. The corps has always embraced change and rapidly adopts new technology, tactics and equipment. Whether it was perfecting amphibious assault operations in World War Two to adopting the helicopter ahead of the Vietnam War, the corps realised it had to raise its game if it was to stay relevant. The American public continue to love their marines, but today's marine leaders realise that this could evaporate if the Marine Corps does not look like it is ready fit to fight and win America's wars.

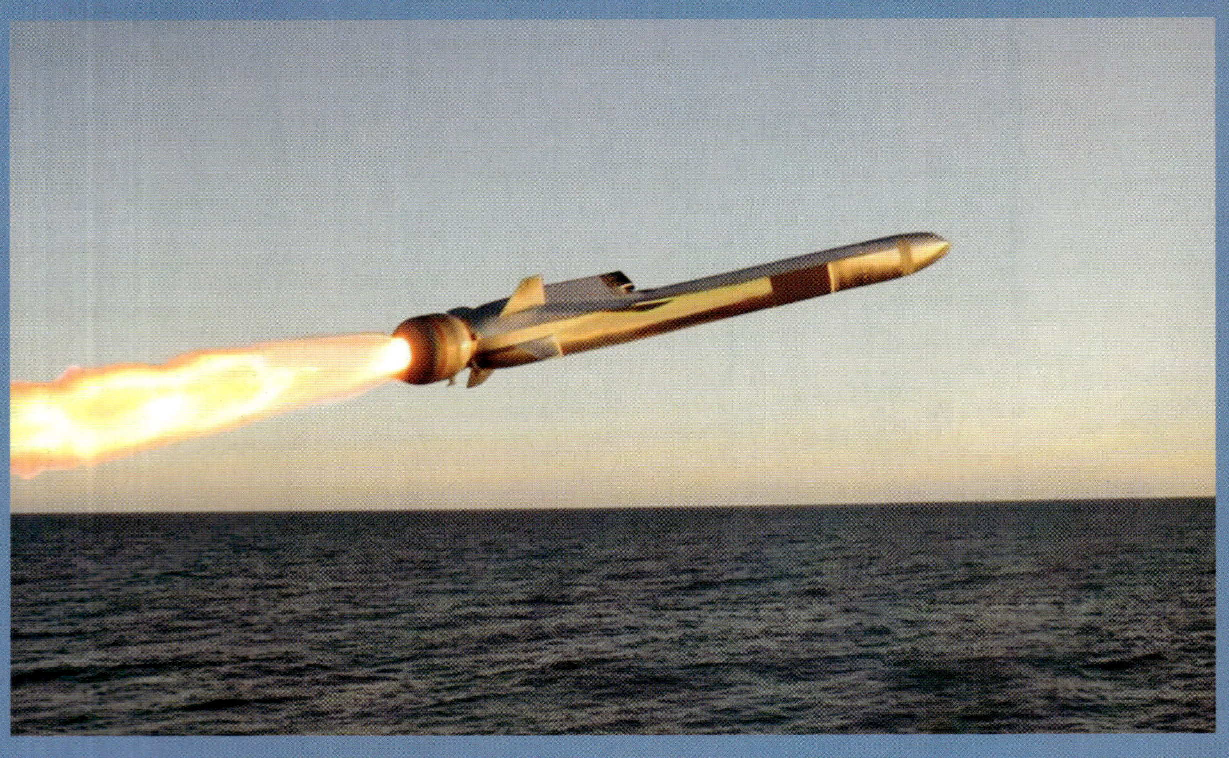

BELOW: The NMESIS is mounted on the unmanned JLTV-based mobile launch platform, allowing it to be dispersed in high threat areas to protect its operators. (USMC)

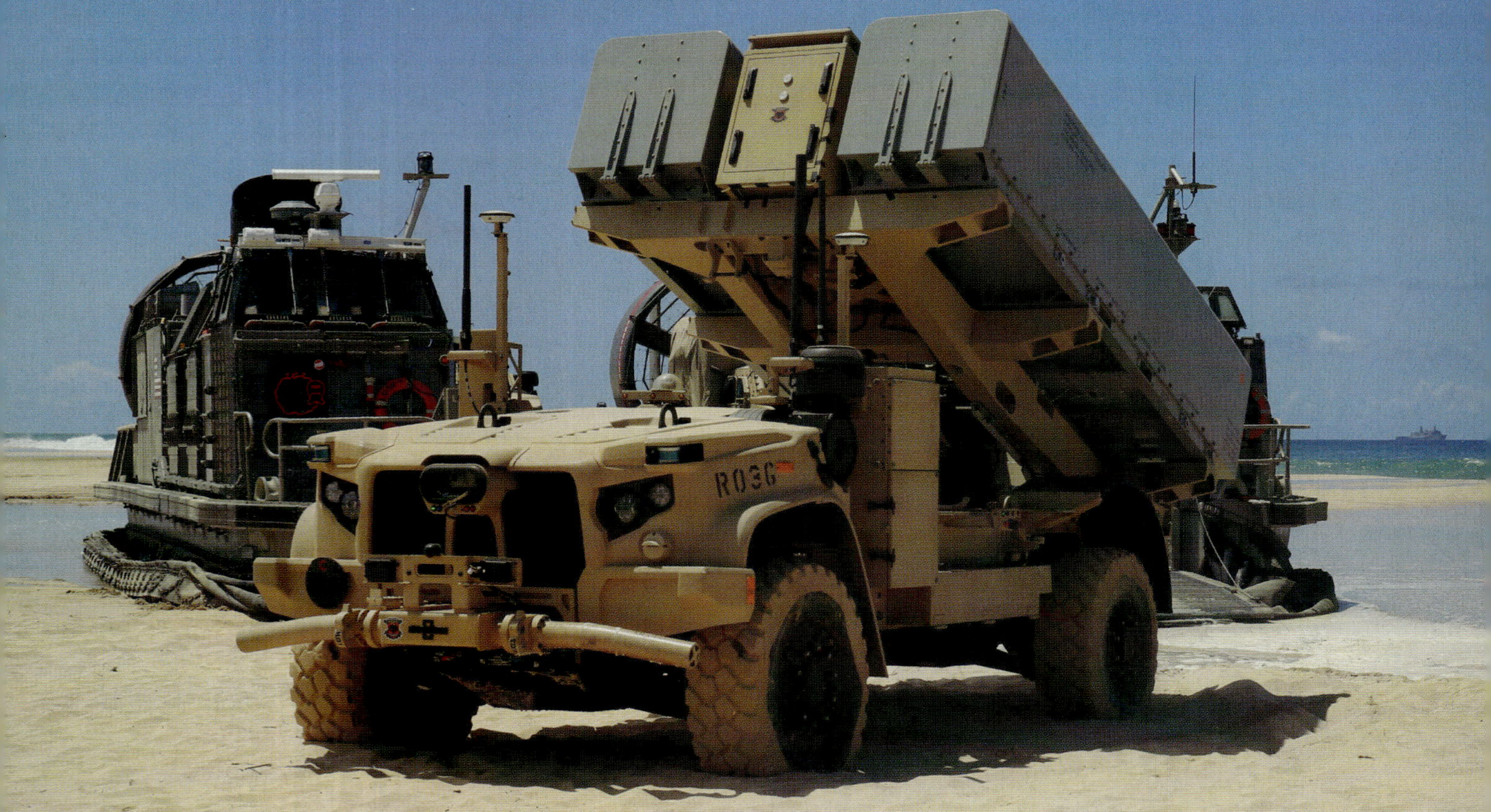